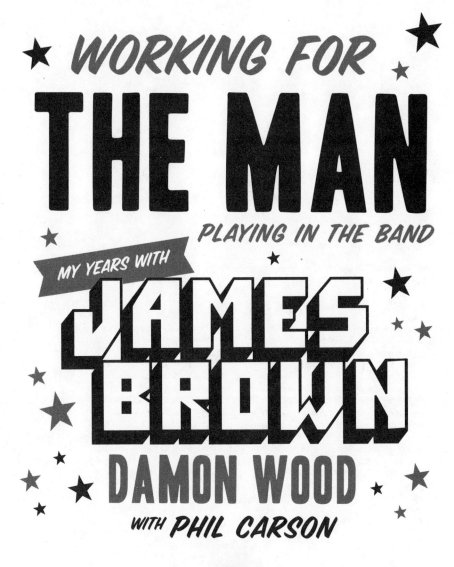

WORKING FOR
THE MAN
PLAYING IN THE BAND

MY YEARS WITH

JAMES BROWN

DAMON WOOD
with PHIL CARSON

EC
W

Published by ECW Press
665 Gerrard Street East
Toronto, ON M4M 1Y2
416-694-3348 / info@ecwpress.com

Library and Archives Canada
Cataloguing in Publication

Wood, Damon, author
Working for the man, playing in the band /
Damon Wood, Phil Carson.

Includes bibliographical references.
Issued in print and electronic formats.
ISBN 978-1-77041-385-6 (hardcover)
ALSO ISSUED AS: 978-1-77305-165-9 (PDF),
978-1-77305-164-2 (EPUB)

1. Wood, Damon. 2. Guitarists—United States—
Biography. 3. Brown, James, 1933–2006.
4. Soul Generals (Musical group).
I. Carson, Phil, author II. Title.

ML419.w874A3 2018   782.42164092'2
C2017-906184-4   C2017-906185-2

Editor for the press: Michael Holmes
Cover design: David A. Gee
Cover photos: Larry Hulst

Unless otherwise stated, all photos are
from the author's personal collection.

MIX
Paper from
responsible sources
FSC
www.fsc.org   FSC® C016245

PRINTED AND BOUND IN CANADA BY FRIESENS   5 4 3 2 1

TO JAMES BROWN
AND THE SOUL GENERALS

"He could be charming, hilarious, kind, thoughtful, scary, intimidating — all at the same time. Plus, he was my boss."

PREFACE

More than a decade after I left James Brown's band, he still appears in my dreams. Sometimes he's brooding and I'm not sure whether I'll get to play the show. Other times he's welcoming me back. At first, I'm elated. Then I'm not sure what the hell is going on. When I awake I realize then he's no longer with us. Yet, he still lives inside me. And I wonder about my former bandmates and whether Mr. Brown lives inside them and occupies their dreams, too.

Racing around the world, playing guitar for James Brown turned out to be the hardest work I'd ever done in my life. And playing music was only part of it. For nearly eight years, when my phone rang, I jumped on a plane and spent anywhere from one night to six weeks on the road with the Godfather of Soul and my bandmates. The business of getting funky took us across the United States, Europe, the

Middle East, South America, Australia, Southeast Asia, Russia — you name it. The Man was in demand *everywhere*. By the time I worked for him, Mr. Brown had long since become an international ambassador of soul. To millions of people all over the world, James Brown represented the very best American export: a funky good time.

I wanted a piece of that and, with a lot of hard work, I got it. Of course, it's well known that working for Mr. Brown could be a tough gig. That was no less true in his later years, when I worked for him. He could be charming, hilarious, kind, thoughtful, scary, intimidating — all at the same time. That was the nature of the gig. You had to *want* that job just to get it. And you had to work doubly hard to keep it. Working for Mr. Brown meant recognizing that he ruled the center of the universe. On stage that was easy, because it was true. Off stage, well, let's not get ahead of ourselves. But I wanted that gig, badly. So did my bandmates. They were all amazing musicians and fun-loving people with the ability to survive and even thrive on the road, despite its rigors. I call on them often in the pages ahead to help tell my story.

Let's be clear from the get-go on my role. I'm not a star. My relationship to James Brown was simple: I worked as a guitarist, a sideman, in the Soul Generals. I was an employee of James Brown Enterprises. I was far from green when my path crossed his, but I'd never been involved with music performance at that level of professionalism until I worked for Mr. Brown. As my bandmates will testify, playing music in that setting produced a pure, exhilarating high. The good times made us swear allegiance to Mr. Brown and his mission regardless of the inevitable drama. Whether it was flying in and out of European and Asian capitals, backing Mr. Brown and Michael Jackson in L.A., or jamming after hours in Paris, we had more than our fair share of fun. The highs far outweighed the lows, until, one day, they didn't.

Don't get me wrong, I was fortunate to land a role in James Brown's band, and I knew it. I understood that I came at the end of a long line of highly distinguished artists who'd held that chair before me. I toiled in the shadows of giants. I could not allow myself to be intimidated by the continuum of great players who came before me and still do my job, but I felt its weight just the same. And I had to come to terms with working closely with this individual who was not just another human being. Think of the profound impact James Brown and his hits, his dancing, his *attitude*, and his *message* had on America and the entire world. The sheer force of Mr. Brown's personality permeated the very air around us. In fact, when we traveled, we had to be constantly on guard. Mr. Brown could be anywhere and everywhere, as I would learn to my everlasting chagrin.

From what I could see, James Brown never gave less than 110 percent, even in his later years. By 1998, when I met him, Mr. Brown was in his late 60s. The man had made his mark. His place in popular music, his impact on global culture, had long been assured. The years had released him from the need for more hits. By that time, the rap and hip-hop crowd constantly sampled his music, bringing it to new, younger audiences. I should point out, on behalf of sidemen everywhere and Mr. Brown's alumni in particular, that that sampling frequently showcased the genius of his kickass drummers, bassists, guitarists, singers, and those who composed and arranged for him, rather than the star himself. But they all toiled under the James Brown brand. Despite his musicians' often astounding abilities, only a handful of them really stepped out of his shadow. Even though Mr. Brown was a modest five-foot-six, he cast a long shadow. He could have put his feet up or gone out occasionally for marquee gigs. Instead, he headed out on the road in every season, often on punishing schedules, making music, making money and, not incidentally, providing jobs for nearly two dozen musicians, singers, and dancers. Working musicians need to work. That's the deal. So hitching your wagon to a global brand who lives to work makes a lot of sense. And it goes a long way to explain why we all endured the difficulties. A musician could make a living by working for James

Brown. And he worked and worked until he passed from this Earth because, as trumpeter Hollie Farris says in the pages ahead, music was his life. Spending too much time at home really wasn't good for him, as a number of troubling headlines in his day attested. The title, "The Hardest Working Man in Show Business," was for real, even in his later years. Few artists have created their very own genre of music and then personally put their band through its paces every night on stage for decades on end, as he did. James Brown was fearless and his energy exceeded that of men half his age. The man was — and is — worthy of our loyalty. I hung on for as long as I could.

Working for Mr. Brown meant that your emotions had more power than your reason. His star power was contagious. Once I experienced the world from a stage dominated by James Brown, once I felt the respect of other, famous musicians because I worked for *James Brown*, once I raced in and out of the world's capitals as a member of his team, I wanted to be part of that bigger world. Once I tasted that life, there was no going back. I wanted to get funky and feel the audience's energy flowing back in return. When the night was right and the band was tight, we forgave the man for anything and everything that had happened that day, and we gave it our all. On certain nights, in our heart of hearts, we knew we were the hottest band on this planet.

I hope the James Brown I knew comes across in these pages. The world may have known him as "The Godfather of Soul" or "Soul Brother No. 1" or "Mr. Dynamite," but I knew him as an actual human being, my mentor, and my boss. I tell this story because I loved that man and all that he did for me, and I still do. Working for James Brown was the hardest thing I ever had to do but it was, and *still* is, the greatest thing that ever happened to me . . . so far.

Damon Wood
DENVER, 2018

ACT ONE
TRIAL BY FUNK

"Welcome, son! We're gonna have a *good time* tonight!"

James Brown called out to me as he approached from across the stage. I'd known him professionally for a little over a year, but I hadn't seen him for eight months. We were on a multi-level stage in the open-air Earth Theatre in Thessaloniki, Greece. Mr. Brown had arrived several days earlier without his two "go-to" guitarists, prompting him to call me to fill in. Mr. Brown, as he preferred to be called, seemed genuinely glad to see me, and he was his usual smartly dressed, perfectly coifed self. In contrast, I wore faded jeans and a nice set of bloodshot eyes, having just flown halfway 'round the world on a moment's notice. I knew that Mr. Brown did not like jeans, but he diplomatically ignored my appearance. He was aware that I'd just spent the better part of a day flying through multiple time zones with only a change of clothes and a guitar to answer his call — "the call" I'd been working for and waiting for all my life.

"We'll tell you what key we're in," Mr. Brown assured me. "We'll give you a few solos. The guys will show you the stuff. You'll be *fine*, son. Don't worry about a *thing*."

Mr. Brown was smiling, clearly at ease, and now he had a guitarist who could deliver the trademark "chank" sound so integral to his funky grooves. Mr. Brown knew I didn't know his whole show. But I'd been on stage with him half a dozen times in the past year or so, and he knew I'd been studying his music. I'd seen several of his shows by then and opened shows for him, backing his protégé and current companion, Tomi Rae Hynie. I'd met most of the band and most of them knew me. They also knew I couldn't be truly familiar with the James Brown show because of how complex and ever-changing it was, even for them. But I was welcome to give it my best, and everyone made me feel like I could pull it off. Mr. Brown radiated so much confidence that I undoubtedly absorbed some. Perhaps he could see that I was a crazy mix of fatigue and nerves. At this point, I knew enough not to ask him what had happened to his two guitarists. Within 24 hours I'd know the story, and over the next seven years I would live my own version of it. But right now I had to get through a sound check. Then I'd clean up, grab a bite to eat, and learn whatever my bandmates could teach me in the two hours remaining before show time. I kept telling myself: I *had* to survive the night. Who knew where things might lead? As it turned out, I rarely looked back for the next seven years; facing forward took everything I had. Only now, nearly 20 years after I joined James Brown onstage in Thessaloniki, does the whirlwind that began that afternoon make sense.

My adventure began in late June 1999. I had been quarreling with my girlfriend at her apartment in Las Vegas, my hometown, when the phone rang. Miss Ware at James Brown Enterprises was on the line. "Can you go to Europe for Mr. Brown?" The tone was like, "Can you do Mr. Brown a favor?" It was the call every musician dreams of. I gave the only answer a sane man would give. "Sure!" Then I added, "W-when?" Miss Ware said, "You fly out tomorrow morning at six a.m." I had a difficult time sleeping that night, but I boarded that plane. I can no longer piece together my route from Las Vegas to Thessaloniki beyond the fact that it included three or four flights and lots of dashing through airports in the course of one very long day. In retrospect, it was like passing through some sort of portal into a new life. My former life faded to sepia tones; my new life most definitely would be in Technicolor. The Thessaloniki gig was 30 June 1999, my first proper gig in James Brown's band. I was 29 years old, a professional guitarist of 10 years standing, and I'd been a few places. Thessaloniki was not one of them.

My arrival in Greece was inauspicious. The organization hadn't sent anyone to meet me. I didn't have much money. I really had no idea where I was going or where the gig would be held. In Greece you can't tell the letters from the numbers. All I had was my Gibson Les Paul guitar, a change of clothes, and a stack of plane tickets I'd picked up under my name at McCarran Airport in Vegas. So I called James Brown Enterprises in Augusta, which had just opened for the day, and Miss Ware, who was typically mean as heck, got us on a three-way call with the promoter, who was literally speaking Greek. Somehow, I grasped that I was to take a cab to the Earth Theatre and have the driver take me right up to the stage. James Brown's manager would pay for the cab when I arrived. The cab ride was brief — my driver grasped the urgency of his mission and obliged by speeding through the hills to the gig. "Judge" Alford Bradley, a tall man with a rakish mustache, paid my tormentor. I attempted a beeline for the dressing room to change out of my rumpled jeans — I already knew Mr. Brown's preference for sharp-looking associates — but "Judge" Bradley said, "Naaaah. They need you up there *right now*."

Out on stage, dozens of musicians, singers, and dancers were arranged for a performance. Indeed, I was the only guitarist. (I learned later that being the "only" this or that carried a certain status within the band.) I already knew most of the band. Robert "Mousey" Thompson, the first chair drummer, was real outgoing and all smiles from ear-to-ear. I made friends with him right away. Mousey had become the band's No. 1 drummer after his predecessor, Arthur Dickson, passed away shortly before I joined. Jerry "Louie" Poindexter played the Hammond B3. He was another really outgoing, crazy person who instantly made an impression on me. I knew Jerry had something special. He could take you to church with his B3. (To this day he calls me "colored boy" and leaves messages on my phone I can't repeat.) These two cats were my solid acquaintances, budding friends, by the time I reached Thessaloniki. Just about everyone in the Soul Generals was easy to get to know and pretty open once we'd had a chance to connect. Even the musicians I didn't know gave me a warm welcome as, suddenly, we were in this thing together. The group included Hollie Farris, trumpeter and band leader — a very physically fit dude — and the nicest guy; he never threw an attitude around. Jimmie Lee Moore was a multi-talented guy who typically played bass but also played a monster guitar. Jimmie was a real showman who could play his instruments every which way and steal the spotlight, a dangerous talent in Mr. Brown's band. It was easy to get to know Erik Hargrove, the No. 2 drummer. Erik was a stand-up guy, even-keeled, outgoing; we quickly became friends. The others I would get to know in the process of gigging across Europe over the next two weeks. As we headed to the dressing rooms after the sound check, the promoter approached Judge Bradley and, within earshot of me, said, "Here's the per diem money for the guitarist who just showed up." Judge Bradley pocketed my money right in front of me. "Don't worry, son," he said to me, realizing that I had witnessed his routine, "you're coming out *way* ahead." That was a famous phrase of his that I love to repeat to this day. In other words, "You're gonna make a lot more money this week than you made last week, so don't worry about the details." Whenever anyone tells you that, they're in your pocketbook. I could see a little greasiness in the organization, but I was too tired to really care, and there was no time to dwell on it.

Had I the time or inclination to grab a newspaper, I could have read the following account of James Brown's arrival in Greece just days earlier. Though I can't vouch for the details, the tone of the article reflects the reverence Mr. Brown could inspire overseas.

> James Brown in Greece for 2 concerts
> ATHENS, 30 JUNE 1999, ATHENS NEWS AGENCY:
>
> Legendary singer James Brown arrived in Athens yesterday for two concerts in Greece, one in Thessaloniki today and one in the Greek capital tomorrow. Mr. Brown [later] gave a press conference.
>
> The 71-year-old [sic — James Brown was 66] funk phenomenon stressed that soul music will continue far after he's gone, "because it comes from the heart and from God."
>
> James Brown arrived in Greece in true rock-star style for his first performances in the country in 12 years, replete with 80 personal suitcases . . .
>
> He had to make do, however, with only a simple Rolls Royce for transport, after organizers convinced him it was difficult to find a seven-meter, six-door white limousine.
>
> Dressing rooms for the soul legend and his entourage will provide the requisite 20 full-length mirrors, 10 steam irons, 78 bath sheets, 30 boxes of shampoo and cosmetics and a fully-equipped press office for the exclusive use of James Brown. Also available will be a ping-pong table and, during his stay in Thessaloniki's Hyatt Regency Hotel, he

will have the exclusive use of a roulette wheel, housed in a room next to the presidential suite, where he is staying.

On standby during the concerts will be two hair-dressers and two mobile hair dryers, as well as oxygen masks and bottles. The fresh juice and soft drinks also on hand will go nowhere near James Brown. His contract stipulates that at least seven bottles of Dom Perignon Champagne be on hand at any one time.

As the gig approached, I thought, "This is going to be *deep*." Think about it. From the moment I entered that venue to show time was less than four hours. My determination to come through was riddled with jet lag and fear. I'd never played that show before. I didn't even have an outfit. When you play in the Soul Generals backing James Brown, you must look sharp. I had to go through the Soul Generals' rack of tuxedos and find — I hate to say this — a dead guy's suit, one nobody else in the band had claimed as their own. A number of Mr. Brown's sidemen literally left the band and life itself at the same time. I found one about 10 sizes too big and rolled up the sleeves of the jacket until my hands appeared. Just before we went on stage, members of the band sat me down and walked me through the show. A few of them remember that moment.

ERIK HARGROVE: We're in the dressing room after sound check and everyone's trying to go over stuff with Damon so he knows what to do. He's heard the tunes before, but he doesn't know the signals, all the ins and outs. A few people were really trying to give him the best advice on what to play. I took a picture of them. We were sitting in a weird World War Two bunker kinda thing — that was our dressing room.

Backstage in Thessaloniki, Greece, before my first official show in the Soul Generals, 30 June 1999, with (left to right) Robert "Mousey" Thompson, Hollie Farris, Fred Thomas, Damon Wood. CREDIT: ERIK HARGROVE.

HOLLIE FARRIS: I didn't have a clue [who would play guitar that night]. Suddenly, here's this white guy with long hair. I said, "Oh, rock 'n' roll." [*Laughs*] And I was *right!* But we sat around — me and the bass player, Fred Thomas, and Robert Thompson, the drummer, and Damon — and said, "Here's the way it goes, here are the keys." And then it was show time. Let's go! We started up and he was in it pretty quick. I thought, "Looks like we'll make it through the show." And we made it just fine. Damon was like a deer caught in the headlights, but he hung in there. And Brown was as happy as he could be. The audience went nuts. That was the thing with Brown. He could pull off a show with an upright bass and a washtub.

JIMMIE LEE MOORE: Now, Damon — that man can play the *hell* outta that guitar. I don't care what color you are, if you can play, you can *play*! James Brown had talked to me about him, said he was going to bring Damon on. He said to me, "What do *you* think, son?" I said, "Man, he can *play*!" I was the bass player. I played guitar when another guitar player screwed up. I play the guitar, but Damon is a *guitar player*. There's a difference. I was happy for Damon. He had been working with Tomi Rae [Hynie] in Vegas and all of a sudden he got his break. I liked seeing the man prosper.

Everything happened so fast that night. I remember tuning my guitar and hustling on stage into the lights and a sea of warm applause. The band was arrayed on the stage's multiple levels, with Mousey in the first drum chair on stage left and Erik in the second chair, stage right. Between them, behind a big rack of "toys," sat George "Spike" Nealy on percussion. Fred Thomas and Willie Ray "Bo" Brundidge both played bass; they too were split stage right and left. Jerry Poindexter sat at the Hammond B3 organ, stage right. The horn players were in a row, stage left: Hollie Farris and Todd Owens played trumpet and Jeff Watkins, Leroy Harper, and Waldo Weathers played various saxes. "R.J.," Mr. Brown's "second," always hovered stage left to jump in for Mr. Brown and pick up any slack in the show's energy. The Bittersweet singing group lined up stage right, opposite the horn players. On this tour the singers included Martha High, Cynthia Moore, Kelly Jarrell, Amy Christian, and Candice Hurst. They added female harmonies or stepped out as lead vocalists, lending class and sex appeal to the show. Three dancers, Heather Hayes (daughter of Isaac Hayes), Dara Wells and Sara Raya, periodically took the stage to add some heat to the proceedings. James Brown always used to say, "I want something on my stage for everyone." So, apart from his all-male sidemen, he had sexy women of all colors, shapes, and sizes singing and dancing for him.

Hollie Farris led the band through a couple uptempo numbers to warm up the audience for the star's arrival. Then Danny Ray, the emcee, wound up the crowd in his inimitable way by calling out James Brown's best-known hits, while the band responded by quoting the melodies and rattling off the signature riffs. "Aaaaaand nooow, ladies and gentlemen," Danny Ray intoned, "it's Star Time. *Star Time!* I want everyone here tonight to call the Godfather of Soul himself — Mr. *Jaaaaames* Brown! *Jaaaaames* Brown! *Jaaaaaaames* Brown!" The crowd in Thessaloniki gave it up as a spotlight found Mr. Brown and followed him across the stage to the lead microphone. His coif was perfect, his outfit impeccable, his smile dazzling. The effect was electric and the crowd rose to its feet as one. James Brown had that star thing down. It was something to see, especially from the stage. But the razzle dazzle was for the customers. I had to ignore James Brown the star and remain focused on James Brown my boss. So I watched and waited for his signals in a frenetic state of anticipation. I knew the performance would be fast and furious and that our responses would have to be near instantaneous. My memory of the show is a bit sketchy, perhaps understandably, under the circumstances.

A few impressions remain: the audience saw Mr. Brown's entrance before the band did, and you knew he was stepping out because the audience let out a big "*Aaaaaahh*," and that energy flowed right into the band. He'd make eye contact with a few of us as he made his entrance, like, "What's going *on*, brother? Let's tear the *roof* off this place!" (Of course, the fact that we were outdoors made no difference. James Brown would rip the *sky* off the place if necessary.) That's all James Brown had to do — just walk out onstage — and the atmosphere became charged. I don't know how many shows create that instant energy from one person just stepping onstage. I know that all stars are loved, but James Brown had a force field around him. He really had a power. And the band felt it, too. Our intensity and our focus multiplied when he hit the stage. The Greek audience was freaking out, playing right into his hands. Mr. Brown started moving to the music, feeling for the groove, shuffling his feet to the beat, inviting the audience to do the same by his example. Dancing and grooving with James Brown — that's what the audience came for and why they spent their hard-earned money to be there.

James Brown's sound is known for a funky dominant 7/9 chord, played by his guitarists. He knew I'd know that. During the gig, I'm jamming along on this funk chord and he comes over and he holds up three fingers with one finger from the other hand placed across the three fingers. It looked like an "E" or a convoluted "A." I had no idea what he wanted — I'd never seen that hand signal before. He finally yelled out, "Thirteen!" He wanted me to play the 13 chord form, a nice funky sounding chord that's a variation on the dominant 7/9. I just put my pinky down on the high E string, two frets up from the 7/9 position, and he smiled back. ("The kid's got it!") His smile radiated a dazzling, almost artificial whiteness under the spotlights. Later, I realized that Mr. Brown had had dental implants. Once, when an interviewer told him, "You have *amazing* teeth!" he responded, "Yes, I bought *all* of them!" (One thing I learned to love about this man was his quick wit and contagious sense of humor.)

Mr. Brown worked that crowd hard until he had them where he wanted them. When he needed a break after a half-hour of pushing hard on the funk, he brought his then-featured singer (and companion), Tomi Rae Hynie, out on stage to lead a few numbers. As she stepped up to sing "At Last," the standard made famous by Etta James, trumpeter Todd Owens came over and threw a chord chart in front of me. He was trying to be helpful, but in my decade-long rock-and-roll career, I had never used a chord chart. I'd never had to stand on stage and use a piece of paper to know how to play a song. So I threw the chord chart on the ground and moved my amp closer to the drummer to make it look like I had something to do.

Just don't expect me to read that chart! I moved my amp like I was a roadie — something you don't do in James Brown's band in a Soul General's uniform, as I learned later. I bet the band was cracking up behind my back.

The fact that I was the only guitarist on stage that night — my first night with the band — was a pretty rare occurrence. If you were the only *something* — the only guitarist, the only drummer, the only trumpet player — even for one night in the James Brown show, you gained a certain status. By showing up with my guitar to provide the chank, I had kinda, sorta *saved* the show. That was a distinction created and honored by the band. Why? At that stage in James Brown's career, he used what I'd call a Noah's Ark approach. He had two of everything. Two drummers, two bassists, two guitarists, two saxes, etc. This approach to touring served several purposes. First, with his incessant touring, he wanted redundancy in his team so that every obligation could be met. People might get sick, have passport problems, miss a plane — anything was possible with nearly 30 people involved. And when, inevitably, he felt he had to fire someone, he could do so and still have a full band for the next gig. No one could get him over a barrel because, with two of everything, he could replace anyone. So being an "only" meant there was a lot riding on your shoulders. James Brown might welcome you for that reason. But he would not allow himself to be vulnerable to your singularity for long. My "only" status lasted all of one night.

That's all I remember about that first gig. What should have been the most exciting night of my life passed in a blur. *I'm on stage with James Brown!* It was trial by funk. Eventually I became comfortable enough in the James Brown show to enjoy my surroundings a bit, even interact with the audience. But that first night was a doozy. A couple times Mr. Brown told me the key he thought the song was in and he'd be wrong. So I'd start playing the wrong chords and the horn guys would signal me. "No! C, not E flat." On that first gig in Thessaloniki, I wasn't involved in the tight little arrangements that

Hollie Farris was leading, so I just watched James Brown. When I got lost I looked around to see if anyone was giving me a cue. If not, I followed the musician's maxim: "When in doubt, lay out." After the gig, I was hanging out with the band, drained and relieved. We were behind the stage, talking with some fans who were smoking hashish mixed with tobacco, as they do in Europe. I joined the party and, because I don't smoke tobacco, I'm thinkin', "Wow, this is *strong*." I exhaled and looked up at the night sky. At that moment, a shooting star blazed overhead. I made a wish. I said to myself, "Man, I want to stay in this band for a while."

That night and for the rest of the week, I roomed with Bo Brundidge, who had joined the band the previous fall. We were the two newest guys in the band, although my status at that point was far from assured. Bo is a real cool, a soft-spoken cat.

> **WILLIE RAY "BO" BRUNDIDGE:** I hadn't met Damon yet. I was new in the band. That was my first time in Greece and my first international travels with the band. Since I was the new guy and he was the new guy, he ended up being my roommate in the beginning. That first night he was telling me what it was like making all the flights from Las Vegas. You want to be in the right airport at the right gate at the right time. So we had that conversation. Just to make the trip and do the gig had to have been wild for Damon. I remember it was a big outdoor festival. There were many to follow. You come to realize that, all over Europe, that's what summer is about. Festivals everywhere! Amazing festivals and the amazing people that you'd meet at them. That whole Greek and European tour, we were on the same bill with the Temptations and the Supremes. Amazing people everywhere.

Bo got his nickname when a Euro-itinerary inexplicably rendered his last name "Bobadino." (Willie Ray is definitely *not* Italian.) Nicknames were common in the band and, early on, mine was "Jesus," due to my long hair and the flip-flops on my feet. When Bo would put new strings on his bass backstage before a show, he'd get 'em stretched out, tuned up, and then would go into this ungodly, Larry Graham–like, slap-bass, funk thing. I thought, "If they'd just let him do that in the show!" Of course, he took some heavy funk solos.

THE END OF "THE ONLY"

The morning after the show in Thessaloniki, having survived my first performance with the Soul Generals, the band drove in a van to Athens while Mr. Brown and his entourage flew. Keith Jenkins, one of Mr. Brown's ace guitarists, joined us in Athens. I'd met Keith the year before when I worked in the Tomi Rae Band and we'd hit it off. Crossing paths with him again meant that I'd be hanging with a guitar buddy and someone close to my own age. Keith and I were in our 20s and everyone else, except maybe Erik Hargrove, seemed much older. I looked forward to Keith's camaraderie as well as his help in learning the show. I mean, Keith's a great soloist. At that time he could solo over the chord changes in ballads much better than I could. He was figuring out how to play the melody, instead of just jamming over a blues progression. Musically, he's a very intelligent player. He'd know the horn parts to all the songs — all three parts. And he could tell other players how their part was played on the original recording or how it changed in a later version. He knew three guitar parts to every song and could make up extra guitar parts that would fit. And he was probably the biggest

James Brown fan in the band. Those two would butt heads quite a bit, but of all the people I've known, Keith Jenkins really was the biggest James Brown fan, and still is, to this day. So I had a lot to look forward to when he returned. At that particular time, however, Keith had other ideas. He was 24 and had been in the band for four years. But, initially, he'd refused to join this short Euro tour. (Thus, I got "the call.") I'll let him tell you about it.

KEITH JENKINS: I'd just quit the band. For some reason, James was getting more and more impossible to deal with. I'd had enough. I thought, "I'm not going to Europe for three weeks with this guy." So I quit that action at sound check at Avery Fisher Hall in New York. The next night, Waldo Weathers, one of our sax players, called me. "Come on back, man." I thought, "Europe is hard enough, even with things being as good as they can be." The extra added stress of Mr. Brown being in a certain awful mode was untenable. So I said, "No, I ain't goin' back. I'm goin' home." I finally got to my apartment in Augusta and slept for a long time. The next morning the phone rang. It was "Rock," Ron Laster, the other guitar player. "Doogie!" he said — everyone in the band had a nickname and I was the youngest, so the band named me after *Doogie Howser, M.D.*, a TV show about a teenage doctor — I said, "What's up?" "*Get up!*" Rock said. "You gotta get goin' on this trip. I'm at the airport and they took my passport. I'm not goin'. You *gotta* go. Just go get the money. They gonna call you as soon as I hang up." Sure enough, James Brown's office called. "Mr. Jenkins, this is Miss Ware. Can you be on a plane to Athens this afternoon?" I reluctantly said, "Oh-*kay*."

I was thinking, "Surely they haven't found anybody." So I went back. I kind of relished the idea of being the "only." James Brown didn't like having anybody in the "only" position, because that's a position of leverage. In my whole time in the band, I was never the only guitar player. At some point I found out that they'd called Damon. I already knew him. He'd been on tour with us in James Brown's opening act in '98. We were already friends. But I'm kinda like, "*Damn*, they *got* somebody. There goes being the 'only.'" I was still feeling arrogant and indignant about the whole deal. I flew from Augusta to Athens via Atlanta and Zurich and arrived in time for the second show on the tour. I knew Damon would be there. I'd made a decision: "I ain't showin' him *shit!*" Nothing against Damon, you understand.

So I went to sound check, met with Mr. Brown. I demanded a big raise. Usually, if you had done what I had done, you'd come back with a big pay cut. Taking a monetary stand with him took a lot of nerve because where money was concerned, that was not an easy topic. You had to be ready to go back home. Ninety-nine out of a hundred times he was going to win that deal. But I didn't care. I'd had all day to work up my nerve. First thing, he walks up to me and said, "You don't owe me no apology." I said, "I'm making *this* much, but I need to make *that* much." He chuckled. "Son, just do your job. You're not going to come up here, demand no pay increase. Get on your job. Don't make that mistake." He kind of defused it. I was prepared for him to be bully-ish, but he wasn't. He brushed it off.

I tried to maintain my attitude about Damon, but as soon as I saw him, I was like, "What's *up*, man?!" For one thing, he's older than me and, really, a better guitar player in a lot of ways. I knew a lot about James Brown's music, but he knew all this other music. So we went through the whole James Brown show in the dressing room before we went on. My whole plan to not help him went right out the window. We had a musical connection, and a personal one. Damon was close to my age. Being so young, I'd felt a little alone my first four years in the band as there was nobody I could really relate to from my generation. Then Damon came along. We'd listened to a lot of the same music. He was maybe five years older than me, which wasn't much of a gap, considering other people were 25 years older than me.

When Keith arrived in Athens he didn't pat me on the back for having handled the Thessaloniki gig as an "only." Keith told me later that he was planning on keeping his knowledge to himself and protect his own job, like most people would. I don't think they made it easy on him to get information when he first started. Anyway, he backed off not showing me anything. Even though he'd just quit and returned, he was still looking out for James Brown. He had the James Brown motivation to put on a great show. And I think Keith realized that, as a new player, I wanted it to be great, too. Once we started hanging out, he ended up showing me all my parts. After that first gig in Athens, Keith and I stayed up until five in the morning after each gig for the next four days, drinking beers and going over the set list. Keith showed me every part to every song that we could possibly be called on to play and more — B sides that not even James Brown pulled out at that point.

The gig in Athens was at the Lycabettus Theater, which is an in-the-round amphitheater carved out of a hilltop in the middle of town. You have to see this venue to believe it — a truly amazing setting above such storied surroundings. I have to acknowledge that I only found out more about the theater's location when I researched the gigs for this book. At the time we played this amazing venue I knew next to nothing about it. Our printed itineraries were sketchy on details. As sidemen, we could not afford to dwell on our where-abouts. Sounds crazy, and it should. All we knew on the road was rushing to the hotel, making the lobby call for a ride to the venue, ironing our tuxedos, and dashing to the stage to deliver 90 minutes of serious funk behind our leader, anywhere, anytime. In Athens, I spent the show lasering in on Mr. Brown and my fellow bandmates, keeping in mind all that Keith had shown me. I still couldn't really appreciate my surroundings just yet. We flew to Vienna the next day and played the Fernwärme Wien in the Open Air district, part of a two-week festival that included Ray Charles, the Supremes, the Temptations, and B.B. King. You get the picture: stars everywhere. It hadn't been that long ago that I'd been scuffling for a "dead leg-ends" gig in Las Vegas, and here I was on a stage trod by the biggest names in soul and rhythm and blues.

As we traveled gig to gig, I got to know my bandmates better. Spike Nealy, the percussionist, was a really welcoming dude. He took me aside one day and privately complimented my solos. Spike would do outrageous percussion solos, using "the toys," as James Brown called Spike's set-up. In the middle of "It's a Man's Man's Man's World," it would get quiet and Spike would hit a chime at the perfect moment. On one gig during that first tour, Spike was get-ting his turn in the spotlight when Mr. Brown called him out front. But there weren't any drums down front. As I puzzled over this development, Spike dropped to the ground and played a drum solo on the wooden stage. Mr. Brown stepped back and Spike played off his microphone stand. He got "major house" — a musician's term for big applause — with that trick.

GEORGE "SPIKE" NEALY: I could tell Damon was the kind of guitar player that when you point to him, he's *gone*. I'm sure James Brown saw that. Mr. Brown would always give you a trial moment to see where you stood with the band. When he pointed to Damon to do a solo on that first gig in Thessaloniki and Damon delivered, I knew right then he was in — he was going to be James Brown's solo man. James Brown knows he has an army. But he has specialists. He was wise. He knew each person's strength. If he needed a quick solo right on the money, he could hit Damon at any time and Damon wouldn't miss. I spoke to Damon after Thessaloniki. "When he points to you, go for it. That's your moment to shine." But I cautioned him, too. Although it's your moment to shine, you're shining on James Brown's show. So do not pull it out of pocket, because it took 45 minutes to get the audience to that point. When you're playing for James Brown, you're playing for James Brown the man, James Brown the music, and James Brown the brand. You're doing a James Brown concert. You just have to remember the context.

The next night, at the Campo Santo at the Orleans Jazz festival in Orleans, France, was my fourth gig on the tour. It rained in biblical proportions. We played outside in a big courtyard. The stage was covered; the audience was not. But nobody went anywhere — they had amazing energy, all in the pouring rain. We had to change into our uniforms in a tent while it poured. I remember going on stage with my shoes and socks soaking wet. But it was a great show because the French are wild for James Brown. I'll never forget one moment. James Brown cued Jerry Poindexter and Jerry started playing this sweet gospel song on the Hammond B3 organ, workin' the pedals, while the rain poured down in sheets. And James Brown started singing this gospel tune, straight from the heart. At the time, I actually thought they were both improvising a spontaneous moment from heaven! I discovered later it was a gospel standard, "Precious Lord, Take My Hand." I'd never heard it before, but Mr. Brown and Jerry had performed it many times.

JERRY "LOUIE" POINDEXTER: Mr. Brown was introducing the band between songs and when he introduced me he said, "How 'bout some gospel?" He turned to the audience. "Does anyone here go to church?" And they all yell, "Yeah!" Just like a preacher's call-and-response. He said, "Well, we're going to church right now." And he introduced me. I made the B3 do that swelling sound, and I started playing "Precious Lord, Take My Hand," one of my main gospel songs. And I ended it on a kind of jazz note. We were really cooking that night. Everybody had that vibe.

Jerry has such an outrageous personality that to hear him get down with Mr. Brown on such a beautiful gospel song gave me new appreciation for the guy. That was one way I connected with my bandmates and learned what made each of them an integral, complementary member of the band. As each of them got called out during a show, I learned something new about them and their amazing talents. Of course, we spent the bulk of our time traveling and hanging out, and you can't travel the road with two dozen people packed tight on a bus without really getting to know them, one way or another. Even though everyone had given me a warm welcome, suddenly joining a score of musicians as the new boy on the block didn't mean instant camaraderie. How could it? Some people were easy to know, others took time. My first connection with someone might be during an irritating, unforeseen incident that required us to work through it. But once I managed a difficult start, I tended to really like that person. In fact, I sometimes didn't realize how much I liked someone until I'd been through an incident with them. Then I'd realize that I loved them as much as I loved all my favorite people. I had a lot of learning experiences of that nature on the road with the Soul Generals. Once I understood the personal dynamics, I could finesse things that might piss them off. I learned to recognize when I was walking on eggshells . . . and when to run.

Meanwhile, I had to step up my game onstage. I was catching on to Mr. Brown's signals and the dynamics of a performance. Some songs had established soloists and, on others, Mr. Brown was completely spontaneous about who he called out. I had to know the whole set and the other guitarist's parts in case he pointed to me. The after-hours sessions with Keith continued. No one could predict what James Brown might do on that stage. The Soul Generals needed two guitars to play James Brown's music, at least in my day. Perhaps our most famous predecessor, Jimmy Nolen, could do it all by himself. Jimmy's credited with pioneering the "chank" — aka the "chicken-scratch" rhythmic guitar sound — that helps define funk. Jimmy joined Mr. Brown in 1965 and stayed until his death from a heart attack in 1983, with the exception of two years after 1970 when James Brown's entire band quit on him. But Jimmy was a giant who cast a long shadow and his influence could still be felt in my day, almost 20 years later. As Keith and I worked together on this tour, we divided the chores for any given song. One of us focused on rhythm while the other played the signature riffs. Keith guided me. He would say, "Okay, you've got a wah-wah pedal, why don't you play this part?" He would show me how that part went — the groove of it. I might listen to the record to pick up a few extra tricks, like how Jimmy Nolen worked the wah on a particular song. Keith gave me tips on how to develop the "chank" to keep that rhythm really tight with the bass and drums. Once I got the chank, I understood its role, how its emphasis came on the downbeat of each new measure and how I couldn't rush the space before it.

HOLLIE FARRIS: Keith and Damon really had their groove going, got it locked in good. All of a sudden, here are two white boys, playing funk, and they were great. Keith could play the funk groove, but he was not a technically rocking guitarist. Damon brought a different thing. He could wail! When it came time for a solo, he'd nail it every time. They had different styles, but when they played together for James Brown, it worked.

FRED THOMAS: The only time you got a chance to really shine, to get noticed by the audience, was when Brown'd call you out to solo. He'd say, "When I give you a solo, step up. The stage is yours. It's time to shine." And Damon always shined. In living color. Damon really played from his heart and he got a great response from audiences. To me, Damon already was a disciplined musician in his own right. He fit right in. Brown could call on Damon, he could call on Keith. He had those two working together, one soloing right after the other, and that heightened the excitement of his show. Brown always pushed us to make the show more exciting. And he always said it's good to have white cats in the band because it makes audiences more receptive. I never put a lot of merit in anything like that. I'm a musician. As a musician I don't give a shit if you're pink. The question is: can you *play*, brother? And Damon could play. I liked that side of him. We had the hook up with friendship, and with music.

THE SWIM TEAM

We flew from Orleans to Paris to Tbilisi, Georgia, in the former Soviet Union, for our next gig. At that time Tbilisi was bidding to emerge from the shadows and become an internationally recognized cultural hotspot. Our gig took place at the Laguna Vere, a swimming complex originally founded to explore the benefits of training swimmers who had their arms and legs bound together, forcing them to swim like dolphins. (True story.) Laguna Vere also served as a local community pool, where the locals could cool off on hot summer days. The concert promoters set up a stage along the long side of a rectangular, Olympic-sized swimming pool, with the audience in bleachers on the opposite side. I remember a sweltering three-hour sound check in the July heat, right above a big blue pool. And I remember Mr. Brown said, "Tonight I'm going in. Y'all comin' with me?" Everyone just laughed. We all knew he couldn't swim.

Our performance went well that night. At the end of the show, we were jamming on "Sex Machine." James Brown had done everything he needed to do. He told the crowd "Goodnight!" and he took the right shoulder of his coat off, looked back at the band, like, "Y'all comin'?" Everyone's like, "Yeah, *right.*" In the blink of an eye he whipped his coat off, threw it down, took a few steps back, ran forward, and *leapt off the edge of the stage.* From where I stood, James Brown had simply vanished. The music was too loud to hear a splash. Once he jumped, he was gone, with his boots on. And he's not a swimmer. My heart sank, but not as quickly as Mr. Brown apparently did. I looked over at Keith, who kept the rhythm going despite the disoriented look on his face. Suddenly, the Soul Generals turned into first responders. Meanwhile, a guy in the audience across the pool saw James Brown sink and *he* jumped in — nice clothes, boots, the whole thing — and started making his way across this Olympic-sized pool to save Mr. Brown. Half the band kept the song going and the other half was just *gone.*

GEORGE "SPIKE" NEALY: Mr. Brown doesn't play with water. He does not swim. Zero — *zeeeero.* I told the road manager, "Please put some reflecting tape three or four feet before the end of the stage, just to give him a warning that that's the end." We go into "Sex Machine." He had this thing at shows. He'd take his jacket off, spin it around like he was going to throw it into the audience, but he'd throw it behind him. I'm thinking, "Okay, the old jacket trick." He backed up and looked up at me and I looked back at him. And when I looked again, he wasn't standing there. He was heading toward the lip of the stage. I said, "Oh, this is going to be a good trick. He's running like he's going to jump." I saw him pass the tape. I thought, "This is going to be one heckuva trick, because he's got me thinking he's going in the water, and I *know* he's not going in the water." Then he went airborne, just like the cartoons: out into the air, hung there, then straight down into that doggone pool. Good thing we had two of everything, because half the band went for him and the other half kept on playing. Amazing! He always wanted to end a show with something that caused people to walk away in disbelief and that was one of those moments.

ERIK HARGROVE: When people ask me, "What's your favorite James Brown story?" Tbilisi comes to mind. It was super hot. All I wanted to do was get in the water and cool off. I'm talking to the promoter and he said, "You know, all the acts who perform here usually jump in the pool." I'm thinking, "That's funny." When Mr. Brown came in for the sound check, I said, "Mr. Brown, the promoter says that a lot of the acts that play here jump in the pool." And he kinda chuckled. During the gig, we're playing "Sex Machine." [When] Mr. Brown ran towards the edge of the stage, everyone expected him to pull back. But he jumped. Everyone gasped. We almost stopped playing. It was like 15 feet down. At first he tried to swim the width of the pool, which was way too far. He cut to the right, where it's closer to reach the edge. Well, those polyester clothes were weighing him down. He's having trouble. So the dancers jumped in and went to help him. I thought, "This is the perfect chance for me to get into that pool." I did a flip on my way in. I'm having fun. I don't realize that Mr. Brown is actually in trouble. Sara Raya yelled, "Erik, *help us!*" So I went over, helped get him to the side of the pool. He was laughing, waving to the crowd.

JERRY "LOUIE" POINDEXTER: James Brown was no friend of no damn body of water. At his mansion in Augusta he had a yacht on a lake. But he never set foot on it. Eventually, it sank right there, at the dock. So when that motherfucker done *jumped off the stage*, I looked down. Man, from that height, he looked like a little ink spot. "Somebody help him!" I said, "Shit, it's a mighty long way down." James is down there, struggling. "Man," I said to myself, "I don't know about this shit." It was hard, man! But I dove off the stage, came up right beside Mr. Brown. I said, "Mr. Brown, it's Louie." "Oh, Louie!" I said, "I gotcha, just relax." I grabbed him from behind, across his chest — I knew that from lifeguard training. Once he relaxed, he just floated like a piece of cork. Man, it took me forever to get him to the shore. We're in a big ass Olympic swimming pool. It seemed like a hundred yards to get out of that damn thing. I sat down, I was tired as hell. I said, "Why the *hell* did you jump offa that thing?!" It just came outta my mouth. He was too tired to say anything. He was just glad to get his ass outta that water because otherwise, his ass was *gone!* When I looked up at the stage, the band was *way* up there. And the crowd thought it was part of the show! We had to get him back up on stage to finish the show. And his hair was like a wet mop on his head. Shit, you should've seen him.

HOLLIE FARRIS: The stage was *way* up there. You could hurt yourself hitting the water if you didn't hit right. He said to me, "Mr. Farris, if I jump in, are you going to jump in after me?" I said, "Of course, Mr. Brown." Because I knew there was no way on God's green earth he was going to jump in. He was deathly afraid of water. He'd almost drowned as a kid. That man never even took a shower. He had a swimming pool at his house that he never went in. There was no way he was going to jump. But, in the back of my mind, I thought, "He might just be crazy enough to do it." And sure enough, he did it. I put down my trumpet and went right behind him. He couldn't swim, but in his mind he was going to swim all the way across to the other side where the people were. By the time I got to him he had a look of fear in his eyes, like, *Please save me!* I didn't ask him why he did it. I knew why. He wanted to swim over to the audience. He was wrapped up in the audience. It was *showbiz*.

Back at the hotel, Mr. Brown threw a big party and, at first, he invited only the people who jumped in the pool. He called them the "Swim Team" and gave each of them a $200 bonus and a steak dinner. Later, he invited everyone else to come down. At this dinner, I remember walking by Mr. Brown and he said, "*Damon*, why didn't *you* jump in, son?" I said, "Mr. Brown, this is my fifth day on tour. I didn't know if it was cool to ruin the suit." He was like, "Aahhh, my *man*."

JERRY "LOUIE" POINDEXTER: Mr. Brown gave us each $200. I was like, "*Two hundred dollars?!* At least give me *a thousand!*" I could've lost my ass jumping off that stage! The next time he jumps off a stage into a pool, somebody else can go get him! $1,000 would've made me smile. $200?

That's a smack in my face! I asked him all night long. *"What* made you jump *off* that stage?! What *made* you *do* that?!" He said, "I don't know. I don't know." Well, *I* know. He was gonna kill us all, making us keep up after his ass!

WILLIE RAY "BO" BRUNDIDGE: I learned that day that James Brown would do anything to top himself. He could've taken a bow and made his exit. But he wanted to blow their minds. He almost drowned himself doing it, but if you notice his whole track record, he doesn't do normal stuff. He wanted to leave you talking. He was a genius at that. We used to do a lot of big festivals and the next day after the festival, the local media featured highlights: pictures, interviews. The question became, "Who's going to be in the paper the next day?" That became a big deal. You had all these fantastic groups, all these photographers, but only so many pictures are going on the front page. It was amazing how many front-page spreads this guy had. Not only was he on the front page, but we'd look to see who in the band was captured in the picture with him. So you made sure to get your morning newspaper, because a lot of times there'd be some nice surprises. That's what drove Mr. Brown to jump in that pool.

In fact, an item did make the local paper after the show.

> The James Brown concert was . . . tricky . . . [with] 38 people on stage and tons of equipment. Brown was pleasantly surprised that so many people had turned out to see him. The concert was incredibly lively and Brown got so into the music that at one point he threw himself into the pool. The crowd went wild! It was incredible! No one will

ever forget that concert. It really went down in history not only for Georgia but apparently for Brown as well, as he had never jumped in a pool at his own concert before!

Next stop: Istanbul, Turkey, for the Sümerbank Müzik Günleri. In the middle of the show, Mr. Brown gave Fred Thomas the nod to sing B.B. King's "Sweet Little Angel" and directed me to back him up. Well, not only is Fred Thomas a great vocalist, he's a great blues vocalist. He'd get "big house" whenever James Brown would let him sing blues. So here we are, in Istanbul, on my first tour, my sixth show, and I'm playing blues solos behind Fred Thomas singing a B.B. King tune. So Fred and I kinda had a connection right there. We were like, "My blues brother!" Fred was an original "J.B.," the band prior to the Soul Generals. He became one of my favorite people in the band. He's on more hits with James Brown than anyone else.

FRED THOMAS: Brown had a way of putting you out there. He would do stuff on a spur of the moment to test the musicians, see what they're made of. Mr. Brown could see the magic in you. And Damon had the magic. So he put Damon out there that night and Damon came out with flying colors. I thought Damon had a great sense for playing blues. It worked. The whole band was all blown away. Damon didn't know anything about me lovin' the blues, and I didn't know he could play the blues. It was a spur of the moment thing.

From Istanbul, we traveled to the Cesme Open Air Amphitheater in Izmir, Turkey, for a 9 p.m. show. Readers can be forgiven for not knowing that Istanbul-to-Izmir is a nine-hour bus ride. I think it was on that ride that Fred Thomas taught me a trick that has come in handy many times over the years. On the road, particularly in Europe, you might find yourself in possession of a few warm beers. I don't mind Europeans' taste for lightly chilled beer, but warm beer? No thanks. You've got a long day ahead on the road and a cold beer just might tip it in your favor. You might not have a fridge but you've got some ice and, possibly, a bucket. You want those beers to be cold, like, *now*. Fred's trick was to place that bottle of beer into the ice and spin it, using the cap on top. Twist it one way, then the other. Just keep it moving. In about three or four minutes, you've got an ice-cold beer. Ice cold! I learned a little science working in James Brown's band.

From Izmir, Turkey, we flew to the Côte d'Azur — the French Riviera — where we played the Arènes de Cimiez at the jazz festival in Nice, between Cannes and the Italian border. How much I appreciated my precise location at the time is hard to say. A band on the road is geared toward relaxing and enjoying the ride. We knew we were on the north coast of the Mediterranean Sea, we just weren't perusing any maps. Then it was on to the Velodromo Vigorelli, an open-air venue in Milan designed for bicycle racing. The Beatles played there in 1965. The Italian promoter of the Milan show was sketchy in the third degree. One of our singers, Kelly Jarrell, wrote in the margin of her tour book: "Slimeball . . ." We saw the Temptations perform, and we ran into Herbie Hancock in the lobby of our hotel. He was playing the same festival. Of course, some of the guys in the band knew him. Running into people of Herbie Hancock's stature and being respected as a member of James Brown's band gave me a good feeling. To this day, having worked for James Brown is a passport for respect and goodwill wherever I go.

After Milan, the tour was over. I didn't know whether I'd made the cut or whether Mr. Brown even needed another guitarist. I'd focused on the job at hand, which left little time to ponder my future. As I left the velodrome gig in Milan, I got my pay for the tour, all in cash. For a broke musician, it looked like a lot of money. I told Judge Bradley, "That was great. Whatever you guys need, I'm down!" He said, "That's all right, son. You done great, but that's it. Go on home." Basically, end of story. Three hours after we got back to the hotel after the last gig, I had to leave. The tour promoter — we called him "Mossi-mo" — was cool. He gave me a wad of lire and said, "This is not much money; don't waste it." I remember taking a cab to catch a bus to hop a train to the airport, at seven in the morning. I flew from Milan to London to New York to Vegas. When I finally got home, my girlfriend was acting squirrelly; apparently, she had "met someone" while I was gone. Everything was in chaos. I went to sleep that night dead tired and confused as hell.

COMING UP IN VEGAS

A brief backstory is in order here. My roots are in a rootless town. I'd grown up in Vegas. Isobel Donaldson, my grandmother, left her husband in Thomasville, Georgia, in 1959, and took her daughter (my mother) and son (my uncle) to Cuba, of all places. She arrived just before Fidel Castro overthrew President Batista with a little help from his friends, including Che Guevara. After the revolution, Isobel returned to the States, looking for opportunity. She headed west to Reno, stopped in Las Vegas, and stayed. Las Vegas, 1960: think Rat Pack, Elvis. The syndicate ruled. (Not that I know *anything* about *anything*, folks!) Isobel worked in the flower shop at the Tropicana Hotel on the Strip and met half the stars of the day, just selling them flowers. Elvis had her send floral arrangements to Ann-Margaret. Errol Flynn invited her to his pool parties. You get the picture. I wished I'd recorded the stories she told when I was growing up. She was matter-of-fact about her life in Vegas's heyday.

My mom's name is the coolest: "Dess." Ann deSaussure Donaldson. She met my biological father, the late Dennis Wood, in

Me, age two, with my first guitar, at home with my father, Dennis Wood, in Las Vegas, circa 1972. CREDIT: WOOD FAMILY PHOTO.

the mid-'60s, and I was born Damon La Grand Wood in December 1969. My folks have a photograph of me at age two with a toy guitar in our living room. I didn't really work at playing the guitar until I was 13 or 14, but it seems the idea took root rather early. My folks got divorced when I was three. I was a '70s kid, raised on AC/DC, Joe Walsh, Michael Jackson, the Cars, Journey — good, solid rock and a little pop. My mom got me guitar lessons when I turned eight, but this boring old jazz guy tried to teach me triads — a bit much when you're eight. A friend, Tommy Madsen, got really good on guitar. He was finger-picking Bach within a year and sight-reading. We thought, "Wow, Tommy's the *man*." That made me really want to learn to play guitar. Tommy let me and a friend, Scotty O'Neal, borrow a cheap electric guitar and showed us chromatic exercises. That got me started.

By the early '80s, we were entering the "hair band" era. I was 14 and listening to Judas Priest, Iron Maiden, KISS, Scorpions, Yngwie Malmsteen, heavy stuff. I remember catching Ozzy Osbourne with Motley Crue in concert. My mom had remarried (my stepdad is Dave Eastman) and my folks got me weekly guitar lessons for a year or so. They were so supportive of my career choice that Dave let my first thrash metal band practice in the room next to his office, with no door to protect him. At 16 I knew it was time to

Me, age 17, around the time I formed my first band, at home in Las Vegas, circa 1986.
CREDIT: EASTMAN FAMILY PHOTO.

start a band. My first, "Barrage," dealt in thrash metal. We had four originals, including "Blood Lust." You get the picture. We never played a show, perhaps fortunately for society. Then Frank Zappa and Yes began to interest me, with their intricate arrangements and lightning-quick changes, and I began to explore prog rock with a new, more mature band we called "Retinal Circus," with my friend, Hal Floyd. When acid came along my appreciation grew for Jimi Hendrix, the Grateful Dead, Pink Floyd, the Allman Brothers Band, and, by extension, Lynyrd Skynyrd and other Southern rock acts. I got my first top-quality guitar, a Les Paul custom model, because Frank Zappa's *Shut Up 'n Play Yer Guitar* album pictured him with that guitar, which featured a cherry sunburst finish set off by gold hardware. I just stared at that picture. "Man, if *that's* how he's getting those sounds . . ." (Actually, Zappa also used a Fender Stratocaster and different amps.) I knew Jimmy Page played Les Pauls; a lot of major people played them. I was like Mike Myers's character in *Wayne's World* — I had to have a Les Paul out of blind devotion. I still own that guitar.

I always knew I wanted to be a professional guitarist. Once, I got in trouble in high school, and a counselor told me, "You'll never succeed at this. Do you know how hard it is? Do you know how many musicians are working on the Strip?" And I thought, "This is not the town I intend on doing most of my performing in." Because Vegas itself is a one-trick pony. If you're a local musician, you could work with some talented people, but it's pretty rigid. It's all about the front person, often an impersonator. Only tribute bands get over. There's not much of an original music scene, at least there wasn't back then. I knew casinos weren't in my future. I already knew what I wanted to do with my life, and I'd take any job I could get until I got good enough to make money playing music. My first gig was a "battle of the bands" in 1987. We sat in our car outside The Moby Grape until three o'clock in the morning, waiting to play. I was 17.

I'd turned 20 by the time I fell in with Jimmie Van Zant. He was a cousin of the three Van Zant brothers. Ronnie and Johnny Van Zant were in Lynyrd Skynyrd and Donnie Van Zant was in 38 Special. Jimmie had grown up in that family, so he'd seen professionalism up close. And he had a lot of talent. He sounded like Ronnie Van Zant and that was his forte. We used Jimmie's name and put together a band with Steve Husson, the drummer from Retinal Circus. We were a new band in Vegas, and it was tough. At one point, Jimmie and I dropped the rest of the band and joined the rhythm section of another band. That's how I met Mike Burdett, a bass guitarist, who showed me guitar harmonies and double leads. Terry Lynn played drums and Roger McGarvie played guitar and

Jimmie Van Zant looks on as I solo.

keyboards. We went out on the road, and over five years we probably played 500 shows in 30 states. We played biker rallies, fairs, clubs. Sometimes at biker rallies we'd alternate sets with well-endowed, bikini-clad women engaged in mud wrestling. Women would flash their breasts at us from the front row. One time, we ran out of beer onstage and made the mistake of announcing that fact over the PA. *Incoming!* Full bottles of beer rained down on us. We even played the Roxy and the Whiskey a Go Go in Hollywood and the Cubby Bear in Chicago. My first gig in Colorado, which became my home in 2002, was at the Iliff Park Saloon, which for some reason paid us thousands for one night! The next two nights at the Little Bear in Evergreen paid just $100 each for the same show. I guess they call that "payin' dues."

You could probably make a B movie out of my years with Jimmie Van Zant. We traveled in a 24-foot motor home with a 12-foot trailer hitched behind. The band's backdrop was the "rebel flag" — that's the Confederate flag — which was not exactly an image with which I wanted to be associated. If anyone makes racial comments, I call 'em on it. That's how I was raised. Anyway, I got most of my early experience in Jimmie's band. We never made much money, but we worked a lot and kept getting better. Everywhere was a party, though it could get a little hairy on the road. After a gig in Pensacola, Florida. I caught a ride back to the motel with a woman who wanted to hang with Jimmie. She had a joint and someone said, "Oh, Damon should ride with you." I wasn't interested in her at all, just the joint and a ride. We jumped in her car and right off she told me, "I don't have a boyfriend." Red flag, right there. We're in a line of cars leaving the bar when someone came to her window and said in a low voice, "He's *here*." Turned out she *had* a boyfriend, there's a *situation*, and he's in the car *right behind us*. She punched it out onto the highway and he was right up our ass at 60 miles an hour. I'm puffing down on that joint, thinking it's gonna be my last. She spun the wheel and headed off on some dirt road, still doin' close to 60 mph. He caught up and started ramming us from behind, over and over. But we stayed on the road until suddenly he pulled up alongside us. I'm yelling, "Slam on the brakes!" thinking we could stop, turn around, and get away. But this guy cut us off and we both ground to a stop, with our car halfway in a ditch. He jumped out and started walking toward us. I looked to see if he had a gun. I'm thinking, I'm a dead man. She threw it in reverse, whipped it around, and hightailed it outta there. "Go back to the bar!" I yelled. And he's on our ass again. She roared into the parking lot and I jumped out and yelled at the security guard, "I hope you have a gun, 'cuz you're gonna need it!" They grabbed him and that was that. Just another relaxing ride back to the motel with a fan.

At one point, the band simply had too many miles on it. Jimmie seemed content to do the same thing over and over. I didn't want to be in a cover band all my life. It was my choice to leave and I did. We were killing it with the Skynyrd tribute, but some of us, including me, wanted more. The Van Zant thing ended in 1995 after about five years. I was 25. We'd had plenty of sex, drugs, and rock and roll, and some feuding as a result, but mostly good times. Now I had to figure out my next move.

I headed to Santa Cruz, California, with my girlfriend, but that didn't work out. Back home in Vegas, I answered an ad in the paper for a guitarist for a psychedelic rock cover band led by Mike Tuttle, who played drums and had a gift for persuasion. He called his new project "Dead Legends," and he was seeking impersonators to play Janis Joplin, Jerry Garcia, Jim Morrison, and John Lennon. I wasn't an impersonator, I'd just play guitar behind them. I thought, "I've played a lot of this stuff already. I can get this gig, if it's gonna pay." The Strip had nothing like it and I thought maybe it would pay off. During the audition I broke a string on the Doors song, "Light My Fire." I transposed the solo and played it all, note for note, with a broken string. Mike told me later, "You were hired when I saw that." The next night, this girl named Tomi Rae Hynie came in from Texas. I thought she was talented, if a bit over the top. She got the Janis part right away. The Lennon guy was good. The Jerry Garcia guy, even though I was a huge Dead fan, was not very good. And the Jim Morrison guy, well . . . he thought he *was* Jim Morrison. Vegas impersonators can get lost in the persona they're trying to be and that can be difficult for all involved. We did some low-paying club gigs and non-paying showcases that led nowhere. The Jim Morrison guy just kept talking shit onstage instead of singing his songs. One night — I think it was our last gig — I just whispered in his ear, *"Can you just sing this fucking song so we can move on with the gig?!"* And he got all pissed off. He had talent, but he was a head case. Our take on that last gig was eight dollars apiece. I left the group and it disbanded.

LEAVING LAS VEGAS

A week later I got another call from Tuttle. We'd split on good terms. Mike told me that James Brown was in town. One of his singers, Candice Hurst, was an old friend of Tomi Rae's. Candice had called Tomi Rae: "Get your ass over to the Hilton, one of the singers just quit. Sing some Janis for him. He *loves* Janis! Maybe you could get in." (Later, Mike told me Tomi Rae had *begged* him for a ride to that audition.) Mike said to me, "You know who James Brown is, dontcha?" I said, "Yeah, he's *huge*." I was bluffing. At that time I didn't have a bunch of his records. I mean, everyone knew James Brown, right? But there's a lot there to know. Beyond the hits I'd heard, I didn't know much about the man or the deeper aspects of his music. Mike said, "James Brown wants Tomi Rae to play at a pre-Grammy party in L.A. next week. She told him she's got a band. Can you play the gig?" At that point I'd heard about a lot of things that were supposed to happen that didn't happen. I said, "Give me specifics. What's this thing going to pay?" Tuttle had Tomi Rae call me. She had plane tickets, cash for tuxedos, the gear would be there, just show up with your guitar. You'll be paid; this is real. Da da da da da.

Well, we get the tuxes. There's an airline ticket booked in my name. It *is* real. At the last minute, we thought we'd better rehearse "I Got You (I Feel Good)" in case James Brown wanted to join us and do something. Like that was going to happen. We didn't know any of his songs and he wasn't planning on performing. He just had a connection with this party he was attending and he got Tomi Rae into the talent lineup. To be safe, though, we figured out a couple of his hits.

On February 12, 1998, we found ourselves at the Hollywood Roosevelt Hotel in Los Angeles. We're wearing these slick-looking tuxes with long tails and apparently we're going to meet James Brown backstage. I'm thinking, "This is heavy. I've never been involved in anything like this." James Brown came in and made the rounds. He's got the gloves, the glasses and the grease. We used to call them the "three Gs." He's got leather gloves on when he shakes your hand. Full suit, dark glasses. And the coif that defies gravity. Just bein' his funky self. All charisma, that's for sure. The room seemed to bend around him. People revolved around him. Once I'd met him, I wanted to know more about him. (One of the first things I learned: you address the man as *Mister* Brown.) We held a sound check and I remember Mr. Brown told us to keep our volume down, because there were just two small PA speakers on stage. Mr. Brown said, "She's gotta come through with her vocals. Don't play too loud." He saw we were a rock band and thought, "Let me calm these boys down. This isn't a rock show." We assured him we were hip to what he wanted. But the keyboard player had this cocky thing, "Yeah, but we gotta play loud enough to get our *tone*. We gotta have our *tone* together." I'm thinking, "Man, if this dude wants a whisper, he's getting a whisper. I don't need my tone. I need a fucking *job*!" Of course, it was up to each of us to handle the opportunity as we saw fit. If the keyboard cat wanted to be loud enough to get a certain tone, and he pissed off our patron and got fired, and I didn't play too loud and ended up sticking around, you can't say I was wrong. Ultimately, you're always trying to please the big boss, whoever that is, if you want the gig. I'd take Mr. Brown's advice. Here's a superstar brand in the music business. James Brown is The Hardest Working Man in Show Business, right? You think he's going to be a pushover? You know there will be many challenges working with this guy. I'm thinking, "Bring it," because I like challenges. I kept my volume in check during the 20-minute set and we put it over.

It was a good thing we'd done our homework, because after Tomi Rae sang her Janis tunes, James Brown jumped up on stage and called for "I Got You (I Feel Good)." We kind of seat-of-the-pants that number. I don't remember James Brown being anything but cool about it. He asked us to watch our volume. He just popped up there and we realized that he was very spontaneous that way. He'd break into things on a whim. That was part of his charm. Later, I'd see him join a hotel lounge band to sing jazz standards.

After the gig, we met up again and he talked with me a little, one-on-one. He took us all out to the Rainbow Room on Sunset Strip. We sat in a booth and Mr. Brown bought us drinks and talked with us. We were a party of seven, including Snowman, his bodyguard (former Oakland Raider Keith Graham), Tomi Rae, Mike Tuttle, singers Amy Christian and Candice Hurst, and myself. Mr. Brown asked me if I wanted a second drink. I hadn't realized yet that he didn't like a lot of drinking around him. So I got a cranberry vodka. As we got up to leave, I still had most of the drink in front of me. I thought I'd discreetly slam it, but Amy caught my hand and said, "Don't do it." It was like a test. James Brown wanted his entourage well-mannered. He was real calm, well-dressed, a businessman. If he was out in public with an entourage, he wanted their overall presentation to be professional and positive. That made sense to me. (Still, I would run afoul of this unwritten rule several years later on the road.) In the limo back to our hotel, we got the drift that James Brown was interested in Tomi Rae for more than just her singing. That's why he was cultivating her. At that time, he was 65 and she hadn't turned 30.

James Brown had been hip the whole time, and meeting him really sparked my interest in his music. When I got the $200 gig money, I spent $65 on *Star Time*, the four-disc box set of James Brown's music released in 1991. The funk and soul on *Star Time* captivated me. Being from Vegas, I'd seen fake and phony up-close and personal. I never had a desire to play anything that didn't really speak to me and make me say, "Wow, there are a million different possibilities with this music." So when I got the box set and really immersed myself in James Brown's music, I *felt* it. Here's this amazing body of work that's *killing* me, and I just met the cat. I knew instinctively that I had to get close to this individual. If I could, things would happen. I hungered for any positive career move I could make, as long as I could feel the music. An association with James Brown could open a whole new world and be a career move to boot. I figured out as many songs as I could on my own. A month passed and I got wind that another opportunity was coming my way.

On April 28, 1998, at the House of Blues in Los Angeles, we opened for James Brown and his band, the Soul Generals. We'd watched the Soul Generals rehearse and perform the night before. I'd never seen or heard anything like it: more than 20 people played full force, creating a massive sound, yet with a precision that stunned me. They ran through amazingly tight changes. Tuttle and I were in awe. After the rehearsal, I talked with Keith Jenkins, one of the Soul Generals' guitarists and my future bandmate. He was a young, white cat from Augusta, Georgia, James Brown's hometown. He was younger than me, and he had a prominent role in the band. Keith was Southern and we'd both played Southern rock, so we had all kinds of guitar stuff to talk about. I also met drummer Robert "Mousey" Thompson and guitarist Ron "Rock" Laster. The Soul Generals were operating at another level, and they were playing James Brown's music. It was enough to give a man ideas.

Jim Belushi's band had been scheduled to open that night, but James Brown had slipped us into that spot and Belushi had to open for us. My first backstage experience at the House of Blues: brushing past Jim Belushi with his shirt off, all sweaty and hairy, being cool and funny but pissy "Who are *you* and why do *I* need to open for *you*?" Belushi did his thing. We set up behind the curtains. Apparently, the audience expected the big James Brown show next.

Expectation is buzzing throughout the room. Those crazy patch-work curtains at the House of Blues parted, we played a funky little intro, bah-dah-dah-dah-dah-dah *BAH!* and . . . it's us, not James Brown. The audience excitement evaporated, instantly. That was humbling. But we overcame the moment and played a fun gig. I met Dan Aykroyd that night, and we chatted. Funny guy, as you might expect. Who doesn't love his work on *Saturday Night Live* and *The Blues Brothers*? As part owner of the House of Blues, he'd always be there when we passed through town in the years ahead. The connection with James Brown had begun when Aykroyd and John Belushi featured Mr. Brown in *The Blues Brothers* movie way back in 1980, when James Brown records weren't selling. Aykroyd sang and danced with James Brown on several occasions over the years when I was in the Soul Generals.

Apparently, Mr. Brown was happy with our set, because we opened for him on a string of four West Coast dates, from Stateline, Nevada, to Seattle, Washington. Being back on the road was a lot of fun, and being associated with James Brown gave the run pres-tige and potential. Then we didn't hear anything for a month or so. Suddenly, James Brown Enterprises announced we were going to Europe and we needed passports so that Tomi Rae and her band could open the James Brown show. A couple of band members dropped out; they just couldn't take off for Europe on a moment's notice. That's a recurring theme in the business. To be fully open to opportunity, one has to be almost completely footloose and ready to travel — despite spouses, significant others, and jobs — and to pay the price if it doesn't work out. You know I was on board.

Traveling Europe that summer with Tomi Rae's band meant riding on the Soul Generals' bus — exciting for us, not so much for them. Suddenly, they didn't have two seats to sit in or the chance to sleep. We were piling in next to them, cramming our stuff on top of theirs. But once we broke the ice, they were all real nice. Keith Jenkins said, "Yo, Wood! Sit next to me, check out these tracks I want you to hear." So it worked out and I got to know many of the Soul Generals on the long bus rides between gigs. My part in the show was easy. As the opening act, we'd do 25 minutes and, boom, we were off. We played one show in Austria and three in Italy. For an encore at our last gig in Asti, James Brown invited our bass player and me to come out and sit in with the Soul Generals. Keith and I did dueling guitar solos on "Sex Machine." James Brown knew I'd be thrilled, and he was right. I went home on a high note. He'd built camaraderie between the two bands and he knew he could count on us to back up Tomi Rae as needed.

I retained a copy of an eight-page contract rider from this period that spelled out James Brown's requirements for transportation and lodging, illustrating the distance between the life of a singing star and his entourage and the working stiffs in the band. Any promoter who hired Mr. Brown had to provide a five-star hotel with a two-bedroom "Presidential Suite," one stretch limo ("black or white, 186 inches long, current year model"), and two hot meals per day. Plus one van for luggage. A professional hooded hair dryer was required for Mr. Brown's dressing room. A baggage handler had to be available to haul Mr. Brown's luggage. He required an oxygen tank and mask onstage. "Insecticide must be sprayed in Mr. Brown's dressing room two days prior to his arrival." The stage had to be 50 feet wide by 40 feet deep. And there was a laundry list of instruments, amps, mics, lighting, etc., that had to be delivered well before show time. The rider for 1998 listed the names of 32 people, not counting Mr. Brown and his entourage or Tomi Rae and her band, which included me. So the James Brown show was akin to an army on the move and getting from A to B and putting on a tight show in well-ironed tuxedos represented a minor miracle. Suffice it to say, Mr. Brown had a lot riding on his shoulders.

When we returned home from that first tour, though, Tomi Rae's band learned that that was it. Mr. Brown — or his accountants — moved Tomi Rae into a featured vocalist spot in his show.

Suddenly, he had no need for the Tomi Rae Band. Back home in Vegas, I got a part-time job delivering posters for the casinos. My girlfriend and I had a place together, but we weren't getting along. One day, we were quarrelling and that's when the phone rang — I got "the call" from Miss Ware at James Brown Enterprises to fly to Thessaloniki, Greece, for a stint in the Soul Generals.

GETTING ON THE BUS

As you know, my first Euro tour with James Brown proved quite a trip. Mr. Brown had established that he was willing to risk drowning to please an audience — now *that's* showbiz — and he'd seen me learn his show on the fly. I'd made that wish on a blazing star above Thessaloniki, but here on Earth, Judge Bradley had sent me home with a pocketful of cash and little hope for the future. When I returned from that first tour to my girlfriend's apartment in Las Vegas, where I'd been living, I slept soundly. That's the way it was after being on the road. Returning to normalcy (whatever that is) would take a day. I'd sleep in, shed the jet lag, get my bearings back. The very next day, though, the phone rang. "Good morning, Damon, this is Miss Ware. The manager wasn't supposed to send you home. There's a gig tomorrow night in Virginia Beach." Something about a soul festival. (FunkFest in Virginia Beach is still going strong.) Domestically, things weren't right. I'd been gone, but still living at my girlfriend's apartment, and I got the call, again. What was I going to do? I took the call and headed to the airport. She said, "Damn, you're leavin' again? You just got here." What could I say? Mr. Brown's organization — and with it, a much bigger world — was calling.

I flew to Virginia Beach to find out that the landscape had changed again. My friend Keith was there, of course, and so was

Ron "Rock" Laster, a 20-year band veteran. The Soul Generals now had its two main guitarists back in place. I'd be No. 3, if anything. The pecking order was understandable. Rock had been the No. 2 guy when Jimmy Nolen had the first chair. I knew Rock when I played in the Tomi Rae Band during the 1998 tour of Europe. He's extremely funny. I always thought highly of him. He is a real funk master and he can play two, even three different parts on the guitar at the same time, and *sing*. Very talented guy. Rock missed the Euro tour because of passport problems. Over time I'd learn that band members tended to come and go — sometimes voluntarily, sometimes not — but they nearly always returned at some point. They might be gone two weeks or two years. But constant demand for James Brown's services meant steady, decent-paying work for sidemen. As a result, a constellation of players revolved around James Brown and anyone in the band who wavered could be replaced with a phone call or two. Mr. Brown made sure everyone understood that. With the Noah's Ark approach — two players for every instrument — Mr. Brown had himself covered. In Rock's case, he was already in the band and, perhaps most importantly, he knew the show. Even though the boss might be miffed at Rock for his passport problems, his getting on the bus and showing up at the gig was one way to return to the fold.

But Mr. Brown had called on me in a pinch for Europe and asked me to play in Virginia Beach, so it made sense to go. It's not like I had better things to do. After our performance in Virginia Beach, Keith said to me, "Just ride the bus back to Augusta. Don't go home. Come hang at my house. I heard about some gig comin' up next week in New York. You might be able to just jump on the bus and stay in the scene. This is your chance. You don't want to lose this, if this is what you want." To this day, Keith's encouragement, friendship, and hospitality still slays me. He is a true brother and I'll never forget that he supported my ambitions despite the uncertainties he himself faced. Augusta — home to James Brown and, of course, James Brown Enterprises — was where the most band members lived in one location. Some lived in Atlanta and the rest of us were scattered across the country. After protesting that Judge Bradley had told me to go home, I reluctantly agreed to head to Augusta with Keith.

> **KEITH JENKINS:** The thing about Damon that I learned the hard way, before I knew him well, is that he did not like to be talked into things. It became a running joke. I'd rib him, good-naturedly, about that tendency. I called him "Captain Contrary." When we finished [in Virginia Beach], Damon said, "I guess that's it. Judge told me to go home." I said, "Why don't you come down to Augusta?" Damon said, "Why would I do that?" "Well, just to hang out and . . . get on the bus." He said, "They didn't tell me to do that." I said, "Well, if you're there, they're not going to tell you *not* to get on the bus." He said, "You think?" I said, "What do you have to lose? Just come down, we'll hang out." I don't think it took too much to convince him. I did twist his arm a little bit. I said, "[Mr. Brown] likes you. We had a good tour. He likes what we're doin' [together]. You've got a much better chance of stayin' around if you just stay around."

When I returned to Augusta with Keith, we were driving in his car and the local radio station — I don't know if James Brown owned it, but he might have — was playing a tape of our performance on the European tour we'd just finished. The station played a live version of "Funk On Ah Roll" and I could hear myself in the mix. We were like, "Wow, we just did that tour and now we're on the radio." That was kinda cool and it stoked my ambitions.

The gig Keith had mentioned was set for Rome, New York, which initially meant nothing to us. I'd never even heard of Rome,

New York. Turned out, James Brown was set to open Woodstock '99. Granted, the festival was a 30th anniversary event, only an echo of the defining original, but it would be a major gig and a real scene. Hell, I didn't care. Wherever that band went, that's where I wanted to go. And it turned out Keith was right: I was on the bus with the band. The day before the gig, we rode the bus north from Augusta all day and all night. The James Brown bus was a 1983 Greyhound Eagle, like the buses you used to see on the highway, crisscrossing the country. Think about it. After nearly 1,000 miles on the road, dozing in an upright position at 70 mph for 15 hours, we got to our hotel near the festival site around 3 a.m., with a 6 a.m. lobby call. We had three hours to compose ourselves, iron our uniforms, get to the festival site and . . . wait for five more hours to perform. A nap was out of the question. I opted, as I often did, to change my strings and practice. I wasn't going to bust a string in front of James Brown, with a zillion concert-goers out there. This would be my tenth performance with the band.

At noon on Friday, July 23, 1999, we fanned out on a massive stage. The audience stretched away over the horizon, beyond our vision. I'd played a few large Euro festivals, but this was crazy. Our road manager, "Mr. Ronnie" or "RT" (Ronnie Tompkins), had tried to not spread us out too much, knowing we could have trouble hearing each other. Even with 30 musicians, singers, and dancers in our troupe, we still had almost too much room. For extra punch, Mr. Brown had beefed up the band with alumni, adding his son, Daryl Brown, on guitar, Joe Collier on trumpet, and Waldo Weathers on sax. The scale of the audience was intimidating, so I kept my eyes on Mr. Brown. Video of the performance catches me like a deer in the headlights. As with the European festivals we'd just played, the audience was predominantly young and white — a new generation of cross-over audience that perhaps had never seen Mr. Brown perform. Headliners among the nearly 100 bands scheduled to perform included a lot of "nu metal" bands as well as established acts such as

Metallica, Megadeth, and the Red Hot Chili Peppers. But first, the kids would get a solid dose of funk.

HOLLIE FARRIS: When I first started [with James Brown] it was a mostly black crowd, maybe 90 percent. That gradually started to change so that [later] the audience might be 90 percent white. A lot of times we played a festival where the kids didn't come to see him at all. They came to see whoever was on the charts at the time. But once James Brown showed up on stage, 99 percent of the time they really loved it. He'd create new fans that way.

Inevitably, the scale of an event like Woodstock '99 puts distance between performer and audience. When you're 20 feet above the crowd and chain-link fences are involved, you don't get the audience connection you get in a club. But the Soul Generals came out all business and got that sea of people moving. Danny Ray gave his characteristic wind up in an impeccable white tuxedo. Tomi Rae sang a few Janis Joplin tunes and I backed her up. The Bittersweet stepped out on a tune. Then the band fell into a vamp on "Ain't It Funky Now" as Danny Ray incited the crowd. "Aaaaaaaaaand now, it's *Star Time*! Let Woodstock '99 call the Godfather of Soul himself, Jaaaames Buh-*rown!*" The Bittersweet chanted: "James Brown! James Brown! James Brown!" Mr. Brown strode out to the mic in a glittering purple outfit and launched into "Get Up Offa That Thing." The Soul Generals two-stepped in unison. When Mr. Brown called out Jeff Watkins to solo, Jeff jumped at Mr. Brown's signal and darted for the lead mic out front. Due to the distance, he barely arrived in time to deliver the first notes of his solo. For an hour, we poured out the hits. During one of his signature ballads, "It's a Man's Man's Man's World," Mr. Brown literally stopped the show. "We want a 30-second round of silence for JFK Jr.," who'd just perished at sea in a small plane earlier that year. And when James Brown bowed his head with this request, he got his 30 seconds of silence from 200,000 partying kids. But even the Godfather of Soul's charisma could not contain the throng. When he called for a round of applause for the Kennedy family — a slightly bizarre request for the first hour of a three-day rock festival — the crowd complied only halfheartedly. But when Rock Laster hit the opening notes of Jimi Hendrix's version of "The Star-Spangled Banner" — an iconic moment from the original Woodstock — and segued into a jam based on "Foxey Lady," the crowd went berserk. Rock's opportunity to blaze, bestowed by Mr. Brown, looked like a big welcome back into the band for him. I sure dug it, but where that left me I had no idea. With Daryl on stage that day, we had four guitarists, and common sense told me I might take a backseat to the boss' son.

Some of us talked about hanging out after our set, but we bolted instead. Staying would have been insane — the day was broiling, we all had instruments and luggage and nowhere to stay. "Mr. Jesse" — Jesse Beard, the bus driver — had that old Greyhound backed up to the stage and as we finished boarding he revved it. Billows of black smoke blew right into the crowd in front of the stage. We were appalled. "Let's go! You're gassin' the kids!" And that was just the beginning of the festival, which two days later ended in anarchy and violence. I flew home to Vegas, and when I reached the apartment that night I saw myself on CNN. Meanwhile, my bandmates who lived in Augusta were still riding the bus. They didn't arrive home until dawn the next day.

Sometime after Woodstock '99, Mr. Brown left me a message on my answering machine. Naturally, I called him right back. Tomi Rae answered and she put him on the line. He said, "*Damon*, what's going *on?* Look what I'm listening to." He was playing a demo tape that Jeff Watkins, the sax player, had given him. And while the demo played in the background, Mr. Brown was in his living room playing keyboards to me over the phone. I thought, "This is *cool!*" Later, I learned something about Mr. Brown: he never told Jeff that he'd listened to that demo, yet he called me and was partyin' over how great it was. I don't think he wanted Jeff to know how much he dug it. It was up to me to let Jeff know. Anyway, Mr. Brown had called me as a gesture of encouragement. He could see I was hungry for the gig, and that I respected his direction. People always say he favored the underdog, maybe because he himself had been (and maybe in his mind continued to be) the ultimate underdog. Although I had miles to go before fully participating in his show, and my status seemed uncertain, I'm pretty sure his phone call was his way of telling me to hang in there.

JAMES BROWN UNIVERSITY

Hanging in there meant that my education had just begun. Phone calls, memos, international travel, and more stage time gradually revealed more of the dynamics of my new job.

Things went quiet for a week or so. Then the phone rang — Rock's passport problems, unfortunately for him, had provided me with another opportunity on a short tour of the United Kingdom in August. Thinking back, other factors might've been involved. Rock was a real showman and the center of attention in many situations. That's a dangerous talent when working for James Brown, who might permit his sidemen to take the spotlight, occasionally, but, as Spike mentioned earlier, we had to avoid crossing an invisible line. Apparently, much later, one of Rock's final transgressions — gyratin' onstage during a James Brown appearance on the Tom Joyner Show — got him fired for the last time. (The irony: it's a radio show, but in front of a live audience.) Rock got "caught up in the hype," as my bandmates would say. I felt for Rock, given his talents and his longevity in the band, but, ultimately, his absences boosted my chance of being accepted into the Soul Generals.

I met up with the band in Atlanta in late August, and we flew to the U.K. Our first gig of the tour was opening the Rose of Tralee Festival in County Kerry, Ireland. Mr. Brown signaled me to take a solo on "It's a Man's Man's Man's World," which I'd been working on, knowing this moment might come. Mr. Brown played it in E flat, which is a somewhat unusual key to work in for a guitarist. At this point, after a dozen gigs with Mr. Brown, I could relax a bit, enjoy my surroundings, and focus on the work at hand. During my solo, I felt poised and I developed a simple, melodic line for this slow ballad. This time, my desired tone came through. On the road, it was so hard to get a sound you liked on the often-battered rental equipment, even if it was the contractually required Fender Twin Reverb amp, whose dual 12-inch speakers typically delivered vintage tone. That night my confidence was up and I hit a few sustained notes and got just the right amount of feedback, the perfect edge of distortion on my solo. I could hear it ringing out of the big-ass PA system. That felt good. And Mr. Brown could tell I was feeling it. That night was a turning point in my confidence. Now I *knew* I could do the job. The next night we played the V Festival in Staffordshire, England. I clearly recall that gig too, for the simple reason that I was forced to go commando (i.e., no underwear) in white pants. I apologize if that's too much information, but it was a memorable evening even though I have no clear memory why I performed in front of tens of thousands of people without underwear on — possibly my luggage had gotten lost? The next night took us to Weston Park in Weston-under-Lizard. (Don't you love British place names?) We wore out those Brits one more time, then flew home. The whole tour lasted less than a week but, looking back, I'd gained confidence and, perhaps, Mr. Brown had realized that I was up to the job.

At the next gig — a one-off in Las Vegas, which was easy for me — the band received a memo from Mr. Brown, the first of several I would receive during my tenure. Looking back, I suppose my receipt of the memo might have reflected my status as an actual band member. With less than two months on the job and the guitar duties still shifting, however, I didn't feel that way. Dated August 26, 1999, the memo read: "Starting today no one will be allow[ed] to be late for the job or rehearsals. If you are late you will be terminated immediately. Thank you, Mr. James Brown." I don't remember what precipitated this memo, but I thought, "Fair enough." We soon received two more memos containing dire language. The first made sense: "We are the BEST!! We want to look the BEST!! No jeans and tennis shoes allow[ed] on the job, [or] traveling. Only at rehearsals. Violations lead to terminations. Thank you, James Brown."

The next memo had to be taken with a grain of salt, given Mr. Brown's well-documented proclivities. "IT HAS COME TO OUR ATTENTION THAT TIME AFTER TIME DRUGS ARE BEING USED AT THE VENUES. ANYONE CAUGHT WITH DRUGS WILL BE TERMINATED IMMEDIATELY. WE WILL NOT TOLERATE THIS KIND OF BEHAVIOR. THANK YOU, JBE [James Brown Enterprises]."

At some point, when I had become a full-fledged band member we received yet another memo. I couldn't locate a copy for its verbatim language, but I clearly recall the memo covered a lot of ground: it reiterated the organization's dress code and drug policy, rambled on about proper behavior while traveling, and included an admonition against telling jokes. Jokes and the laughter that went with them had been banned, according to the memo. Joking and laughing was what the band did to stay sane and to deal with the curveballs of being on the road and working for James Brown, so someone in the band immediately created a fake memo to spoof the original and circulated it, providing us all with a good laugh. So, obviously, that memo didn't get much traction with its intended audience.

In early September we flew to Buenos Aires for another week-long overseas excursion. We played two sold-out nights at the 8,000-seat Luna Park soccer stadium in Buenos Aires. I don't remember much about the trip. Flying overseas, taking a bus to a gig, then playing a "90" — a 90-minute set — is out of this world. We were dog-ass tired. The amazing thing was, though, that no matter how tired or sick I felt — if I thought I might puke or not be able to play the show — when I walked onstage the energy made me forget everything else. After our performance in Buenos Aires, I got word from R.J. that a young woman wanted to meet me. When I arrived at his room, he was working on a steak in his bathrobe and two local women were hanging out. One seemed to be with R.J., while the other one invited me back to her apartment. But she mentioned in broken English that she owned seven cats, and I decided that might be six too many. The next night we stayed in town and, equipped with all-access passes, got to listen from backstage to Yes, the British prog-rock group. They put down a killer set to a sold-out audience. As Steve Howe came off stage, I called out, "Good show!" to one of my guitar heroes. We moved on to play the Olympia Theater in Sao Paulo, Brazil, but another gig scheduled for Santiago, Chile, was canceled due to poor ticket sales. I knew that many of the countries we traveled in — just like the United States — had haves and have-nots. But traveling with a touring band meant we were in a bit of a bubble. We were tightly scheduled, traveled by plane or chartered bus, and stayed at good hotels, so we didn't see the nitty-gritty side of South American cities.

Back in the U.S. we played the venerable Fox Theater in Detroit for an older crowd. This was a heavy place where James Brown had a lot of history. The Fox is a particularly sumptuous venue — you have to see it to believe it. I found out later it had opened in 1928, just before the great stock market crash, billed as a "Temple of Amusement," part of the Fox movie theater chain of the Roaring Twenties. Today the Fox holds 5,000 concert-goers and remains one of Detroit's crown jewels. In my time with James Brown, we played quite a number of historic venues akin to the Fox in other American cities. At the Fox gig, Mr. Brown stepped away from the microphone and had the band break it down so low that he sang "Prisoner of Love" to a full room without amplification. The audience hung on every word, spellbound, as the band comp'd behind him at whisper level. That's how quiet that band could go. I began to understand the deep bonds that James Brown had forged with his audiences over the years and how simple dynamics could foster that sense of intimacy. He could take the energy to a peak, but then he'd break it down to the shortest distance between his soul and the soul of every single individual in the room. To make that connection, he needed absolute control over his band and their dynamics, and the band willingly gave him that control. (In fact, if you couldn't play at a whisper, you didn't get the gig.) Mr. Brown told me directly, even before I was in his band: "Do you know how your stereo goes from 1 to 10? Well, my band goes from 1 to 100." The Soul Generals could play loud or soft at any little notch and up and down a carefully calibrated scale of dynamics. Now that I was playing in the band I learned the truth. We could, and would, take it down to a whisper, so that Mr. Brown could sing unaided and connect with his audience. And then we'd take it up to the peak again. So you had zero to 100, right there. It wasn't just about volume, of course. When Mr. Brown wanted a whisper, every musician's approach to their notes — the "attack," as it's known — became gentler, softer. James Brown loved that power and his art depended on it. He knew how to make it so funky you just had to dance, and he knew how to take it down and confess his heart and soul until you felt the need, too.

KEITH JENKINS: We played a lot of really nice theaters. We did the Paramount in Oakland, the Paramount in Seattle, the Apollo in Harlem, the Fox in Detroit, the Wang in Boston. Those places were cool. But because some of

those rooms were [originally] designed for opera, they
weren't that great for a big band with a loud PA. They
were designed for unamplified sopranos to be heard
in every corner of the room. You could easily be too
loud in a room like that, and that played right into Mr.
Brown's hands. No matter where we played, the thing
that cracked me up was, there was always a reason not
to play loud. Mr. Brown would say, "You see this room?
Y'all don't have to play loud in here." He'd say that
whether you were in a club or an arena! "Y'all don't
have to play loud in here." I thought, "Well, when *is* it
okay to play loud?!"

Of course, Keith is joking — kinda, sorta. As musicians we
understood that James Brown's stagecraft required him to hear his
own voice in performance, regardless of the venue. In all my years
with him, he never used floor monitors — the speaker wedges at the
base of the main microphone that deliver the singer's voice back to
him so he can hear it above the band. Instead, Mr. Brown based his
perception of how his voice and the band were going over on the
sound of the house PA, as speakers on each side of the stage filled
the room with sound. In later years, he also had "side fills" — PA
monitors on either side of the stage pointing at the band — which
also helped the band hear his voice, all the better to lock in on. I
think he just wanted a clear, powerful signal from his microphone
that wouldn't feed back, as monitors sometimes will. With the band
playing at the right volume, in support of the singer, he'd hear his
voice come back from the room itself. This forced the band to be
sensitive to his every gesture, because he might take a song down
from high energy to intimacy with the flick of his hand. If he had
trouble hearing himself sing, he'd keep breaking us down, down,
down, until the volume felt right and he was comfortable singing
over it. Our amps would be aimed toward his microphone from the

sides of the stage, so with just a little gesture he could regulate both guitar players' volume while singing straight at the crowd. He'd let us know which part he wanted louder, which instrument he wanted louder. Maybe he heard everything more clearly because he didn't have floor monitors shooting his voice back at him. As players in the band, however, we couldn't always hear everything just right. Our road manager, RT, strove to get a consistent set-up wherever we performed, but each stage was different. We could be in an intimate theater like the Fox in Detroit or we could be on a festival stage, with little or no natural acoustics to work with. I'd often be situated near Mousey, who played drums on the bulk of the set in my time, and watching his snare hits helped me time my rhythm playing.

Still, I really couldn't afford to take my eyes off Mr. Brown for more than a split second. To prove myself I had to "learn the show," a phrase with multi-layered meanings. On one level, that meant learning dozens of songs, both the hits and the B sides. It meant being familiar with the other band members' parts, to know who did what and when. Then there were what I called the "bits," the most musically demanding passages in a performance. These were "head" riffs, percussive accents, segues, endings — short, sometimes staccato bursts of notes, matched to rapid drum hits. The bits, and the way Mr. Brown signaled them, was a deeper layer in learning the show. To maintain or punch up the excitement he'd signal us to play one of these bits. Learning the show meant understanding, even anticipating, his vast repertoire of vocal cues, hand gestures, and body language that told us what he wanted at the precise moment he wanted it. And two dozen players had to simultaneously deliver it. Some patterns emerged, certainly, but a James Brown performance was his to create every night and we hit the stage without set lists or expectations. The bits added razzle-dazzle to the proceedings and offered Mr. Brown the means to change direction or pump up the show's dynamics on the fly. If you watch a video of James Brown and his band in performance from any era, you'll see what I mean.

He could redirect us to the chorus or verse of the song we were playing or he could signal another direction entirely. An important move, that we used consistently, was to return to a segue riff, or "bit," that gave us a moment to go anywhere. He'd time it perfectly. The band would hit a da da da, dut, dut, dat dut dut daaa! And it would give him a moment to decide where to go next. To milk the moment, he might point one arm to the side for us to play an ascending riff, da da da *dat*! The band would stop on a dime and the crowd would go crazy. We could go anywhere from there. At that point, Mr. Brown might point to Keith or myself and that usually meant we were going into "Doing It to Death." And off we'd go, havin' a funky good time.

Mr. Brown directed these bits on stage, but he didn't author all of them. Often his band leader or another arranger in the band would create them. In the past that was often Fred Wesley Jr., who wrote a great book on his lifelong experiences as an arranger and sideman, including his time with James Brown titled, *Hit Me, Fred: Recollections of a Sideman*. Another bit was called "T.J.," written by Tyrone Jefferson, who played trombone and created arrangements for Mr. Brown in the 1970s and '80s. (Naturally, as with most alumni of the James Brown organization, Tyrone rejoined our troupe as band leader on occasion.) Our percussionist Spike wrote a great intro that James Brown employed for years. (Spike was a good example of the amazing talent in the Soul Generals. He's featured as one of the music teachers in the movie *Drumline*, about the great drumming corps at historically black colleges in America and their annual competition.) Spike wrote a killer intro with a Da-da-da-ding! Da-da-da-dah! Bom-bom-bom-bom! It's James Brown–esque but unique and original. It incorporated bits of James Brown's hits and led into his opening song, "Make It Funky." Spike's bit would climax with the singers going, "Aaaaah, make it funk-ay!" — a chant they would continue until Mr. Brown came out and took the spotlight. I once wrote out all the bits in an effort to become intimately familiar with each, so I'd never be caught off guard. I think I counted more than 60 songs and dozens of bits that I had to learn. To this day I still have that cheat sheet. Just the simple act of writing them out helped get my mind around what could have been an overwhelming challenge. Plus, these bits were often fast intricate riffs with abrupt accents that were sometimes intensely percussive. There was no room for error, or you and your guitar would be left hanging out there on your own with the band looking at you. I did not want to be that guy. So, to "learn the show," I had to be ready for anything — obscure songs, covers, mysterious hand signals, subtle body language, those intricate "bits," you name it. Every show had a new twist.

To emphasize his primacy in this complex picture, Mr. Brown took me aside early on and said, "You can't really learn my show. You have to be *taught* it." He meant that I could study his records to learn the correct keys and chord changes and signature riffs and learn all the bits, but that did not mean I could perform his music to his satisfaction. Only spending time on stage, focusing on Mr. Brown's direction, soaking up how he delivered his moves and how the band anticipated them and acted as one in response could help me complement a performance. Surprises were to be expected. He would command changes to the existing arrangement for a song while we were playing it on stage. He had to feel the music to perform it, and if he didn't feel it he'd change things up right there and then until he *did* feel it. And he'd directly interact one-on-one with most of the musicians on stage — sometimes face-to-face — to get *that* feeling. James Brown never phoned it in the whole time I was with him. I don't think he was capable of faking it. He was a master showman and he knew how to pace a show and put it over. I couldn't help but take this all in as I learned — that is, as I was taught — the show. The method was osmosis, soaking it up.

ROBERT "MOUSEY" THOMPSON: It was on-the-job training [when I joined]. At that time, Arthur Dickson played drums

— God bless him, he passed. That first year, I'm not playing a thing! I'm like a football player, ready to come in. Mr. Brown told me, "Son, it's going to be a little while before you play with us. You gotta learn the show." He knew what he wanted and he knew how to present a show. We sometimes questioned what he was asking for, because he'd take you places you never thought you'd get into. But people loved his shows.

Personally, I wasn't questioning anything quite yet. But I remember early on during a rehearsal, Keith — who'd studied James Brown's recordings in detail and knew the keys, the changes, and the riffs like no one else, including Mr. Brown — led a song just as it was played on the record. Mr. Brown stopped everyone and demanded an explanation. Keith calmly said, "We're in G, just like on the record." Mr. Brown snapped: "They cut it wrong." So learning the show also meant deferring to the boss, whether he was right or wrong. Of course, as the boss, he was right even when he was wrong. No matter how crazy his logic, you didn't question him. Keith's response was the right one: it was best to state your case and let him correct you. If James Brown wanted you to play a certain way, you played that way. Understandably, he wanted you to morph your strengths to suit his music and his way of playing his music. As you changed your style to suit his purposes, however, you could lose your footing, your instinct for where to go and how to play in the heat of battle. Later, he'd ask you, "What happened to all the things you had when you came here? What happened to all that *fire?*" More than once he told me: "Y'all done lost your *thing*, man! What happened to your *style?!*" I thought, "Well, *you* made me stop playing like that!" But I held my tongue. He just wanted me to take what I had before and fit it into his music. The pressure to complement his music made me an infinitely better player, but it also pulled me out of my comfort zone where confidence could propel a clean, thoughtful run of notes. And, to be sure, there were times when nothing was good enough to please Mr. Brown. We could be the baddest band in the world, but he'd tell us: "Y'all just really can't play this funk." He meant everyone in the band, including 30-year veterans.

Comments like that might sting, but James Brown looked at himself as Coach Carter — the tough guy who pushes you to be your best. He might have seemed like a hard-ass at the time, but he really tried to offer something deeper than most stars would. He took an interest in new players and he knew how to cultivate talent. As the boss, he wanted the most he could get out of every player in his service. So he made sure you knew what he wanted from your playing. And to get the best performance from the entire band, he'd use every psychological trick in the book: divide and conquer, intramural competition, the works. He'd put you and another guy on the same instrument into direct competition. Just before a show, he might casually say, "So-and-so cut you last night." He did it to motivate people. A little comment like that might fire you up. You'd go out wanting to play that show so tight that he'd think, "No one's ever played my show that tight." Not that he'd ever say that. Sometimes during rehearsals he'd praise you in front of the band and you had to gracefully acknowledge the compliment, all the while wondering if he was setting you up, making your colleagues resentful. In front of an audience, he was always gracious and professional and called your name after you soloed. That could be heady. Over time, though, the boot camp approach — break 'em down then build 'em up to serve the James Brown mission — had another, perhaps unintended, effect. As I learned to play his music to meet his demands, I also found myself further developing my own personal musical identity. Playing Mr. Brown's music the way he wanted it played started me thinking that someday I'd play my own music just the way I wanted it played. It took a while, but, in time, I began writing my own songs and developing my own sense of how to put them across. It would be years before I fully understood how playing James Brown's music had led me to playing my own, but a seed was planted early on and it grew.

ACCEPTANCE

By the fall of 1999, I'd been with, if not "in," the band for four months and played more than 30 gigs. The band had more or less accepted me as I dedicated myself to the Soul Generals and the show. And it seemed like I'd made the grade in Mr. Brown's eyes. By this time, Rock Laster was in and out of the band, and Keith and I formed the most consistent guitar lineup. I'd certainly received the memos on band behavior, and I began to receive the tour itineraries and stacks of airline tickets that marked the advent of each tour. Apparently, I had become an employee of James Brown Enterprises, but it dawned on me that there would never come a moment when I'd be declared an official member of the Soul Generals. There'd be no congratulations, no induction ceremony, no contract, no nada. To the contrary, holding down your spot in James Brown's band was a tightrope walk without a net. You delivered or you fell to your demise. Possibly, you could deliver and still get pushed from your perch. In fact, in the past Mr. Brown had at times abruptly fired a number of his longest-serving musicians for no apparent reason, sent them into exile, then rehired them weeks or months later. Of course, no further upward movement was possible. Certain trusted band members had been designated as band leaders, but they too came and went with an alarming degree of regularity. The only possible movement from your chair in the band was down and out. I had the job and it was mine to lose. I'd earned only the opportunity to continue to prove myself. There'd be no nameplate on a bus seat, no name tag in a uniform, just opportunities to shine or tumble from the heights.

Despite this rather tenuous existence as a member of the Soul Generals, the band's core members remained pretty stable throughout my own tenure, a remarkably long time in James Brown's universe. At this point in his career, I think he looked for team players and, when he found them, he'd take them under his wing. He knew from experience that sidemen could get big egos and visualize themselves on their own. He'd seen his share of bands get big heads and leave him. In my era, team players were important to him. I think he saw that in me. I was ready and able to take his advice. He was loyal to people, too. If they returned that loyalty, they might have a long, if at times tumultuous, career with him. I think Fred Thomas might have been with the band 30 years when I joined. Yet, as events will show, anyone could be the target of Mr. Brown's wrath, despite exemplary service. The boss took charge, as in most jobs, I suppose.

As an employee of James Brown Enterprises, I had a few practicalities to address, like getting paid, riding the bus, and keeping my guitar together. I still have a payroll sheet from a one-off gig in fall 1999 that has seemingly innocuous, standard entries marked "Date," "Venue," "Social Security No.," "Salary," "Loans," "Terms," "Fines," "Amt Rec'd/Misc," and a spot for a signature. But nearly every category comes with a story.

The category marked "Salary" remained elusive. To this day, none of us know how much money the others made, except me and Keith. (As you'll see, that came about for the wrong reasons.) Players who'd been with Mr. Brown a while seemed to be making pretty nice money. I minded my own business. Mr. Brown probably had a separate deal with each and every band member based on their relationship and history, and perhaps longevity in the band. Mr. Brown always paid me well. (If you overlook the sporadic, organization-wide pay cuts that sometimes popped up.) In

Thessaloniki, when I started, he told me the average base starting pay and — maybe because I flew in on a moment's notice and was able to handle the gig — he started me at a nice little chunk above that. In fall 1999, three or four months into my tenure, I received another bump in salary. Looking back, that was probably the most tangible sign that I'd landed the job.

"Fines" have a long and notorious history in traveling bands, and James Brown had a hand in making that a fact. When James Brown began leading his own band in the 1950s, he used fines to exert total control over his sidemen. Back in the day, each band member paid for his own motel room and meals. If a guy in the band was making, say, $200 a week, he might spend most of it just staying alive on tour. In my time, it was band lore that Mr. Brown fined his people with alarming regularity. In fact, fines might have figured into his business plan to, say, reduce overhead, like salaries. The alleged transgression might be hitting a clunker note or some perceived infraction in on-stage behavior. On a tour, a few fines could rapidly eat up a man's take-home pay. If James Brown picked on someone using fines as punishment, they might want to quit, but they wouldn't be able to afford to get home. So they'd have to cadge meals and floor space off their bandmates until their fortunes improved. Band lore had it that not a few players returned home penniless after touring for weeks. Those dark tales of the early days made my time seem rosy, at least financially. In my time with the band, fines were no longer used like a blunt instrument. In fact, they'd become pretty rare. First of all, Mr. Brown had two of everything. If he had a real problem with you, he'd just fire you. Still, fines did happen on occasion. If you made an obvious mistake during a performance, he'd wheel around, look right at you, and open and close his hand rapidly to signal $5 increments. If he flashed his hand five times, you owed him $25. I received the dreaded hand signal a few times, but it turned out to be more of a warning because he never took it out of my pay. So, at that point, it was symbolic, more like, "I gotcha! Now keep your shit together!" But the fact that "Fines" remained a category on the payroll sheet served as a regular reminder that Mr. Brown could levy one if he was so inclined and spoke volumes about the business we were in and who we worked for.

I saw this punishment in action when Mr. Brown took umbrage at what he called someone's "monkey shines." One night at Heinz Hall in Pittsburgh, in November 2000, Jimmie Lee Moore had a long cable for his bass guitar, and he was hot-doggin' around the stage during "Sex Machine," our last song of the night. He was having too much fun and he got kinda outrageous. Jimmie Lee was kinda outrageous anyway and everyone loved him for that. But every stage belonged to James Brown and, in his eyes, Jimmie Lee got caught up in the hype that night. *Bam!* Mr. Brown levied a $500 fine on the spot, a very heavy hit. It must have been delivered verbally; that'd be a lot of hand signals. RJ came to the dressing room afterwards: "Bench warrant for Jimmie Lee Moore — the king wants to see you." Jimmie Lee went to Mr. Brown's dressing room and apologized, and Mr. Brown reduced the fine, but apparently the boss felt he had to take something from Jimmie Lee to teach him a lesson. The worst-case scenario was to be sent home without pay, which happened to Jerry Poindexter before my time. As Jerry recalls, this backfired, big time, on Mr. Brown.

JERRY "LOUIE" POINDEXTER: Early on he sent me home one time
without my pay. I had to have my mother send for me.
I was a grown-ass man, 23, 24 years old. My mother
didn't give a shit who I worked for. "You get paid," she
told me. "Don't let anyone use you. Ever." Mr. Brown
called my house, probably to tell me to come on back.
My mama said, "Give me that damn phone." She cussed
Mr. Brown's ass out! I raise my right hand to God,
may he strike me dead. My mama said, "Who is this?"
"James Brown." "Well, let me tell you something, Mr.

Brown. If you ever use my son and make him play and don't pay him, you're going to be dealing with me. You don't call here until you pay my son every copper penny and nickel you owe him." And she hung up on him. I said, "Oh, there goes my career . . ." An hour later the phone rang. It was Miss Ware, with James Brown Enterprises. "We want to let Jerry know he can pick up his money at Western Union." And he quit messing with me. Two weeks later, I'm back on tour, we're playing in Cleveland, Ohio, at the Front Row, not far from Youngstown, where I grew up. I wanted Mr. Brown to meet my mother. He said, "No, no. I got to stay away from that." My brothers and sisters came up for the show, but she wouldn't go. But I told Mr. Brown my mother had arrived with them. He said, "No, no. I can't see her." He didn't want to meet no real people who would cuss his ass out!

The payroll category "Loans" referred to any "draws" we received before or while on tour. Being from Las Vegas, I have to say that "Loans" is a loaded term, and it reveals another angle on working for James Brown Enterprises. If we'd been off work for a while and just jumped on a lengthy tour and we wouldn't be getting paid for a while, Hollie Farris, the bandleader, would tell the road manager, "Hey, the cats need a draw." We might receive $100 or $200 each against our payday at the end of the tour. While the organization in my day covered travel, accommodations, and, often, food, we still needed spending money on the road. After a show we often went out to get a meal, chill out, and mingle with the locals. Typically, dinner was provided for the band a couple of hours before the gig, to ensure the musicians could perform. Breakfast might be in the promoter's contract as well, but if we'd hit the hay around, say, 4 a.m., then we'd miss a meal. We'd be starving after a show. So we always needed a little cash just to handle a tour. On long tours in expensive foreign countries, a series of draws could eat up a chunk of your paycheck before you got it. So the "draw" was a necessary evil.

Early on in my tenure, the band got paid in cash after a tour or a one-off gig. That seemed a bit old school. The tour manager — i.e., the "bagman" — would be the paymaster. I don't pretend to know how these things work, but it seems that in the old days, touring bands and the venues they played operated on a cash basis. Inevitably, large caliber guns were involved. The artist would be paid in cash before the performance. Someone would have to babysit the cash through the gigs, run payroll, pay expenses, and transport the proceeds all the way back to Mr. Brown's "bank" in Augusta. (I put "bank" in quotations because Mr. Brown was famous for operating on a cash basis.) On paydays, typically the end of a tour, we'd line up at the tour manager's hotel-room door to get cashed out. That might be Judge Bradley or Mr. Charles Bobbit — though I hesitate to group their names together; Mr. Bobbit was first class, in my eyes. The paymaster would call names. Each of us got an envelope and a pay-roll sheet. As we walked out past the line, we would smile a knowing smile at our bandmates. Our unspoken thoughts were basically the same: "Hey, we're workin' *and* we're gettin' paid! Ain't life grand?"

My main concern as a responsible employee of James Brown Enterprises was getting myself and my guitar to where we needed to be. At first I traveled with two guitars, concerned about the vagaries of travel and the risk of a guitar malfunction. That only made sense. Most touring musicians bring backup instruments. What if something happened to my guitar over the course of a multi-week, 10,000-mile tour overseas? But managing two guitars and a small suitcase proved unwieldy. Soon I was down to one guitar and a bit of nagging low-level anxiety. At first I kept my Les Paul in a big flight case and I'd have to check that as luggage — I couldn't carry it on the plane with me. As I toured more, I realized I had to bring a guitar that I could fit into the overhead bins so my one instrument never left my side. But a guitar in an overhead bin might get slammed around. With the Les Paul (as with Gibsons in general), the head-stock angles back from the neck, and if something gets forced into the bin on top of that, the neck can snap. In that sense, a Fender Stratocaster is better because it lies flat. I used a soft gig bag instead of a hard case so it would fit more easily into an overhead bin. I really couldn't afford to let that instrument out of my sight. My job depended on arriving at the gig with a working instrument. But sometimes I had to gate check it. I'd plead with them. "I play for James Brown and I'll get fired if anything happens to that guitar!" Jimmy Page famously had one of his favorite Les Pauls stolen in an airport because it left his sight and went through the baggage system. I had to consider these things. I'd fly halfway around the world with my one guitar and a change of clothes, meet up with the band and off we'd go for a couple of weeks. After a while I didn't even bring guitar tools. At first, I'd take a few wrenches, in case something went wrong, and wire cutters for stringing my instrument, but they'd all be confiscated at the first security check, especially after 9/11. Before I left home I'd try to make sure every nut and screw was tight. If anything happened in London or Paris or Munich or Barcelona, I might find an electric guitar technician to help. Tbilisi, Georgia? Not so much. Miraculously, in seven years and hundreds of thousands of miles traveled, I never experienced a major problem.

HAVE GUITAR, WILL TRAVEL

In fall 1999, we performed two shows at the gorgeous Paramount Theater in Seattle, and a month later, in mid-November, we did a one-off at the Maritime Hall in San Francisco. The sheer variety of venues we were playing gave me a lot of experience and made the job more fun. On a James Brown tour, we would play big festivals, tiny clubs, and ornate theaters in America and Europe. Casinos and the House of Blues in the U.S. were our bread-and-butter gigs. In fact, casinos all over the world kept us working, and not too hard, actually. A typical James Brown performance might be 90 minutes, but the casinos that wanted the most exciting entertainment brands to dazzle their customers would typically want only 45-minute sets, maybe an hour tops, so the gamblers would return to the tables. Apparently, hiring James Brown and his 30-plus piece traveling troupe to perform for an hour cost peanuts compared to the house take on a night of gambling.

KEITH JENKINS: Touring with James Brown, you weren't confined to any one thing. Some bands go out and play an arena tour. Some bands do a club tour. Some do a theater tour or a festival tour. Our tours would be all that — you'd do a festival, then you'd do an arena, a theater, a club, a hotel ballroom, a casino, all in a given week. It was never the same venue over and over again. We'd go to Italy and play in a field! They'd put up a stage on the side of the road. Once we played on a $60 million yacht for a sheikh in the Mediterranean Sea. The sheikh said, "I want James Brown to play on my boat." We worked out a quick deal and the next day we played on this dude's boat, a private show right on the water for a few hundred people. That was a trip. If something wasn't cool, you'd say to yourself, "Okay, tomorrow will be something totally different."

Keith's right — whatever kind of night we had, the next day we'd be on the road to a new city and another gig. The possibilities seemed endless. The Soul Generals traveled with their instruments, a change of clothes, and little else. Drummers brought only their sticks, a snare drum, maybe a few cymbals. Everything else — drums, amplifiers, microphones, the PA system — was the promoter's responsibility, whether we were in New York City or French Guiana. Sometimes a promoter would have to obtain the contractually required gear from a sound company in another country hundreds or thousands of miles away. Or slip us the equipment they *could* obtain. On one gig in Turkey, I didn't get the Fender amp that provided a clean sound and, instead, the promoter had only a Crate Red Knob amp that was missing some of the knobs. With all due respect to Crate, their amps do not produce the fine, vintage tone of a Fender Twin Reverb that fit Mr. Brown's show. We never knew what to expect when we arrived for a gig in out-of-the-way places. One time, in French Guiana, I got a horrific burst of nasty distortion coming through my amp in the middle of a song. James Brown wheeled around with "the look" on his face and hissed, "*Somebody kill his amp!*" I thought I needed a new amp but RT said, "They don't have another amp. You'd better change the battery in that wah pedal and hope that's it." Fortunately, and to my embarrassment, that *was* it. Looking back, how could anyone expect a promoter in French Guiana to have two Fender Twin Reverb amps (one for Keith, one for me), let alone a spare? We'd get into places and be aware on some level of the poverty or the off-the-beaten-track nature of the place and how difficult it must be to get proper equipment shipped there. We simply couldn't expect uniform quality gear everywhere we went. And we went everywhere. Many, if not most, top international acts would have roadies toting all their own equipment, everywhere, just so they could reliably produce a uniform quality show with no surprises. That was not the case with James Brown Enterprises. That's not a criticism, by the way. I respect the fact that the show came together with amazing consistency no matter where we went, and I am grateful to have been involved. It's just worth observing that, even in the 21st century, the James Brown gig was a real old school, fly-by-the-seat-of-our-pants production.

That extended to personnel. On the road we had RT, our every-thing man, or, at least, our man who attempted to do everything. Except for a couple of brief stretches, we brought no dedicated soundman, and we never had instrument technicians or equipment roadies. You might think that a global superstar with a relentless schedule of high-profile gigs and endless road dates might invest in some help, but, in the case of James Brown Enterprises, you would be wrong. It's simply amazing how, despite the odds, things seldom went wrong. Mr. Brown's approach worked, though I'm sure it took a toll on RT. I'm tempted to believe that it did work because Mr. Brown had supreme confidence that it *would* work.

I make our domestic travels sound quite simple, at least on paper: Detroit, Albuquerque, Houston, Seattle, San Francisco. No big deal, right? Well, domestic tours often strung together distant des-tinations just days apart on the schedule, which meant riding the James Brown bus all the way. Consider, for a moment, this ancient practice. Back in the day — which is to say the 1930s, '40s, '50s, and early '60s — a small band of black musicians traveling the Chitlin' Circuit would all cram into a car or two and head out for weeks on end. Same with white rock 'n' rollers in the 1950s and '60s. Big name bands might ride in buses, for prestige but also for efficiency's sake. Only the biggest names in entertainment could manage such an expensive luxury. You can get a sense of the prestige from con-temporary publicity photos that captured a band leader and his men standing alongside their fabulous transportation, with the star's name emblazoned on the bus's side. In his autobiography, *Blues All Around Me*, B.B. King recounts his rise on the Chitlin' Circuit and how he'd finally become popular enough to maintain a large touring band, which necessitated the financial risk of getting a bus for the road. Today, top touring musicians often travel in luxurious motor coaches, outfitted with private rooms and the latest com-forts, primarily because it's more reliable, comfortable, and private than flying. The James Brown bus I rode was a throwback to the old days, and the practice appeared to be focused on economy alone, if you catch my drift. It wasn't dilapidated, but it was a 20-year-old Greyhound Eagle, an aging version of those buses you still see hammering down the big interstate highways, which is precisely what we did in ours. Most of the band lived in Mr. Brown's hometown of Augusta, and they had to ride that bus everywhere but across the Atlantic Ocean. Those of us who lived elsewhere hopped a plane and met the troupe at the first gig, where we joined the bus ride. Our driver was an Augusta-area gentleman, Jesse Beard, who we referred to as "Mr. Jesse." Danny Ray told us that when we traveled the Continent — which meant Mr. Jesse wasn't working — Mr. Jesse would poke a pin in a voodoo-doll version of our Euro bus to make us break down. (We did have a few mechanical problems with that Euro bus, leading Danny Ray to swear the curse was real.)

In the fall of 1999, the band rode from Augusta, Georgia, to Detroit, Michigan, an approximately 900-mile ride that took a solid 12 hours. I flew from Las Vegas to Detroit and grabbed a seat on the bus, reuniting with bandmates after a break. We played the gig and got back on the bus and rolled to Albuquerque, New Mexico — more than 1,500 miles and 24 hours away. From Albuquerque we headed to Houston, burning up another 900 miles. At the end of that short tour, I just hopped on a plane for Las Vegas. But Augusta-based band members, who'd already logged about 3,300 miles, still had another 1,000-mile ride to get home. Don't get me wrong. Riding the James Brown bus with your bandmates could be a lot of fun, and we certainly made the best of it, but travelling thousands of miles over the course of a week or so could have a major influence on your state of being, as my colleagues will testify.

ERIK HARGROVE: We learned early on that the bus *was* the gig. We would get on the bus in Augusta and drive anywhere in the United States. We could go from

Augusta to Seattle, rattling on for three days. The truck stops became a Pavlov's dog thing. Whenever the bus stopped, it was time to eat, and stock up for the trip, because we didn't know when we were stopping again. Most of us would gain a few pounds before we hit the gig. That was especially hard on the women in The Bittersweet, having to fit into their tailored dresses. Sometimes the bus driver was told to drive slower, so we didn't get to the hotel too early and cause the organization to pay for an extra day's stay. That meant we were on the bus longer than we needed to be. Also, Mr. Jesse, the driver, could not read a map. People in the band would read the map for him. Plus, we had to make sure Mr. Jesse stayed awake. At night somebody in the band always stayed awake with him. Anytime there was a little jerk in the wheel, everybody's head would pop out into the aisle to see what was going on. God was with us on that bus. These things affected us before we even hit the stage. If we had to go straight in off the bus, do the sound check, do the gig, it was hard to keep level, to give a great performance. Yet you still had to, because James Brown demanded it. And James Brown did not want to hear anything about that bus. "Just do your job." That was it. You got on the bus and rode to the gig, or you didn't. There was just that one bus and it came from a little bus company in a little town outside of Augusta. That was James Brown's tour bus, which James Brown did not travel on.

JIMMIE LEE MOORE: I rode the bus. I was one of the ones who did not like it. I'll just be transparent. I did not like that bus. That bus was unsafe. Sometimes the air conditioning would go out in the middle of the desert. Or the heat would go out when you were freezing. It was a hazard, an accident waiting to happen. It was just crazy. Man, I hated that bus. Because I lived in Miami, Mr. Brown would fly me in, because I just refused to ride that bus. I said, "No. Oh no. I'm not going to do that." I was on that bus when the brakes went out on the curve coming down outta Lake Tahoe. I thought I was going to die. *No brakes?!* I'm like, "This is it! I know I'm not going to see my mom again." So I'd start prayin'. We scraped the wall till the bus stopped. Lake Tahoe is tied to the clouds, you know what I mean? If you lose it, you're gone. Ain't no sense in even lookin' for ya. That happened more than one time. Hey, I've been in that bus when a tornado turned it upside down. I woke up upside down with state troopers around us. I hated that bus. However, Mr. Brown was not moved by complaints about the bus because he didn't ride it. [*Laughs*]

KELLY JARRELL: In 1995, two days before we were to record the third *Live at the Apollo* album, I went to Mr. Brown in a panic. I said, "Mr. Brown, I'm so sorry, but I cannot ride that bus anymore. The bus is unsafe." We went careening off the road one time after Mr. Jesse fell asleep at the wheel. So I told Mr. Brown, "I can't do it. I just can't do it." And Mr. Brown said, "That's okay, Miss Kelly, no problem." I was so relieved. I thought, "This is great!" But as I left Mr. Brown's office, Miss Ware handed me my passport and said, "Thank you so much, your services will no longer be needed." I got fired for telling the truth and sticking up for 24 lives! So I missed singing on *Live at the Apollo.* That was my punishment. When I finagled my way back into The Bittersweet, I'd find out where we were performing and I'd fly there on my own dime.

ROBERT "MOUSEY" THOMPSON: Man, riding that bus — you'd think you were going to Bingo. We might ride from Augusta to Oakland, sitting up straight. People talk about "payin' dues" in a funky band. They need to come check us out, because by the time we got there, we *were* a funky band. You're kinda smelly and pissed off and you want to get on that stage and do what you know how to do. So by the time you got there, you're ready. There was a strategy to James Brown's game. For those who didn't understand the road, it gave us something to complain about. But nobody was going anywhere. You had to find your comfort zone. I would get off that bus and just take a walk, get myself together.

WILLIE RAY "BO" BRUNDIDGE: I came into the band as a "flier," although, I enjoyed the bus rides. When we did an American tour, hitting little cities in the South or crossing the country, there'd be a bus ride from here to there. I enjoyed that. You're hanging out. We could watch DVDs and have music in the back of the bus. We had a cooler, so we had munchies and beer. It was a big party, from city to city. You're talkin', hangin' out with your friends. I loved it. Now, Augusta to Oakland, that's a lot of bus time. After a tour, when everyone said, "I'll see you next time," I headed to the airport. Within five or six hours I was home. If you rode the bus, you might not get home for another two days. The people who lived in Augusta eventually accumulated enough frequent flyer miles so that they could jump [on] a plane, too.

In time, Mr. Brown urged me — as he urged everyone, apparently — to move to Augusta. He would extoll the virtues of Augusta, but I could see where he was going with it. That's where he lived, that's where James Brown Enterprises had its headquarters, that's where other band members lived, and that's where the bus ride always started from. It would have been cheaper for James Brown Enterprises if I lived locally and just hopped on that bus, which wasn't exactly a strong incentive for me to move. Besides, I liked living in Las Vegas near my folks, I had friends in my hometown, and I was well positioned to fly anywhere in the U.S. or make international connections. I did not need additional time on the bus. But, as Erik said, "The bus *was* the gig." If you couldn't hack serious traveling and all its twists and turns, you'd best find another way to make a living.

CELEBRATING Y2K IN BEIRUT

The new millennium was ushered in with two gigs overseas, one in Lisbon, Portugal, on New Year's Eve, the other on the second day of January 2000 in Beirut, Lebanon. (Yes, you read that correctly.) According to the *New York Daily News*, Jeff Allen at Universal Attractions said that Mr. Brown received $500,000 for the gig at the Hotel Estoril in Lisbon, if you can believe that. The *Daily News* also referred to what it called "Millennium Fever." If you recall, the end of 1999 and the beginning of 2000 inspired fears of widespread computer-based chaos, dubbed "Y2K." Planes might fall from the sky due to computer glitches, reports suggested at the time. Jeff Watkins stayed home — although I never asked him why — and he got some backlash for it. Anytime you missed a gig you'd be set back, somehow — you'd be left off some jobs or your pay got cut. The gig demanded 100 percent devotion. I never missed anything that I was asked to do. I mean, why would anyone want to miss flying into Beirut during Y2K? What could possibly go wrong?

We flew into Beirut on New Year's Day for Lebanon 2000, a celebration that ran from the day after Christmas through the first week of January. The brochure I saved painted a rosy picture of modernity in a region known for strife. "Step into the 3rd Millennium at Lebanon 2000, with impressive shows of cosmopolitan caliber, artistic creativity, and state-of-the-art technology . . . Enjoy live performances by famous Lebanese, Arab, and Int'l Stars, with the magnificent interplay of Giant Imagery, Powerful Lasers, Lighting Effects, Sound Effects, and Water Fountains; all in all, the marvelous impact of 200 tons of Show Equipment and dazzling Fireworks. A once-in-a-lifetime chance to experience breathtaking laser effects, beamed by some of the most powerful laser equipment in the world . . ." During the show, Spike did one of his trademark freak-outs on percussion, which ended with him triumphantly tossing and catching a drumstick. That segued into an alto sax solo by Leroy "Funky" Harper, another one of my favorite people in the band — he's a family man, three kids, super-funny guy. James Brown would say, "Use the little horn!" and Leroy would grab his soprano sax and whistle you up into the heavens. In Beirut Mr. Brown called Leroy to the front of the stage, and Leroy quoted that Hollywood ditty that snake charmers supposedly play. The afterparty must have been fun, because I don't recall anything else about that particular night. But the next day, we were alarmed to learn that the Russian Embassy had been attacked with rocket-propelled grenades to protest Russia's war in Chechnya. Events had unfolded on the streets below us.

ERIK HARGROVE: We saw where 25-millimeter rounds had gone through buildings [in the past]. That's a nice size hole. If you make a circle with both your hands, those are the kinds of holes you'd see in some of these buildings. So we played the gig. It's the next day. We're hanging out, getting ready to leave. It came on the radio that there'd been a bombing. The airport had closed. They said, "Everyone stay in your hotel, don't go outside." We look outside and saw armored personnel carriers going up and down the street. We stayed an extra night. But the circumstances were unnerving. James Brown flew out, and we didn't. I don't know the exact circumstances. Technically, he left us. The fact remains, he flew and we stayed.

When I got home from Beirut, there was a letter in the mailbox from The New James Brown Enterprises, headquartered at 1217 West Medical Park Road, Augusta, Georgia. Inside was a letter and a check.

> Jan. 6, 2000
> To: All Band Members, Dancers and Background Singers,
>
> Happy New Year!!!!!! This is James Brown. I hope this year is as good as last year, if not better. I appreciate and love every one of you. Here is a $250 bonus. Sincerely, James Brown

You might think that check was rather modest for my six months' work on three dozen gigs in as many different countries and states. But as a working musician, as well as a new band member, I thought a bonus was cool, a nice thing for our employer to do. It's the thought that counts, right? Besides, the letter had been addressed to "all band members." That's about as official as it ever got, for me.

Being in the Soul Generals meant you were always on call. I'd get the tour itineraries in the mail, but if anything came up suddenly, a gig got added or canceled, I'd get a phone call that could put me on an airplane in 24 hours. You had to get used to dropping everything; people who didn't make it to the gig were in hot water — they'd have their pay docked, get passed over for a few gigs, maybe even get fired. When you were home, you were expected to be available by phone at all times. And this was just when mobile phones were coming into fashion. That made it difficult to hold down a side job, including gigs as a musician, if you were so inclined. Not to mention the strain on relationships.

Following our escape from Beirut, we had about a month off before heading back out on the road. The first six months of 2000 were less intense than the last six of 1999. We played casino shows in Nevada and California. A brief Southeastern tour in April took us to Richmond, Myrtle Beach, Norfolk. Then things picked up in May and didn't let up for the rest of the year. May and June blended together: we played with Tower of Power in Oakland and gigged in Anaheim, Santa Barbara, and Visalia in California, over to Sedona, Arizona, east to Annapolis, Maryland, back west to Las Vegas for a three-nighter at Caesar's Palace, out east to Atlanta, over to Birmingham, and northwest to Seattle for the Experience Music Project. And yes, we covered a lot of that territory, if not most of it, on a bus whose route wove a cat's cradle of highways criss-crossing the country. Perhaps you can picture riding a bus — the James Brown bus — from California to Arizona to Maryland, back across the country to Nevada, back again to Georgia and Alabama, and then clear to Washington in the Pacific Northwest. I'm not sure the imagination can do justice to the reality.

In Seattle we were scheduled to play at the celebration that opened Paul Allen's Experience Music Project, the Microsoft millionaire's homage to Jimi Hendrix and his hometown's place in American music. When we arrived inside the museum, on a giant digital screen above our heads, we could see a video of James Brown and the Soul Generals performing. We'd spent four days rehearsing at the Imperial Theater in Augusta the previous November, which was filmed to create a digital montage for the Experience Music Project. The rehearsals had been fun and low-key, with lots of friends and family in attendance. I was reminded of the last time we were rehearsing at the Imperial, when Mr. Brown did his famous move with the microphone stand — toppling it toward the audience, then snatching it back. But this time the mic stand tilted and then remained in place at a 45-degree angle, standing on the edge of its round base. To Mr. Brown, who'd used that mic stand maneuver countless times in nearly fifty years of performing, it might have seemed like a sign. Of what? That there's magic in the world? That he had powers? We all marveled at it and people began snapping pictures. Amy Christian moved to get her camera, and her footsteps suddenly seemed loud. *Easy, don't knock it over*, Mr. Brown pleaded. He wanted to savor an amazing moment, a freakish outcome of pure chance that seemed like it could be an omen. But of what, or for whom, it was impossible to know. Reading Mr. Brown's tea leaves was not a task for mortals.

At the Experience Music Project opening, we were joined on the bill by the Original J.B.s, which featured a devastating lineup of former James Brown bandmates. The Original J.B.s included Fred Wesley Jr., Maceo Parker, Pee Wee Ellis, Bootsy Collins, his brother, Catfish Collins, Jabo Starks, Marva Whitney, Vicki (Byrd) Anderson, Bobby Byrd, Johnny Griggs, and possibly others, all of whom played major roles in James Brown's recorded hits and road bands in the 1950s, '60s and '70s. They'd recently recorded an album of their own music, something the Soul Generals yearned to do. Though Mr. Brown often told us that playing for him "made" us for life, the players in the Original J.B.s had had such an influence on him, his music, and his success that that statement might be applied both ways. In any case, Mr. Brown apparently did not approve of the Original J.B.s getting their groove thing on. When our current bassist, Fred Thomas, was invited to join the Original J.B.s on stage because he had been one of them, Mr. Brown gave him a choice. Fred, who'd worked 30 years for Mr. Brown at that point, could play with the Original J.B.s, no problem, Mr. Brown said. But if he did, he'd have to walk. Fred decided to keep his day job.

We were in New York when the Associated Press ran a story oddly titled, "Brown is gearing down now." (Though Mr. Brown's performance schedule had occasional lulls, to his last day he never geared down.) Reporter Patrick Casey asked Mr. Brown five questions. Dig the answers, particularly the last one.

PC: Why do people call you the hardest working man in show business?

JB: I really don't have to work no more. I work because I love music and because God made me somebody who can do some good things. I want to do these things.

PC: How special is performing in New York?

JB: I like to come to New York at any time because people from all over the world are here. It's always good to play where people know you.

PC: How are you doing these days?

JB: We're great, fantastic. I am not bitter about anything. I just want to keep on doing and I enjoy doing it.

PC: What about past troubles?

JB: Everybody has troubles, son.

MELTDOWN IN VISBY

For decades, Europeans sustained James Brown by keeping him in constant demand, just like they rescued American blues in the early 1960s when it wouldn't sell here. People overseas didn't seem to care about Mr. Brown's personal ups and downs — everybody has troubles, after all — and they loved the man, his funky soul music, the show he put on, the whole package. That explains why we made several trips a year to Europe, especially in summer, with its bounty of festivals. In July 2000, we flew over for a short, intense festival tour. That tour ran from the 6th to the 16th of July. We were scheduled to play 11 shows in as many days: six of them in England, with stops in France, Spain, Germany, and Sweden, before a final performance at the Essential Festival in Bristol, England. Even by the Hardest Working Man in Show Business's standards, that was an ambitious schedule. Although, from a scheduler's point of view, it was a dream: not one day without a paying gig and no downtime.

The rapid-fire nature of this tour was magnified by geography and festival scheduling. We started with a 9 p.m. show in Reading, England. We flew south the next day to Bordeaux, France, for a 10:45 p.m. show, a pretty late start. We moved on to Montereau's Parc des Noues south of Paris to play the Montereau Blues Confluences 2000. We returned to South London to play Brixton Academy, where I witnessed James Brown doing the splits. Mr. Brown invited to the stage 16-year-old Michael Mwenso, a fabulous singer/dancer/trombonist born in Sierra Leone, West Africa, and raised in the U.K. Michael got his groove on, then did some of Mr. Brown's own dance steps, including a nice split and the Mashed Potato — that one-footed glide across the floor. (YouTube has a video of this performance.) Then Mr. Brown returned, danced a duet, showed off a bit and incited the audience to shower Michael with more love. Yet, he had to one-up Michael, so he went down into a split, three times, sliding into RJ, who had to literally lift him back up off the floor. Mr.

Brown could still *get down*, he just couldn't get *back up*! Honestly, most people would never attempt a split at any age — Mr. Brown was 67 years old. The motivation couldn't be more clear: just as he, the non-swimmer, leapt more than 15 feet into a deep pool and tried to swim, fully clothed, to his fans, he wasn't about to let a teenage sensation beat him at his own game. No sir. Mr. Brown answered the challenge with triple splits. I remember seeing a subsequent interview with Tomi Rae, who described how painful these antics were for Mr. Brown, who never flinched onstage. I had to admire the man for his consistent hunger to go over the top.

If Mr. Brown was hurting, though, he didn't show it the next night in Liverpool. We headed south next, to the Real Ale and Jazz Festival in Chichester, south of London, near the English Channel. Next we were off to Vigo, Spain, to play the Os Remedios, a huge soccer stadium, at 10:30 p.m. The next day we moved on to Vilshofen, Germany, by bus (that's 1,000 miles) for an 11 p.m. performance for the long-running festival, Jazz on the Danube. At that point, after seven shows in a row (in three countries), we were tired as hell. We'd been driving all night and all day from the last gig. When we got to Vilshofen, it was already night time. We ate quickly and ironed our suits. Turned out Mr. Brown was in a great mood. He was in a bathrobe, backstage, getting his hair done. Then he dropped in on the band. "Well, guys, no curfew tonight, we can play as long as we want to," he said. I'm sure he knew we were dog tired. But he was the oldest one among us, so if he could do it, we should be able to do it. That night he led us through a performance that lasted more than three hours without a break. No intermission. The equivalent of two 90s back-to-back. And this is the James Brown show, so we're moving the whole time. If I remember correctly, we were in a scalding hot tent. We were at the limit of our endurance. But James Brown never took a break. You could put that on his tombstone: "James Brown: He Never Took a Break." Even when he had someone else in the spotlight, he rarely left the stage.

He'd play keyboards, hang out, coach the band, coach the singer on her verses. The next day we were off for Visby, Sweden, the tenth consecutive day and show of the tour.

Visby is a port town on the west side of a large island in the middle of the Baltic Sea. It was just another day for the band. Nice hotel. Looked like a nice outdoor festival gig with several bands and maybe 25,000 kids out there. We drove by the venue on the way to the hotel. We're thinking, stereotypically: Sweden — hot blondes. We were looking forward to a great night. This would probably be my only night in Sweden in my entire life. We're at the hotel, chilling out before the show. Suddenly, word came that Mr. Brown was completely pissed off. Apparently, after rolling past the concert site, he felt his fee did not reflect the size of the festival and, perhaps, his stature as an artist. Big festival, big fee. Bigger festival than he'd been led to believe, bigger fee. In his mind, apparently, he'd been deceived. I'm piecing this together from what little I heard. Then, really bad news: Mr. Brown was so pissed off, he canceled the gig — the only time in seven-plus years and hundreds of shows that I ever saw him miss a performance. I don't know what he said or to whom, but his attitude apparently led to further difficulties. The Swedes, understandably, did not take kindly to his cancellation or to the way he handled it. It soon became apparent that James Brown wasn't going to listen to anyone, even his entourage, about anything. I have no doubt that Mr. Bobbit and Tomi Rae tried to calm him down and to see things reasonably. This was just another gig. Fees averaged out over a tour. Why go out of your head over a perceived slight when it was easier to do a 90 and move on to the last show of the tour? But Mr. Brown didn't need to be right to win an argument. He just had to have his way. I won't speculate on the factors at play in Visby. The cause, as always, was moot; we were concerned only with the effects. If James Brown decided he wasn't going to perform, we would not be performing. Mr. Brown could be volatile and, being a star, he surrounded himself with people whose typical response would be, "You're right." At some point, not even a friend can say something as simple as "Could you at least look at this situation from another point of view? Because I think you're making a mistake here." And when everyone knows better than to question anything, the star is setting himself up to fall, to lose the respect of the people who work for him and the audiences that support him. So it was in Visby.

Next thing we knew, Mr. Brown announced, "We're outta here. Tonight." We had just flown in. Visby's airport had maybe four gates. It was small. Apparently, he made demands. "Get the pilots, make 'em fly us outta here." To which the authorities replied, "It's late on a Saturday night and the airport has closed. The pilots are on a standard schedule. They are not returning to the airport." The Swedish authorities were saying, politely, "You can bark and woof all you want. You're not flying out of here. It doesn't matter who you are." Of course, Mr. Brown, in his state of mind, thought he had the power to make anything happen. He made us all pack, go to the airport, and be ready to depart. We had gotten to the Visby airport at four o'clock in the afternoon. By eight o'clock that night we had returned. The airport officials calmly explained again — as officials do when they know they have you beat — that no flights were leaving the airport that night. It wasn't gonna happen. I'm sure they also knew that James Brown had just canceled his performance at their festival. He'd essentially told the entire town, the entire country, to piss off. But no one was going to "Wake up those bums!" as Mr. Brown referred to the pilots in front of everyone, including the band. Mr. Brown berated the officials, to no avail. We heard screaming. But we weren't trying to witness too much. We were embarrassed. For all his power to heal through music, to be a funky ambassador for America, here he was, acting like the quintessential Ugly American. We could tell something wasn't right. He had dark glasses on. We couldn't see his eyes.

I remember sitting in the airport bored out of my mind. At that moment we could have been taking the stage and heating up the crowd, including all those Swedish blondes I had dreamed about. "What the fuck is this all about?" I asked myself. "This is not right." But I caught myself before a sense of outrage got the better of me. I literally told myself: "Shut up and deal with it." I went to the bathroom to shave, having nothing better to do. When I returned, someone had brought food for the band. We're the only ones in the closed airport. There's a big box with hamburgers and a big box with individual servings of French fries. I'm a vegetarian. The other vegetarian, Amy Christian, one of The Bittersweet singers, was kind of repulsed. I thought, I've dealt with worse than this before. So I walked over to where they'd set up the food, grabbed a pack of fries, and sat down on a little bench with my guitar. I'd have a nibble and wait to see what happened next. Suddenly, James Brown ran up to me. He had mayonnaise smeared around his mouth. He got in my face and yelled, "LET THE LADIES SERVE YOU! LET THE LADIES SERVE YOU!" As if the female members of the troupe would turn into waitresses and bring the food to the men. He was completely out of his head. I don't know what got into me, but I yelled back in his face, "I DIDN'T KNOW! I DIDN'T KNOW! I'M JUST GRABBING A PACK OF FRIES!" In his agitated state, it seemed like he was ready to kill me. The whole thing lasted a split second and it was over before I fully realized what happened. Then he backed off and walked away.

That night, back at our hotel in Visby, I told Keith, "I don't want this anymore." I wanted to quit that night. Keith said, "Man, we've all had that exact same feeling at some point. As your friend, all I ask of you is don't make any decisions right now. Sleep on it. Think about it tomorrow. Make a decision then." We went out for drinks, and we met some nice people. But they were a little less receptive to us than if we'd just played the concert. That was one of my early dark experiences with James Brown. I'd heard the rumors and I'd read the newspaper accounts of his periodic misbehavior. Boom!

Here it was — my first "I-don't-know-if-I-want-this" experience. Keith had been through several such episodes by that time and no doubt the other band members had had their moments as well. The Visby airport scene was my turn.

The next day we flew over Sweden and the North Sea to England and drove to Bristol for "Roots Day" at the Essential Festival. I took care not to bump into Mr. Brown. I didn't want to interact with him, except onstage. My desire for that one-on-one time cooled considerably. At least on stage I could count on him behaving professionally. Having raised my voice to him, I had to be on my toes to ensure I hadn't created a negative vibe between us that could get me shit-canned out of the band. Taking care of business helped neutralize the weirdness. Once we were onstage at the Essential Festival, it didn't appear that my behavior, let alone his, even stuck in his mind. I was grateful for that. In Visby he'd pushed me too far and my sudden outburst had shocked me. That was the most pissed I ever got at him. And we both let it go. Looking back, it was a wake-up call, the beginning of a conscious need to balance the opportunity, the upsides, and the downsides of working for James Brown. The gig, like many relationships, would benefit from my resiliency. As long as the pros outweighed the cons, I was in business. If he could shrug off his behavior, I had to as well. When we returned home, we had two weeks off, and that helped. Then we headed to Japan for a week.

Japan came to be a very special place for me, though I only visited three times. Maybe it's the contrast it represented, maybe the shared pop culture. The country is an island, I grew up in the desert. The culture is deferential, so different from free-wheeling America. Yet the Japanese love American music and pop culture. The night-life in Japan seemed exotic, and it inspired me to write music and develop my part in the James Brown show. This first tour, however, was marred by the same demons that had pushed James Brown over the top just weeks before in Visby. We rehearsed in Tokyo, then played an amusement park in Fujiyoshida (named Fuji-Q! I kid you not) at the base of Mount Fuji, and the Summer Sonic Festival in Osaka. In Osaka, according to my itinerary, we took the stage at 6:20 p.m. sharp, as scheduled. (The Japanese don't fool around.) The Soul Generals were warming up the crowd with "Network," one of our most powerful, intricate, set-opening arrangements. Suddenly, we heard discordant sounds in our mix. We looked stage left and saw Mr. Brown playing an electric bass guitar in the wings, where the audience couldn't see him. "Network" is a very intricate piece, and I guarantee you he had no idea what notes to play as we worked through it. But he was over there, just wailing away, and it was loud enough for all to hear. He was in that special state of mind where he thought he could do anything, even play the bass over the most complex part of the show. In short, he was feeling omnipotent, and he likely had assistance. I knew then we were in for a long night. Later in the show he had a conniption — legitimately, some would say — when an idiot in the audience threw a large (though empty) plastic water bottle on stage. (This is captured in a YouTube video titled "James Brown . . . Pissed," shot by a member of the Jon Spencer Blues Explosion.) Mr. Brown stopped the show and threatened to end it if anyone threw anything else, which I could understand. Still, it was just an empty plastic water bottle.

One day on that Japan tour, Mr. Brown and RT, our road manager, got into it so bad at sound check that RT left Japan and returned home. (Like so many others, he'd soon be back.) RT really had too many roles to play and too many jobs to do. He didn't need James Brown losing it on him. I don't recall the specifics, but at our sound check, RT said, "Well, I'll just go then" and Mr. Brown said, "Then you just go." But to demonstrate how Mr. Brown's mood could change, for better or worse, we performed that night in a crowded Japanese theater. Mr. Brown was talking to the audience, which was doting on his every word. Suddenly, he stopped. He looked over the audience's heads to the back of the theater, first with a surprised look, then a terrified expression. He suddenly pointed to the back of the room and shouted: "Godzilla!" And then he laughed that laugh of his. "Heh heh heh! I'm sorry, I had to do that." The guy had an outrageous and irreverent sense of humor. Things could go from bad to worse to genuinely hilarious in one night. We finished the tour with a show at Roppongi Velfarre, "the largest disco in Asia," with a capacity of 1,500. I remember clearly the runway that extended out into the club audience — it was maybe four feet wide and 12 long and going out there put the performer right in the middle of the club audience. Mr. Brown took full advantage of the opportunity, then he called a few of us out to solo. I got a turn and Jimmie Lee Moore and Leroy Harper got called out as well. Let me tell you, when Jimmie Lee Moore got down with his bass, everyone knew that cat was born to be on stage. He could play guitar or bass behind his back, over his head, between his legs — every which way — and the crowd ate it up. This time there was no danger of getting caught up in the hype — Mr. Brown had invited us to put on a show. Afterwards, Erik Hargrove ran into the actors Susan Sarandon and Tim Robbins, who'd caught the show and said they were blown away.

The tour ended well, despite a rocky start. But over time, Mr. Brown's unpredictable nature could wear you down. He could make you laugh out loud with an outrageous joke or put you on cloud nine with a compliment. Or he could explain to you, after years of toil, why you weren't cut out to play funk in his band. He might declare his pride in the prowess of the entire band one night and, the next, remark on our utter incompetence. Not knowing which Mr. Brown you were getting elevated boss-watching to a new level. Each and every day, an important factor was the word on Mr. Brown's mood. If it was good, you could get with the groove and your interaction with him promised to be really cool. If the word was not good, you'd be walking on eggshells all day. You wondered what the atmosphere at the sound check would be like, how the gig would go. Like any job, you had to consider the big picture. Forgiving and forgetting paid dividends. The gig was intoxicating, and the time spent on stage, participating in James Brown's connection with his audiences the world over, was an amazing experience. All the traveling, the preparations, the sound checks, and, finally, strutting out on stage into the bright lights to receive an audience's warm embrace — it's difficult to put into words what a thrill that is for a working musician, especially when James Brown, the icon, led us in doing his thing. The other thrill, of course, was being paid for it. I had to keep in mind that Mr. Brown was the leader of a diverse enterprise, the lead singer, the leader of the band, the global brand personality, and the CEO of his own business. He employed dozens of people and supported many families. That's a lot of pressure. Imagine dealing with 20 musicians, each with their own personalities . . . there's all the stress anyone could handle right there. Usually if he was in a bad mood, it was because something about the show had been bugging him. On a given night, he might be tired, although he never showed it or complained. Nothing could stop him. I don't remember ever seeing him hold back anything in the show because of an ailment. Band lore included a story about him playing the *Dick Clark Show* in the old days. He went backstage after his set, pulled off his shoe, and showed Dick Clark that his foot was all bloody, all messed up. Yet he still did all the splits, went down on his knees, pulled off all his dance moves. Dick Clark was astonished, "Wow, how did you . . . ?" And James Brown just said, "I had to. That's what I do." When the man needed it, we had to cut him some slack. Most often, he was a very lovable character, funny, charming, and charismatic. So you made that deal with yourself.

HEARTBREAK IN AUGUSTA

That fall we played a couple of sold-out nights at Caesar's in Lake Tahoe and one at the Sunset Strip House of Blues. We could always count on the casinos and the House of Blues and their good-time audiences to keep us working. A big show in Mr. Brown's hometown of Augusta was coming up — a homecoming of sorts. The week prior to the gig, Steven Uhles interviewed Mr. Brown for an article titled, "James Brown Feels Good About Local Show," for the *Augusta Chronicle*.

"We go around the world and sell out everywhere we go, but Augusta hasn't seen James Brown's show in a long time," Mr. Brown told Uhles. "I want the people to realize that we do a clean show; a show without vulgarity. This is a show for the whole family. This is a wholesome show and we're proud to be a part of that.

"There's something about the fact that I was once shining shoes right out there," he said, pointing out the picture windows of his radio station on the corner of Broad and the aptly named James Brown Boulevard. "I want my kids, my grandchildren, and my great-grandchildren to be proud of Augusta. I want old ladies to be able to cash their checks without getting mugged, and I want the drug-infested areas cleaned up."

On October 12, 2000, the day of the show, only 1,700 tickets had sold out of 9,000 at the Augusta-Richmond County Civic Center, and the bill included the Chi-Lites, the Stylistics, and others. I had never witnessed a James Brown show with that many empty seats. One never really knew the reason that attendance might sag at any given show. You could read too much into the sparse attendance in Augusta that fall. People who lived in Augusta at that time will tell you that although James Brown was a global cultural icon, back in his hometown he was not universally adored. His prominent local arrests on unsavory charges over the years might have grated on his fellow Augustans. Scuttlebutt had it that Mr. Brown did not pay local merchants on time. But I will say this: those 1,700 people got a show. Mr. Brown and the Soul Generals delivered the goods. As an old-school entertainer, Mr. Brown believed in performing for the people who *had* showed up, and he would not be daunted by those who had *not* come to see him. In fact, the old-school approach meant that an entertainer of Mr. Brown's stature would work twice as hard for a smaller crowd. In his 25 years with the band, Hollie Farris had experienced this scenario before.

HOLLIE FARRIS: When I joined in 1975, he'd been on the charts for so long — and you know how fickle Americans are — [fans] finally just got tired of him. He just fell off the charts. On the first gig I played with him at the Coliseum in Macon, Georgia, there might have been 200 people in the audience, but the place probably seats 10,000. There were several of those gigs the first couple of years I was with him. Anytime we played out of the country attendance was fine, just fantastic. But in this country, he'd been around so long, it was really hit and miss. He was used to putting his name out there in the newspaper and thousands of people would show up. All of a sudden, that wasn't happening. We played a lot of gigs where there were a hundred people, 50 people even. But I gotta say, he'd put on as good or better show for 50 people than he would when there were 50,000 and give them way more than their money's worth. I'd never seen anything like it.

Steven Uhles, at the *Augusta Chronicle*, laid it all at the community's feet in his post-concert review, "To Its Shame, Augusta Snubs Musical Legend."

"While I'm sure Mr. Brown was disappointed with the crowd, I felt more sorry for Augusta as a community," Uhles wrote. He'd heard local complaints that national acts didn't stop in Augusta. "After seeing how few turned out for Mr. Brown, a local resident and authentic music legend, I can't blame artists for avoiding Augusta. I'd stay away, too," Uhles stormed. "I have to wonder what was more important to Augustans than seeing Mr. Brown, an artist who sells out much larger venues everywhere he plays and has built a reputation on spirited live performances . . . As a community, we cannot expect to attract top-caliber acts if we are unwilling to support them . . . Mr. Brown didn't let the paltry showing affect his performance . . . Leading his instrument-toting troops into battle like a funky field marshal, the gold bedecked Mr. Brown and his scarlet-clad warriors leave an audience gasping . . . Mr. Brown's current company consists of crack players who gel as a band and function admirably when asked to solo." (Thanks for calling out the band, Steve!)

About this time, Keith Jenkins got a rare call at home from Mr. Brown. On a lark, Keith recorded it. Many years later, while I was working on this book, Keith shared the tape with me. Mr. Brown was in a good mood and it seemed that my work had made an impression on him, even if my name had not. (For some reason, Mr. Brown liked to call me "Damien Woods." I never corrected him.)

KEITH JENKINS: James Brown probably called me personally, at home, about a half-dozen times in the 13 years we worked together. So one night the phone rang and it's him. He just wanted to talk. I had just appeared with him on the VH1 Vogue Fashion Awards show at Madison Square Garden and Mr. Brown had just seen it on television.

JAMES BROWN: I just called to tell you I love what you did and I'm very proud of you.

KJ: Well, I appreciate it. Thanks for lettin' me do it.

JB: God bless you, and I'll see ya on the gig.

KJ: Okay!

JB: Well, look-ee here, we gonna wear 'em out.

KJ: We gonna wear 'em out!

JB: Probably just gonna be you and, uh . . .

KJ: And Damon . . .

JB: Damien [on guitar] . . . Let Jimmie [Lee Moore] play a little in between, when we need the rhythm, you know?

KJ: Right, right . . .

JB: That's who you're gonna have, so you might wanna start thinking that way.

KJ: Yessir.

JB: You ever talk to Damien when you off from work?

KJ: Yessir, we talk all the time.

JB: Did he see ya? Did he see the show?

KJ: Oh, he saw it. He called me right after he saw it. Yeah, he's the only one that called me.

JB: Cause he ain't jealous.

KJ: Nah.

JB: That boy can play.

KJ: Yeah . . .

JB: He don't have to be jealous of nobody. He's got his own thing.

I'd be lying if I said I wasn't thrilled to hear this exchange, so many years later. A compliment from the man himself, from beyond the grave, as it were, still goes straight to my head. Looking back, that call took place after I'd spent 18 months in his band. Not only had I gotten a raise or two and a lot more solo time, but Mr. Brown had personally noticed and approved of the job I was doing. He didn't tell me directly, of course, but he told someone who might mention it to me.

NEW YEAR'S IN VEGAS: MELTDOWN REDUX

In November we returned to Europe for a week-long dash through France, Switzerland, and Germany, standing room only at every stop. No mistaking the adulation overseas. Upon our return, we stepped off the plane in New York and proceeded directly to a two-night booking at B.B. King's Blues Club. B.B.'s was a fun room to play because the fans stood close to the stage, which gave us that face-to-face contact with the audience that we craved. Often at festivals and larger venues, the audience might appear like a sea of humanity, a dozen feet below us, rather than as individuals. Even at some theaters, the audience might sit a ways back from the stage. So we thoroughly enjoyed that up close-and-personal contact at B.B. King's, the House of Blues, and other small clubs. Unfortunately, those smaller places typically didn't have sufficient dressing-room space for the star and a troupe of two dozen people. From New York we rode the James Brown bus to Pittsburgh to play beautiful Heinz Hall, a show you can catch on YouTube.

When we returned to the road after a short break, we played the Warfield Theater in San Francisco, where I had the great pleasure of meeting Chet Helms, the legendary concert organizer. Back in the mid-1960s Chet had created Family Dog Productions, which was instrumental in staging San Francisco bands when the Jefferson Airplane, Grateful Dead, Quicksilver Messenger Service, and Janis Joplin were homegrown sensations. Hanging out with him, talking about the old days and the current scene meant a lot to me, as many of my musical and cultural roots trace to that place and time. (I caught up with Chet Helms again, at the Bonnaroo festival in 2003, and we had another chance to hang.) Chet is gone now, may he rest in peace. After a one-nighter at the Warfield we headed north to Canada. It was December. We played the Queen Elizabeth Theatre in Vancouver, the Pengrowth Saddledome in Calgary, and Rexall Place in Edmonton. I caught a bug on that Canadian swing and was deadly sick. I tried to keep it to myself, but I accidentally coughed up blood onstage while Mr. Brown sang "White Christmas." The show must go on, right?

We had two weeks off for the holidays before we reconvened in my hometown for a three-night stand culminating on New Year's Eve at a jazz club called the Blue Note, inside the Aladdin. Three hundred bucks a ticket, five hundred seats in the house. Cozy, but expensive. An advertisement in the local papers played up Mr. Brown's stature in the pantheon of stars:

> The Blue Note Proudly Presents: James Brown! Other
> singers were more popular, others were equally skilled,
> but no other African-American musician has been so

influential on the course of popular music in the past several decades. What more can one say? An ultra-rare club appearance!

The first two nights went well. But the holidays seemed to wear on Mr. Brown. There may have been many reasons for this. I knew that his late wife, Adrienne, had died in early January four years earlier. On New Year's Eve, the third and final night of the run, Mr. Brown fired Todd Owens, one of our trumpet players. Then he jumped on our bus — the James Brown bus that he did not travel on — and told us that if we didn't "clean up all this mess" everyone would be fired, and this and that. Again, though we could have speculated what the cause of this behavior was, we mostly focused on its effects. After unnecessarily getting into Jerry Poindexter's face, Mr. Brown looked out the window of the bus where thousands of people streamed past, celebrating the holiday. Las Vegas had closed down the Strip to vehicles; it was only pedestrian traffic that night. Mr. Brown ranted at what he saw: "*Look* what they're doing to our country! *Look!*" I thought, "It's New Year's Eve in Las Vegas. Lighten up." Naturally, I kept my mouth shut.

The night, and Mr. Brown, unraveled from there. While we were ironing our tuxedos backstage, Mr. Brown was out on stage, in his bathrobe, "interacting" with the audience. The man who never appeared in public except when he was impeccably coifed and dressed to the nines was wandering the stage in his bathrobe, apparently talking nonsense to the crowd. At some point he left the stage, and we headed out to start the show. Suddenly, Mr. Brown reappeared, still in his bathrobe. He started talking trash and doing strange things, way too close to the dinner guests in the front row. Mr. Bobbit whispered, "Keith, just start a song." Keith fired up the band and then BAM! Mr. Brown stopped us with a hand signal. Those hand signals were in our blood by that time and there was no way we could disregard them. When James Brown gave the cue that the song was over, it was over. All he had to do was wave his hand. Mr. Bobbit was just trying to keep the show going and possibly distract the audience from Mr. Brown, who was obviously upset, for reasons only he knew. If he wanted to talk, he was gonna talk. And if the tickets for this special New Year's Eve show were $300 apiece and he felt like talking in his bathrobe, no one could stop him. I remember he told the crowd that he had done "two years in prison for nothing." "America has let me down," he said. "And the show is over because I'm not feeling appreciated." He kicked Keith off the stage for not smiling. (Go figure.) Keith, cool as usual, just rolled up his guitar cable and withdrew. Mr. Brown fired another half dozen people, on stage, in rapid succession.

> **ERIK HARGROVE:** I don't know how to explain it. It was one of the strangest experiences in my life. This is James Brown being way out of sorts, just random, mentally and physically random. He took something out of his pocket that looked like crushed tea leaves and he sprinkled it on people's food on the tables by the stage. People were shocked — mouths wide open and jaws on the floor. Judge Bradley told us after the gig that we weren't getting paid. The band was naturally upset about Brown's demeanor and the gig itself and then we're not getting paid? People were super upset and going off.

After sowing tea leaves and chaos, Mr. Brown left town. We weren't paid for any of the Vegas gigs. But the band stayed because we had an upcoming show within days at the Mirage, a Monster Cable sales rep party for 3,000 people. Jimmie "J.J." Walker, the comedian, would open for us. The afternoon of the gig, Mr. Brown showed up at sound check. He was downright hostile. After all his craziness at the Blue Note gig, he walked up to each person in the band, got in their face, and demanded, "Do you *like* your job? Do you *want* your job?" Obviously, there was only one correct answer, and most of us managed a "Yes" without groveling. His grudging response: "Then you can stay." Rather than acknowledge his behavior or his failure to pay us for our work, he went on the offensive. He was intent only on flushing out anyone who held a dissenting opinion, on anything. He could feel heavy (and certainly justified) resentment from a few people and he sent them packing. That was the ultimate test of our ability to forgive and forget. Most of us had already decided that we wanted to hang onto our jobs, so we steeled ourselves for the task. I remember being pretty nerved out by events. I had partied pretty hard the night before with local friends, just from anxiety over what was going to happen the next day.

My anxiety was justified. As Jimmie Walker finished his set, he introduced us with a somewhat long-winded tribute to James Brown. I didn't understand it at the time, but Mr. Brown was ready to go onstage right on time that night. Even while Jimmie Walker was extolling his virtues, Mr. Brown got so pissed that he told the Mirage management, "If we don't go on at ten o'clock — not ten o' one — and you don't have him off that stage, I'm not playin'." It was heavy. I was thinking, "Why such a big deal all of a sudden?" At the time, I just chalked it up to a bad mood. I took the stage at the Mirage that night with the remnants of a hangover, sufficient to make me sluggish in response to Mr. Brown's cues. Five! Ten! Fifteen! Twenty! Twenty-five! came the hand signals for a fine, with Mr. Brown looking me right in the eye in disapproval as he voiced the numbers. When I got paid for that gig, however, no fine was deducted. I'd gotten a warning; maybe he'd forgotten the incident.

But recent events brought on a fresh round of rationalizing my gig. Everyone knew he'd had a tough upbringing. So tough that perhaps no one other than he could have risen so high. I knew only the barest outlines: born to a 16-year-old mother in a shack in rural

South Carolina; moved into an aunt's brothel in Augusta, Georgia, at age four or five; abandoned by his mother not long afterwards; he learned to dance, play several instruments and box by age 16; sent to juvenile lock-up for robbery before he turned 17. Daunting hurdles, to be sure. Yet there he was, in turn, using the slave mentality on those he could inflict it on. Keith handled this stuff better than anyone, from what I could see. When Mr. Brown upbraided us at the sound check, and Keith had dutifully said he liked his job, Mr. Brown told him pointedly that he could have his job back — without the week's pay. Keith dissented at that point. Mr. Brown retorted, "I'm cutting your pay down by one-third." Keith said, "I have a wife, a family, a mortgage. I can't accept that. I thank you for everything." And he calmly rolled up his guitar cord just like he always did when he was about to leave. Keith was one of the only people I knew who could say "No" to James Brown. By doing so, he was looking out for the band. He'd acknowledge that, perhaps, "things hadn't worked out," shake James Brown's hand, maybe give him a hug, and wrap up that guitar cord. Keith's ability to stay cool under duress was a sight to see. He was a master at wrapping that guitar cord up in a nice, smooth little circle even though, underneath, he was pissed as hell. And James Brown blinked. Maybe he saw that his show was going to be undermined by the loss. Mr. Brown said, "Son, *what do you want*? You want all your money back, just like that?" Keith said, "Yes." And James Brown gave in and paid him and, if I remember correctly, the rest of us, too. No pay cut. That boy Keith has some balls.

Getting back on stage again, taking care of business, helped us in the forgive-and-forget department. When Mr. Brown flashed me the hand signal that he was fining me, at least he was back to caring about his music. And that helped me to get back to it, too. His demeanor said, "Let's get back to business." There was nothing to figure out, just something to get over. Shit happens. Deal with it.

We knew crazy shit had happened before, we knew crazy shit would happen again. But right then we had a show to perform. That's a big part of the job of a sideman. Just get on with it, *do your job.*

Back in the real world, however, for those not beholden to James Brown Enterprises, forgiving and forgetting would take time. As you can imagine, Mr. Brown's behavior did not escape the attention of the Aladdin's management or the local press. Two days after the Aladdin debacle, the headline, "Blue Note Crowd Sees the Downside of James Brown," appeared above Norm Clarke's "Vegas Confidential" column in the *Las Vegas Review-Journal*. Norm Clarke recalled more details than I did, and they were not good.

> Legendary soul man James Brown provided a New Year's Eve fireworks show of his own. His bizarre behavior stunned a high-brow crowd at the Blue Note jazz club with actions that included: an on stage rant in a bathrobe; diving into the crowd to confiscate a front-row showgoer's camcorder; angrily throwing a patron's chair a la Bobby Knight; and saying he had been communicating with the pope . . . Things started going badly early.
>
> Doors [had] opened more than an hour late. Two hours later, Brown could be seen in a bathrobe, just off stage, having a heated argument with "management." Moments later Brown "had words" with women at a table by the stage. When the women left, Brown went to their table, tossed one chair and kicked the other. Then, with his arm, he swept everything off their table: beverage glasses, party favors, etc.
>
> At 10:15 p.m. Brown returned to the stage in his bathrobe, demanded management turn down the sound and told the crowd that they had probably noticed he was "pretty agitated because these people are trying to take

advantage of me." He mentioned that he had been paid $30 million for the performance but that he had given back 'all the money.'

When he eventually came on stage in a suit, he dressed down his drummer at one point, and raised more eyebrows when he said the pope had contacted him and said that he — the pope — was no longer going to hold audiences with people because he couldn't attract the number of people "that James Brown could."

"Brown's whole behavior was not part of the program," said Lee Vlastaris, club manager. "It has a tremendous effect on the paying public, and people were obviously displeased."

ACT TWO
GETTING TO KNOW "THE MAN"

Despite my rationalizations, Mr. Brown's "performance" in Las Vegas on New Year's shook my faith, again. As it turned out, though, my faith was so closely tied to my job that it tended to be pretty durable. I was devoted to being a member of the Soul Generals. I'd gotten the hang of the funk. I liked my bandmates. I liked the lifestyle. I loved it when the energy and the music in a performance sent us all over the moon. I was simply reminded that my job included handling a little turmoil. I wasn't going to be shaken loose from an opportunity on that scale just because my boss could go stone crazy at times. In fact, after 18 months on the road with Mr. Brown and the band and seeing the world, the wish I'd made on that shooting star in Thessaloniki had come true: here I was, a young man from Las Vegas, working for a global superstar in one of the music business's hottest bands. And I was making a living. When I stacked that up against the alternative — obscurity and limping along, playing half-assed gigs — I simply acknowledged that handling the James Brown gig meant dealing with a few hazards. That's how the trade-off worked. I chalked up Visby and Las Vegas to experience, and I didn't dwell on the thought that there might be more to come. My buddy Keith helped me understand what we might call the "sideman's deal."

> **KEITH JENKINS:** Damon went through it all. The excitement
> about having that gig meant you overlooked a whole
> lot. You're new, you're not making waves. You're excited
> about what you're doing, so your tolerance for bullshit
> is really high. That wears off. Then you get to a point
> where *everything* gets on your nerves. Your tolerance is
> really low. Your nerves are really raw. Anything could set
> you off. After Damon got a few doses [of James Brown's
> abuse], he'd express his chagrin with certain situations.
> Everybody had to be talked down, at some point.
> Somebody had to say, "Calm down. Drink this."
> I was that person for Damon and Damon was that
> person for me.

Born into extremely adverse circumstances, James Brown sang and danced his way to self-respect, fame, and prosperity. He made revolutionary music at a time when the world needed it. He stood up for his people and preached economic empowerment. And he'd even transcended all those roles by the sheer force of his personality to become a global ambassador of soul.

That's the James Brown story from the outside looking in. Now that I was in the band, I had a chance to see things from the inside. The opportunity to hang out with Mr. Brown and his band constantly reminded me of the greatness of his art and his artistic staying power. Decades after he created it, his music still made people wanna get up and move. There's a magic trick going on there. I'd see it every night when the audience leapt out of their seats at the sight of him. I never figured out how the magic worked but I had no doubt that James Brown was an utterly unique human being, and because of that, the music remained my focus — to survive, it had to be.

Thanks to my bandmates, I had raised my level of musicianship and my participation in the show to the level expected of a Soul General, and Mr. Brown seemed pretty happy with me on stage, where we spent the most time together. He'd point me in on solos with increasing frequency and, afterwards, call my name out to the crowd, just as he did with the rest of the band. I'd enjoyed positive one-on-one interactions with Mr. Brown over the past year or so. He definitely liked to know his people well and that took time. If there was any distance between us, part of it had to be the employer-employee relationship — how close would one ever get when your boss is James Brown?

Another part of it had to be me, getting over my awe and humility as a musician to deal with James Brown as an actual person. The guy just oozed charisma and personality and talent. I'd be in the same room and he'd give off this 30-foot wave of power. He wasn't trying to use it in some negative way on anybody. He'd just be chilling out, but he couldn't help but project an aura of other-worldliness. Naturally, because he was my boss, I watched myself when I was around him. I watched what I said, particularly if the word on his mood-of-the-day wasn't rosy. Everyone who worked for him wanted to maintain a friendly relationship even if real friendship was unlikely, based on the circumstances. It seemed like everyone had their own style of relationship with James Brown, perhaps based on their shared experiences and longevity together.

A personal relationship with Mr. Brown probably grew quite slowly and ultimately depended on a lot of stage time and a lot of personal interaction over the years. I had to continue to be open to that, despite a few bumps in the road. Certainly Mr. Brown had personally reached out several times to encourage me, even if a sense of full acceptance was slow in coming.

> **ERIK HARGROVE:** The guys in the band accepted Damon long before Brown probably did, because we knew Damon already, having traveled with him when he played for Tomi Rae's band. We had accepted him as a "cat" already. If you're a "cat," you're acceptable to be in the band. I think Brown accepted him as someone who came to do the job at first. And it became deeper later.

I noticed that Mr. Brown dispensed praise in several ways, both direct and indirect. After someone soloed in performance, Mr. Brown called out their name to the audience's attention — *Damien Woods! Damien Woods! Damien Woods!* — which really stroked the ego (even if he mispronounced my name). Later, when I encountered him one-on-one, he would say something like, "Hey, you really killed those solos. I'm glad I can count on you." Or, more likely, you'd hear from someone else that Mr. Brown had said, "Oh yeah, Damien — he can go all night! He doesn't run out of ideas when I lean on him." Like the indirect praise he shared with Keith on that phone call. Or like that time Mr. Brown called me up and was jammin' to Jeff Watkins' latest CD over the phone. I had to tell Jeff what happened because he wasn't going to hear it directly from Mr. Brown. That sort of stuff was sprinkled throughout my tenure with Mr. Brown, as it was for everybody. Whether you were doing something new musically that he appreciated or whether he just wanted to touch base with what was going on in your personal life, when he had a moment, he'd talk about it with you. If you were on the road and you'd been playing well, the conversation could drift to your efforts. All these things represented the upside of my gig.

I received a little of that direct appreciation one night when I had to "go long" for Mr. Brown, which tested my ability to think on my feet. At that performance at Heinz Hall in Pittsburgh in late 2000, Mr. Brown called me out to the lip of the stage to solo on "I'll Go Crazy" and I seized the moment. I laid down what I thought was a respectable solo, thinking that maybe he stepped behind me to play his keyboard. But when I looked over, Mr. Brown was headed off-stage. Unbeknownst to me, he was going to make a costume change in the middle of the song. I kept my solo going, thinking furiously, starting to perspire, but still no sign of Mr. Brown. I found myself consciously digging deep — and deeper — to keep my solo interesting. In the back of my mind I was waiting, praying, for the audience's *ooo-aaahhh!* that signaled Mr. Brown's reappearance on the stage. Perhaps four or five minutes went by, enough for a very quick costume change but a maddeningly long guitar solo, before Mr. Brown finally returned and thanked me in front of the audience. I'd just had the ride of my life. Five minutes is a *long* solo if it's any good and an eternity if it's not. Afterwards, Keith said I could have passed the ball to him, but the thought never crossed my mind. Mr. Brown signaled me to solo, so I soloed! Later, Mr. Brown duly remarked to someone in the band that he was pleased how I could "go all night."

It was around this time that Mr. Brown called me back to his dressing room so I could work with Tomi Rae on "At Last," which was a big hit for Etta James in 1960. Tomi Rae needed to practice her vocals for her part in the show. He knew that she and I had been friends in a band that fizzled. We weren't great friends, but we respected each other. She was a talented, smoky blues singer, but he wanted her to cover the Etta James hits and jazz standards that he loved. She did well at adapting to it, though I felt for her. I thought, "Man, he's making her sing something that's really out of her bag."

It's one thing to play a little guitar behind a front man. It's much harder for the guest vocalist who has to sell a song to the audience while the star of the show is catching his breath. Tomi Rae's slot in the evening's performance was not an easy one to handle. Some ticket holders did not want to see a guest vocalist in the middle of a James Brown show, even though that had been tradition for four decades. Sometimes people would love her, sometimes the reception was rough. As Tomi Rae worked through her songs with me in his dressing room that day, James Brown sat nearby, scarfing a cheeseburger, drinking orange soda and burping relentlessly — like a monster. I thought, "I *love* this guy! He's *human*." Moments like that put me more at ease with James Brown the person and helped me realize that stars are actual people, too. Uninhibited moments like that could go a long way. That afternoon, chilling with Mr. Brown and his cheeseburger, replenished my faith in what I was doing and gave me fresh motivation to excel. Looking back, maybe he saw that I'd been daunted, even spooked, by his behavior and needed a shot in the arm. If so, it worked.

That one-on-one stuff was cool. At other times, Mr. Brown would drop in on the band before or after a gig, just to hang with his boys. He'd let us know by his demeanor that business could be set aside for the moment. Despite the ups and downs, James Brown was a very lovable character. He deserved the camaraderie of his band. His sheer personal drive and devotion to business meant we were working. When he'd chill with us, we could relax around him and see *him* relax and actually get to know him. I think he enjoyed the opportunity to set aside *James Brown* for the moment and become one of the boys in the band. That went a long way to smooth the rough patches.

ERIK HARGROVE: Those moments stood out. There was a cool vibe. Most of the time we were just listening, because wherever he was he commanded the stage. He'd open up a bit and he'd let us interject our opinions — about life, certain visions, concepts of music. It could be anything. If he came into the dressing room and saw somebody's uniform that hadn't been ironed yet, he would tell stories about how they used to use a hot light bulb to iron their uniforms. That's the way they'd have to do it when they all piled into a station wagon and played the Chitlin' Circuit, places where there were "White Only" dressing rooms and they had to use a bathroom or a storage room, where they had to iron their uniforms with a light bulb.

WILLIE RAY "BO" BRUNDIDGE: Oh yeah, he'd tell jokes and hang out. He'd take out a wad of cash and say "Guess how much money I've got here." If somebody guessed right, he'd give the money to him. Or he'd say, "It's a number between one and a thousand." It was like a quick raffle. He'd just walk in with a handful of money and whoever guessed the closest, he'd give it to him.

JIMMIE LEE MOORE: I think he enjoyed having the band around. He liked company. When he hung out with the band, of course, he did most of the talkin'. Didn't nobody else do too much talkin'. He'd allow you to have your say-so about something. We talked about weird stuff, like spaceships and all kind of weird stuff. He was very paranoid, to me. I understand that. When you have that kind of money, you don't know who's your friend. Everybody wants something.

GEORGE "SPIKE" NEALY: Everybody had their moments with James Brown. He would know right off the bat if something was wrong or if you felt nervous about something. We were doing a show in Rio de Janeiro, with four opening acts — huge percussion line acts. Drums for days! He knew that my mind might get pulled into doubt. So he came into the dressing room before our set, didn't say what he wanted. He just said, "Mr. Nealy, you havin' a good day?" I said, "Yessir, Mr. Brown, everything's all right." He said, "These people love funk just as much as you love what they do. You go out there tonight, do *your* thing." And he turned around and walked away. In so many words, you're doing James Brown's show. Stay on your thing, stay on that funk, and you'll have nothing to worry about. That's one of those little encounters I'll always remember.

We had fun sometimes, however, for the most part, Mr. Brown traveled on his own schedule with his entourage, while the band rode the bus or flew coach. That's the natural order of things for a star and his band and, for the most part, that worked for us. Close proximity to the star posed its own hazards, as I would come to find out years later in an episode that would go down in Soul Generals history. The star's schedule and the band's schedule tended to dovetail only for rehearsals and gigs and little else, which, it turned out, was ideal. With an exhausting schedule of gigs and travel, mental downtime was welcome.

WILLIE RAY "BO" BRUNDIDGE: Overall, he was a fun guy to work with and we had a lot of fun. In New York, he'd be at the Trump Palace, we might be at the Edison. It was a nice hotel, in the middle of everything. Whether James Brown was there or not, when you got to a fancy hotel, you'd better wear dress pants and shoes. The boss wanted everybody looking good. We had rules. At a hotel, you can't be wearing jeans. That's a no-no. At one point, it used to be coat and tie. Still, if he's watching, he's always inspecting. And he'd find stuff. Mr. Brown could walk over to you and say, "Hey, man, I got this idea." And he'd hum you a part. "Remember that part!" Later, he might ask you about it. "Remember that part? Let me hear it!" Sometimes you didn't want to be so close. You wanted that little getaway.

ERIK HARGROVE: Out of sight, out of mind, was probably best, because you didn't know if he was going to come at you with something good or something bad. Most of the time you expected it to be something bad. I'll say this, if he was staying in a nice hotel, I wanted to stay in a nice hotel, even if he was there, too, because some of the places we stayed were just horrific, to say the least. Now, at the airport, a lot of the time he went around security. So if you were chatting with him you could sneak in with his entourage and skip security. After a few times he caught on to what I was doing and he started laughing. [*Erik drops into his J.B. voice*] "No, no, Mr. Hargrove, you go over there with everybody else. Nah, nah, not this time, you go over there."

GEORGE "SPIKE" NEALY: When we weren't at his hotel, we had more freedom. We could relax and let our guard down, because the press was not there. The press followed *him*. When you've just done a series of long shows and long nights, you want to relax, put on your tennis shoes. When you're staying at the same hotel as Mr. Brown, the presentation that you give must be A class. Even though the press is interviewing *him*, they may have a question for *you*. So you're never going to catch a member of the band in a pair of jeans and tennis shoes. Make no mistake. When you see the band, you know it's his band. We had to dress the part. At no time should a camera catch you where you've got to explain yourself to Mr. Brown.

PLAYING IN THE BAND

After playing for James Brown for nearly two years, my learning curve remained steep. The breadth of knowledge needed to be merely competent seemed to have no end. James Brown dipped into a vast songbook on a whim, so you were on-your-toes every second. You focused solely on Mr. Brown on that stage, but you had to mesh with 17 other players, sometimes more. Besides locking in with the drummer and bass player to propel the rhythm, I worked hard with Keith to split up the guitar duties in a way that made musical sense. By this time, Keith and I were good friends and a pretty tight musical unit. On stage we were often situated so that we flanked Mr. Brown at the front. Looking back at photographs or videos of some of the shows, I still chuckle. The camera looks up at Mr. Brown, who stands dead center, looking larger than life at the microphone. Flanking him on either side: two young white boys — one with a ponytail —on guitar playing their asses off. Keith was the mastermind of our complementary guitar parts, so I'll let him give you a sense of the interplay we developed.

> **KEITH JENKINS:** I tried to be as authentic as possible and play the parts from the original record, where that was the best thing to do. When the original had only one guitar, Mr. Brown might have a part that he wanted played or there might have been a standard second part that had evolved over the years of live performances. Or it might

have been up to us. I'd try to come up with something that worked. I tried to cop that feeling from those original guitar parts. One guitar would do what we called the "stroke," on the chord, like the nine chord. The other part would be a single note line we called the "figure." If you listen to the records — "Hot Pants" is a good example or "Doin' It to Death" — one guitar's playing the stroke, the other's playing the figure. Some ballads had a single-note line, some would be chord-based, so we'd try to play different inversions — different positions of the chord — and different rhythmic patterns. We just tried to mix it up and leave a hole for the other player. Sometimes Mr. Brown would say, "Whatchoo playin'?" I'd say, "I'm playin' what's on the record." He'd give me his famous line, "They cut it wrong!" Or he'd say, "Don't worry about that. You play what I tell you to." And he'd come up with parts on the spur of the moment. Some things he didn't mess with. Other times he'd demand that you play something he made up on the spot. Some songs he'd constantly tweak. Like "Sex Machine." He'd constantly play around with it to the point of it becoming unrecognizable to the audience.

Dividing up the parts was just the start. James Brown's music might have a lot of simple, well-defined parts that fit together like hand-in-glove. But as a guitarist, I might be vamping on a set of changes for minutes at a stretch, and so within that part, I'd need to be constantly embellishing, adding a little energy. Jeff Watkins would spur us on in the rhythm section. He'd say, "When I come out and solo, and you guys bring it down for the soloist, it just lays there. You gotta keep it *alive*. It has to *percolate* or else I got no juice to feed off of when I go up front to the big mic to take a solo in the spotlight. So when I go solo, you gotta give me some *nuts*." Jeff was right, so I started to embellish my little wah-wah parts without taking away from the groove. I'd take a simple, repeating vamp and keep it in a state of constant improvisation. From then on, when Jeff was up there taking a sax solo, or whoever was blowing his horn, and that player took a moment to breathe, I was listening to that cat and playing this soft pad while he's playing his notes. Then, when he took a breath, I'd give that rhythm just a little more push, one that fit into that space. A small window opened up where I could deviate slightly for a split second, move my sound almost to the forefront, then drop back when the soloist resumed his phrase. Little things like that added to the overall vibe. That's what funk is all about, so I was learning. I wasn't born with it, you might say, but in James Brown's company I found it within myself.

It's not always easy to put feelings into words, which is what talking about funk entails, but the subject deserves the effort — especially in a book on James Brown. As a guitarist, I'd play that chank rhythm, which repeats itself without being repetitive, if it's done right. I'd immerse myself in the rhythm, listen to the drummer and the bass player, and feel their sounds within my chank. And my chank would start to morph. It would move from a one-dimensional, repetitive theme to a circular, ever-evolving groove with a lot of space in it. It was like spinning in the Mad Hatter's teacup ride — I wouldn't hit the sides the same way every time. The effect would be contagious, because the band was listening to me as I listened to them. A certain groove might be simple, but constantly embellishing itself. And when I was feeling it, my playing began to draw on a wellspring of soul. That took time. My ability to play the chank with true nuance and feeling did not happen instantly. When I first joined the band, I worked hard just to be competent. It took years before I really began to understand how funk *breathes*. And I got advice. James Brown talked about it, Jeff Watkins talked about it, the drummers, Mousey, Erik and Spike, all talked about it, Fred Thomas talked about it. Keith talked about it. Over time, they each told me about their approach to funk and what it meant to them. All these cool guys explained all this cool stuff and, after a few years, it began to sink in, and I could feel the funk from the inside.

ROBERT "MOUSEY" THOMPSON: The guitarist's place in funk is definitely rhythmic. Shop-a-dop-bee-dop, shop-a-dop-bee-dop If you can get that right, then you can take it somewhere else, just by playing accents. If you have "that thang," you're gonna make it. I call it "that thang" because I don't know what it is, but if a cat's got it, you say, "Man, he's *got that thang*." You don't know what it is, but you can feel it. Damon had that thang. And he became part of James Brown's chemistry because he'd be creating something new with whatever he brought to the table. Brown was a Baskin-Robbins of musicians, with many flavors. So with Damon we became another flavor of Brown.

WILLIE RAY "BO" BRUNDIDGE: Funk is repetitive. It's hypnotic. If you notice people in a club or at a festival, first they simmer, then they boil. Sometimes you're looking out at thousands of people groovin' to the music. That's the magic of music at work, right there.

HOLLIE FARRIS: I have a degree in music, so I had learned "the correct way" to play. Brown used to call it the "*key*-rect way." But when you play funk music, correct is not always right. What makes funk in the first place is that not everything is exactly right. It's not exactly on the beat, it's not exactly off the beat. It's somewhere in between, where there's this free-flowing feel . . . and that feeling *creates* the funk, that's what it's all about. Playing in a horn section is especially demanding because you have to play in a certain way that's not exactly correct. But you have to play it as a section. Where the guitar player can play his own thing, the horn section — all four or five of us — had to be together. That's the challenge for horns. Sometimes we'd discuss it, sometimes we had to rehearse it. But sometimes it was easier to get there by feel. You can just hear what works and what doesn't work. Trying to describe it is impossible. You have to hear it. When a band is playing a funky song and it's not funky, you can tell. Maybe the drummer is just a tad ahead on the snare, the bass player is rushin'. You can make someone hear the difference, but you can't explain it logically. It's all about the feel of music. So if you've got somebody who can play all styles of music, you've really got something. Damon could do that.

With advice and encouragement from my brethren, I finally got that feeling for funk. I actually had an *Aha!* moment one night. "So *that's* what I've been trying to understand for two years." I recall telling myself. "*That's* what these guys do naturally and I'm starting to get it." Finally, I'm on this wave that the rest of the band has been on all these years. Did it take longer to learn this because I'm white? I'm sure it did. Of *course* it did. Did the brothers in the band ever tease me because I'm of the Caucasian persuasion? Of *course* they did. That was part of the deal: plenty of ribbing. Everyone had a good sense of humor. We had fun with it. Think about it: here's a primarily black band that's been together a long time and they've had white players from time to time and they're all friends. So everybody knows how to get along. And I'm not glossing over anything. I heard stories that there could be racial tensions within the band, but that James Brown wouldn't stand for that. But he'd get in on the ribbing about skin tone. I still laugh about the time

Me, Keith Jenkins, Fred Thomas.

Mr. Brown told me pointedly that I couldn't play funk, that I wasn't a "Funkster" or a "Funkateer," but that that was okay — because I was Caucasian and had that clarity when I soloed.

It seems that in the history of James Brown's bands, there were a few white guitar players but never any white drummers. There was one white bass player, Tim Drummond, in the '60s, but there was never another. I read somewhere that at that time, the Black Panthers were giving James Brown grief for employing a white man. And James Brown would reply, "He's not a white man, he's my bass player." Music brings people together, and it was the music I was exploring. These were styles that I had very little experience with. Funk? No experience. R&B? No experience. Jazz? No experience. Playing with horns? That was brand new. I did love blues, always had. Of course, funk, R&B, and jazz come from blues roots. That helped me get on board. Improvising over I, IV, V progressions was familiar, so I had a basis for learning something new. Can you imagine a better situation? I'd entered a world of new music with people willing to share it. You can see why, after putting in a couple years to get that feeling, I wasn't going to let a little of Mr. Brown's craziness deter me.

Gaining acceptance into the band meant a lot to me. By this time I'd played nearly a hundred shows with the group, so I'd earned some band respect and some self-respect for handling my part. Performing the show was a kind of pass/fail test. In contrast, life off stage presented a whole other challenge: getting along with two dozen people while traveling, performing, and hanging out. That was more of a qualitative test. Just getting to know that many people one-on-one was a logistical challenge, but in the process I made a few real friendships. Every night after the gig, a few of us would gather in each other's hotel rooms and have a drink. Occasionally, Fred Thomas would fry spam on a clothes iron or a hotplate. Who'd want to miss out on that? Or we'd grab a few of our favorite people and head out on the town, if it wasn't too late. Naturally, I became tighter with the people I hung out with after hours, just based on time spent and shared experiences. Some band members preferred to rest up in their rooms after a gig or didn't want to be part of a constant, roving party. But by early 2001, I pretty much knew everybody. My party pals in the band were also the people I exchanged musical ideas with and who I learned from the most.

Leroy Harper had all these Johnny "Guitar" Watson recordings with him, so I'd hang with Leroy and marvel over the music. Johnny "Guitar" had been a pioneer of electric guitar in the early 1950s and he could play blues and funk. His song "A Real Mother for Ya" was a favorite of ours, and when I formed my own band later that year, I included it in my repertoire. (Johnny "Guitar" died on stage from a heart attack at a club outside Tokyo two years before I joined James Brown.) On the road, Keith brought incredible mix tapes of rare tracks and the hippest funk artists like Maceo and All the King's Men, composed of former James Brown sidemen like Maceo Parker, his brother Melvin, Jimmy Nolen, Sweet Charles Sherrell, the Griffith brothers. All the King's Men had recorded a couple of very heavy albums in the early '70s. I hadn't really been exposed to this type of music yet, so I was broadening my horizons while at the same time appreciating my bandmates and their musical tastes. Jeff Watkins would talk to Keith and me about music theory, teaching us when to use, say, a minor 6/9 chord — an eerie-sounding chord — to end a song.

Every relationship was based on something slightly different, something you'd done together or a private laugh you'd shared. Of course, everything wasn't consistently groovy, but even a little friction presented opportunities. I'd occasionally run afoul of someone over nothing important, just a traveling irritation or an awkward incident. Stepping up to smooth things over often led to an even better appreciation for that person's good points. And learning to make a righteous gesture to reestablish good terms made me a better person.

WE'RE GONNA HAVE A FUNKY GOOD TIME

After the Vegas debacle, we headed out on a series of U.S. dates in Boise, Denver, and Houston, followed by casinos in California and Nevada. In early February we all booked into the Ritz Carlton in Washington, D.C., to play the NBA All-Star Jam Session. That's when Yonna Kari joined us as a dancer. She was a trained dancer who'd worked with the NBA's Minnesota Timberwolves and for Prince, the musician. She and I always had a good rapport.

YONNA KARI WYNNE: My audition was a show for the NBA
All-Star Basketball weekend in Washington, D.C., in
February 2001. I was nervous. If they liked me they
were going to keep me and if they didn't like me they
were going to send me home. Well, I stayed for six
years. At first it was a little overwhelming to be in the
presence of James Brown. And the band only had a few
women. However, I fit in well because it was a tight-knit
family. Everyone welcomed me with open arms. Damon
and I had a good connection. He's my "Saj brother"
and I'm his "Saj sister." We're both Sagittarius and we
think along the same lines. We're both creative, hard
working. Because of that — and Damon being Damon,
a nice, creative guy — it was cool with him. He's always
learning something new, trying to better himself. He's
kind of a perfectionist, which I am as well. We want to
do the best we can do. I found Prince and James Brown
very similar in their work ethic and what they expected
out of the people who worked for them. I think Prince
actually got that from Brown. Prince modeled a lot of
his onstage moves after Brown. Same with Michael
Jackson. I've been onstage with all three of them. James
Brown liked to surround himself with beautiful women
of all types, shapes, stripes. The dancers took over when
he couldn't make certain dance moves. He'd call out
a dancer to do the camel walk or we'd do the "James
Brown split" when he could no longer do it. He loved
that we brought it back to life. Of course, having two
hot girls up there is always eye candy for the audience.

Winter turned to spring as we crisscrossed the country, playing
outdoor festivals like the Riverfest in Columbus, Georgia, or the
"Jam on the River" at Penn's Landing, Philadelphia. I remember

the latter show well. At one point Mr. Brown jumped behind the Hammond B3 organ, then dashed to his Korg keyboard, pointing people in on solos right and left, generous with the spotlight. He was on a roll that day. He cued in Hollie Farris during "Heavy Juice," an intense instrumental featuring the band. "Do you *love* your horn?" Mr. Brown asked Hollie through the PA. "Then *make love* to your horn!" (That's a tall order, especially in public.) Leroy Harper took a turn in the spotlight. Mr. Brown must have been happy with his band, because he kept yelling, "Soul Generals! Soul Generals!" into the microphone. The Bittersweet sashayed, the dancers did their thing. The James Brown production was going full strength with two dozen people serving up a blistering funk groove. Then Mr. Brown broke it down into his wrenching ballad, "Prisoner of Love," ("I'm just a *priz-nah!* I'm just a *priz-nah!*") with The Bittersweet on the chorus. Cynthia Moore sang a smoldering "Candy." Sara Raya came out and rapped and danced while Jeff Watkins wailed on a killer solo. Finally, the energy came down and we all exhaled. Mr. Brown broke into an emotional rendition of his classic ballad, "It's a Man's Man's Man's World." I'd been playing on a riser next to our first-chair drummer, Mousey, and now, suddenly, Mr. Brown called me down front.

I grabbed my long cable and started for the front of the stage. I'd been completely focused on playing rhythm. Suddenly I'm in the spotlight, in front of thousands of people, not to mention my colleagues. Mr. Brown kept rapping to the audience. "I'm gonna get *down* tonight! And this young man is gonna play his *heart* out." A typical stage moment: I had no idea what to expect. This would be yet another completely improvised, unique situation. I ripped a few leads on my Les Paul to provide the response to Mr. Brown's call. Mr. Brown turned to me as the band simmered in the background. "Do you know B.B. King?" he asked into his mic, so everyone could hear. I smiled and nodded. Of course. Everyone knows B.B. King. "Oh, you *know* B.B. King?" James Brown was grinning ear to ear. He had me! Of course I didn't *know* B.B. King. I knew his *music*. And thousands of people watched and laughed as James Brown pulled my leg. I cracked up a little, too. This was one of Mr. Brown's classic routines, though the audience couldn't know that. Still, Mr. Brown was capable of anything, and inserting moments like this into his act absolutely delighted him. "What's the name of your guitar?" Mr. Brown asked, for all to hear. "Matilda," I said. It was the first stupid name that came into my head. B.B. King, of course, famously named his guitar "Lucille." "Play like B.B. King!" Mr. Brown commanded. At least I knew this part was coming, so I managed to pull off a classic B.B. riff and then turned the solo into my own. Just another day on the job, working for The Man. It tickled me and the rest of the band to see James Brown having that much fun. When grooviness reigned, his vibe infected the band and audience alike, and smiles flashed all around. Few people could resist James Brown's charm, onstage or off. He had an innate ability to get a good time rolling with the band and take the audience along with us.

Later that month, however, on May 7, 2001, we all received a terse memo by mail from The New James Brown Enterprises that killed any smiles: "Due to rising costs of the economy in the entertainment business, we must cut down 27% in salaries. Thank you for understanding, James Brown, Godfather of Soul." Cutting our pay by more than one quarter was a bitter pill to swallow, and it really tested everyone's resolve to remain with the gig. We really couldn't know whether Mr. Brown was busting us all down for no good reason or whether the The New James Brown Enterprises was shaking down the band to fatten its own profit margin. Coincidentally, there were often 27 people in the band — admittedly an enormous overhead to carry. No doubt costs were high. Taking the Noah's Ark approach to the band to ensure redundancy and reliability was unusual and expensive. But Mr. Brown was used to having his way and, if he wanted a big show with lots going on, he'd have a big show. Maybe management stepped in to prevent costs from sinking the show. But a 27 percent pay cut for a working musician (or anyone) is tough to take. I remember Amy Christian, one of The Bittersweet singers, left at that time, though she'd return in less than a year. For my part, the cut stung — it basically eliminated the multiple pay raises I'd received — but by the spring of 2001, I was way too into the gig to consider jumping ship. We made up songs about "27 percent" and sang 'em on the bus on the way to the next gig.

We didn't stop traveling for any appreciable length of time between spring and summer. I think Tomi Rae had left the show at that point. (She gave birth to James Brown Jr. on June 11, 2001.) I remember a pair of nights at Oakland's Paramount Theater, a spectacular Art Deco palace, on a bill with the Tower of Power, a venerable, horn-driven soul group. We played the Greek Theater in L.A. the next day and the Tower shared the bill again. Later that month we headed north to Anchorage, Alaska, and then to Fairbanks, where the Soul Generals leapt at an opportunity for an after-hours jam. We seized any chance to play a local club after the gig, without Mr. Brown. Through the years we managed to play a handful of club dates that way. We always had to be stealthy about it, though. It couldn't be advertised for fear of competing with the actual gig and, frankly, we didn't want Mr. Brown to know we were stepping out on him. Mr. Brown had had enough of players with big heads, thinking they could move "beyond" James Brown, and we knew he frowned on freelancing. As a band, though, a real unit, we naturally relished the opportunity to get out from under his thumb and do *our thang* and receive a little love for our prowess and recognition in our own right.

HOLLIE FARRIS: When we played after-hours gigs, we would knock it out of the park. Still, if it didn't have that James Brown name behind it, maybe nobody would've shown up. But it was great to realize that we could actually play. Because, according to him, we couldn't play. Sometimes he'd say we sounded good, but most of the time we needed work and all that. But once we'd go out and hit a club, we'd think, "Yeah, we *can* do this. We are a *band*!" We knew we were a band behind him. But when we'd do "us," it became a whole 'nother thing. Whoever was singing the song, whoever wrote it, would lead it. We worked it out as a group. There was no leader, per se. Damon wrote songs, Keith wrote songs, I wrote songs. Everybody contributed.

ERIK HARGROVE: I think Brown realized at one point that he'd actually built up some of the people in his earlier bands — Maceo [Parker] and Fred [Wesley Jr.] and those guys — so high that they felt they could talk to him any way they felt like, that they could do what they wanted to do, and screw James Brown. So I think that was in the back of his mind when he came to deal with the Soul Generals. By that time he was thinking, "I'm going to keep my thumb on every single one of these people and I will only let them rise up when I need them to, for show business purposes, but then I'm putting my thumb right back down on 'em."

ROBERT "MOUSEY" THOMPSON: Hamburg, Paris, Fairbanks — you name it. We were trying to jam after hours wherever we could. We just wanted to have fun. We'd always play some James Brown music, though — that's the funny thing about it. But we would play it the way we wanted to play it, just letting off that steam. Then we could go back, "What do you want *now*, boss?" We'd be ready for him.

Shortly after our return to the Lower 48, Mr. Brown went to the White House to be recognized in ceremonies celebrating Black Music Month, hosted by President George W. Bush. I did not share

Mr. Brown's comfort level with President Bush or the Republican Party, to say the least, but naturally I understood that his infatuation wasn't my business. In fact, Mr. Brown *was* a Republican, due, I think, to that party's rhetoric about self-sufficiency. Mr. Brown had always preached economic self-empowerment. He'd endorsed Richard Nixon for president in 1972 — enraging Black Power advocates — and, in 1999, in response to a question from *Rolling Stone*, he'd named segregationist Senator Strom Thurmond as one of his heroes, blowing just about everyone's mind. But his politics were idiosyncratic: he expressed admiration for the Kennedy family as well. And Mr. Brown obviously enjoyed his invitations to the White House, whoever held office. In fact, I believe his first invitation came from President Johnson, a Democrat, in 1968, when Mr. Brown helped avert violence in Boston following the assassination of Dr. Martin Luther King. Whether the president was Republican or Democrat, Mr. Brown's repeated invitations to the White House were a point of pride for the man. I mean, if the White House calls, you're probably heading down there, right? And the James Brown I knew would be entirely comfortable with being honored by lesser mortals such as the president of the United States. He couldn't be intimidated. In fact, I'd bet it was the other way around when W. met James Brown. This man — the Godfather of Soul — had a presence to match his moniker. Wherever he went, others would need to step up to *his* level.

ERIK HARGROVE: It wasn't just limited to the music on stage. That was him, wherever he went. It was a freaky thing. If you had your back to the door, you knew when he entered the room. If we'd be out somewhere, you knew when he was around. I can't explain it. He had something about him. People could feel it. Big movie stars would come to see him and their whole demeanor would change, their body language would change.

Elton John. Dan Aykroyd. Pavarotti. You could see the humbleness in front of James Brown. It was the way Mr. Brown carried himself. He was The Man. And he projected that. That was a great reminder to us about why we were there and just who we were performing with. Here's a man who changed music forever. Think of all the adversities he had to overcome to get to that point. When you have younger people coming up in your band, you want to show them that times weren't always easy. You put out a little tough love — if you can call it that — to show them it's not all cake and pie. At times he went overboard being that protective parent. And sometimes he just wanted to be an asshole.

SUMMER 2001

In the dog days of summer 2001, we flew to Europe for a rapid-fire tour of nine cities and festivals in ten days, across the United Kingdom, Germany, Monaco, Belgium, and France, then back to England, Scotland, and Germany. Touring Europe at that speed was taxing, mentally and physically, but it offered us the opportunity to play an enjoyable mix of clubs, theaters, and open-air summer festivals. We opened the Gosport Summer Festival in Hampshire, on England's southern coast, then flew east to Cologne, Germany, for the Blue Moon Jazz Festival, the next night. We headed south to play the next two nights at the Sporting Club in Monaco. The audience in Monte Carlo was your basic Euro jet set enjoying the high life on the French Riviera. We had to dress the part just to get to the gig; some of the guys wore full-on business suits. Not exactly my neighborhood. We didn't have big money to throw around, of course, we were just peons in a band, entertaining rich people. As musicians, we were used to that fact and, anyway, we knew damn well that the audience wasn't necessarily any better off than we were. Everyone gets the blues. In fact, nobody jumps out of a window because their gig gets canceled. Yet people jump out of windows when the stock market crashes. Anyway, we played the Sporting Club many times over the years, and people like Elton John and Van Morrison would jump onstage with us. With James Brown on the marquee, you never knew who might show up. I'm sure the Sporting Club paid Mr. Brown an ungodly amount of money to entertain its wealthy gamblers with a couple of hour-long sets. From Monte Carlo we headed north to Colmar, France, for the Alsace Wine Festival, where we headlined one night, and Robert Plant headlined the next.

KELLY JARRELL: After our gig in Colmar, France, it was just me, Damon, and Keith. We went to see Robert Plant. Damon and Keith were going to just stand in the back with the crowd, and I said, "No, no, no." Keith used to call me the "Self-appointed VIP of the World." So I led them down front, where security remembered us, and we moseyed over to the front of the stage where only the photographers hang. We had our James Brown passes on. Afterwards we went backstage and talked to Robert Plant like we'd been friends for a long time.

Knowing that we worked for James Brown, Robert Plant treated us like comrades-in-arms. He asked if we knew "where they keep the beer," and I told him that after our gig the night before we had had to stick our heads in a little backstage window of sorts and request them. Next thing you know, Robert Plant is halfway through that window, passing beers out to everyone. He said he'd caught our show the night before. "So, I'm looking up at your boss," he said, "and I'm thinking that when you're real young, you wear your pants up high. When you grow up, you move 'em down around your waist. Then when you get old, I guess you move them up high again!" (Mr. Brown indeed positioned the waistband of his suit way up on his belly to accommodate his rounder physique at that point.) Though Plant's comment isn't a real screamer on the page, we laughed our asses off when he said it — maybe it was just a relief to hear someone we liked and respected make good-natured fun of the boss. Plant talked about how he'd fairly recently made a pilgrimage to Clarksdale, Mississippi, after he'd studied the old blues guys like Tampa Red, a famous Delta slide player who'd passed in 1981. And he told us a few Jimmy Page stories that can't be repeated. When it was time to leave, someone asked him about a beautiful girl in his entourage. "Is that your daughter?" Plant said yes. Keith didn't miss a beat: "Looks like the mailman might have been involved!" Plant didn't miss a beat, either: "The iceman cometh!" We all laughed and said goodbye. On the way back to the hotel, we had to pinch ourselves to make sure it wasn't a dream.

I'm pretty sure we jumped on a bus for the 200 miles to Leuven, Belgium, just east of Brussels, to close the three-day Marktrock festival. The scale of the crowd — 75,000 — surprised me. The Fun Lovin' Criminals — an alt–hip hop group from New York City — opened for us and rocked the crowd big time; we watched from a monitor in our dressing room. Clearly, the pressure was on for us to bring it. And, as I recall, we brought the funk. Sometimes those seriously large crowds could be daunting, but mostly we rose to the occasion. The next day we hopped on a plane to head over the English Channel to London to play the Hackney Ocean, a venue north of the city. The very next day we took a short flight north to Aberdeen, Scotland, then jumped on a bus to 16th century Crathes Castle near Banchory for a performance. The following day, we flew over the North Sea en route to our final gig of the run at the Open Air festival in Ahaus, Germany.

I subject you to the details of "we flew here, we drove there" to paint a picture of life in a touring band. Economics and logistics called for packing as many gigs as possible into the shortest time-frame with the least downtime. That meant the band could be in perpetual motion for nearly two weeks. That may not sound like much on paper, but this is the backdrop to performing to James Brown's standards at each and every stop. In some instances, we had to leave for the next gig directly after an evening performance. Other times we'd arrive to our destination city with just enough time to check into a hotel and head straight to the venue, where we'd crowd into a small backstage room, iron our tuxedos, and get ready to dash out on stage. Sometimes I'd be lucky to have just enough time to change my strings before heading out in front of thousands of people. We might not have had five minutes to practice all day. There'd be a little pressure. Sometimes they'd have adult beverages set up backstage, which could take the edge off, but we couldn't let James Brown see us drinking alcohol before a performance. And he could pop up *anywhere, at any time.*

Sometimes just getting all the bodies on the bus on time presented a challenge. On my first overseas trip, I realized the exceptional logistics of moving two dozen people around the world in a timely fashion. We had just come off a long overseas flight and took a long bus ride straight to the venue for a sound check. When we got to the hotel, we had about 15 minutes to take what we called a "hooker bath" — just enough time to sponge off the worst B.O. — get dressed again and get our asses back on the bus to the venue. This led to one of my first experiences with RT, our road (and everything else) manager. The troupe gathered in the lobby, but a couple of bodies were missing. RT said, "Look, there are people who ain't out here yet. If they are your roommate and you care about them, you will go get them, because this bus is about to leave. And it will leave their ass behind if they ain't in it in five minutes. Y'all take care of it." You couldn't blame him. He'd been babysitting people

— musicians, no less — for years, and there was immense pressure on him to move two dozen people to and from gigs in an endless number of foreign places on a very tight schedule. Occasionally, I caused a problem. I'm sure everyone did, at some point. Back in those days, Jimmie Lee Moore had a bit of a time management problem (particularly early in the day). He might stay out late after a gig with the local friends he was able to make wherever he went. In the morning, it'd be time to go and, let's just say, his things were not quite in the suitcase. The rest of the band would sometimes break into a couple of choruses of "Where's Jimmie Lee Moore?" to the tune of "Gimme Some More" as we waited for his appearance. The band regaled me with a great story along these lines. It seems that one time, Jimmie literally refused to get on the bus at the end of a European tour to get to the airport to fly back to the States. He wasn't ready to go. His portfolio was in disarray. Eventually, he made it to the airport but, of course, he had missed the band's flight. The whole band is gone. He was understandably a bit upset and not sure what to do. A man walked up to him and asked, "What's the matter, man? You okay?" Jimmie explained the situation, and the man bought him a ticket to the United States. Turns out this guy was some kind of record mogul or rich businessman. When they got to New York, the guy took Jimmie around in his limo. By the time the band arrived from its trans-Atlantic flight and hopped on a bus to the hotel, Jimmie was already sitting in the lobby, waiting. This is the same cat who once took off on a Jet Ski with nothing on but a bathrobe. It's band folklore. He used to wear capes in his hotel room. (He told me he had a thing for them.) Fantastic bass player, great guitarist, a real brother and an amazing character. Really, rock 'n' roll to the T.

We got home in late August and had about a week off before we reconvened for a few one-off gigs around the country, which didn't necessarily line up geographically. We played the Gerald Ford Amphitheater in Vail, Colorado, on August 31, flew east the next day for a gig that night at the Calvert Marine Museum in Solomons, Maryland, returned west for a gig a day later at the African Festival of the Arts in Chicago's Washington Park, and moved on to the West Coast a few days later for the San Diego Street Scene. The evening at the Calvert Marine Museum in Maryland marked a milestone in my journey. For some reason, Mr. Brown gave me an unprecedented five solos that night. That surprised me, but I pulled it off and had something to say each time. I felt I'd met the test and even enjoyed it. But who knew how Mr. Brown felt? After the show I got word the boss wanted to see me. The manager came to the dressing room, as he often did to call somebody out if the boss wanted a word, and said, "Damon, you've got a bench warrant." That meant the King wanted to see me. I didn't know if that was good or bad, but it wasn't likely to be indifferent. So I went to Mr. Brown's dressing room. I don't remember much about the setting. He might have been getting his hair done, which was typical after a show. I remember Mr. Brown said to me, "Son, do you have pockets in your pants?" I said, "No, sir." I politely reminded him that Danny Ray had designed some uniforms with the pockets sewn shut so we could not use them. (Band lore had it that Mr. Brown thought having things in our pockets would detract from looking sharp on stage.) Mr. Brown said, "Well, here's $400 bonus money. I didn't know you could *play* like that." He told me, "Stick it in your sock, son." I probably looked like a kid on Christmas morning. He could pump up one of his people real nice when he wanted to and, apparently, it was my turn. We'd had a few ups and downs. I'd been in the band for two years now and, for the most part, I'd kept my mouth shut and worked hard. Mr. Brown's appreciation meant a lot to me, and that cash in my sock felt good.

Looking back, my skills had improved immeasurably. Still, as a guitarist, I found it challenging to switch from rhythm to lead the second Mr. Brown whipped around and pointed me in. I had to be ready for anything at any time. I couldn't really prepare any solos ahead of time, because the show was too dynamic and fluid. I'd do my damnedest to play something lyrical and inventive on the spot. Jeff Watkins and some of the other guys did that pretty well, but I found it difficult to switch gears like that. I tried to develop phrases for each song that, roughly speaking, could be repeated. James Brown really liked people to build to a high note at the peak of a solo, so I knew the arc of what he wanted. But I never knew when he'd throw me the spotlight. And at the Calvert Marine Museum in Maryland that night, James Brown gave me a gift and a test. Thank the gods, I delivered.

Later, when I shared my James Brown bonus story with my bandmates, most of them had similar stories to tell.

WILLIE RAY "BO" BRUNDIDGE: We were playing a casino in Wisconsin. I had a Fender Jazz bass. Mr. Brown gave me a solo and I came out and played. Afterwards, he called me to his dressing room. I thought, "Wow, maybe he didn't like that solo." He said, "Ray, you're a good guy." There's this long pause. I'm thinking, "What? *What?!*" "You're a good guy, but . . . you need a better bass." "A better bass? What do you mean?" "Go get yourself a better bass and I'll take care of it." The next big city was Chicago. Jeff Watkins helped me find one. We went to eight stores in Chicago on a day off. Finally, we found one at the last store, in the back, in a box — a Marcus Miller Jazz bass, on sale for $900. I could have found a more expensive one, but I just wanted one I could work with. I was making enough money to buy any bass I wanted, so it wasn't like Mr. Brown had to buy it. But I was glad for his generosity. The more he talked to me, the more he got to know me and the more I got to know him. Usually we were in a working situation. After a show, if we were on the same plane and everyone else was crashed out, he'd still be up talkin', so I'd join him. I'd get to one-on-one rap with him.

JERRY "LOUIE" POINDEXTER: I had a child support problem. They came at me, said I owed money. I told Mr. Brown what was goin' on. Mr. Brown's secretary called me the next day, said "Hold for Mr. Brown." "Mr. Poindexter?" "Yes, boss?" "How you feelin'?" "Doin' fine." "I know they're tryin' to get you, Louie." He had nicknamed me "Louie," because I helped take care of things. We were like father and son rather than boss and employee. "People messin' with you and I don't like it," he said. "How much you owe, son?" I told him. He said, "All right. I'm gonna lend you money, you're gonna pay me back. Miss Ware will make the arrangements." He paid off my child support. It was in the thousands. I paid him back. In fact, I overpaid him. His office called me and said, "Mr. Poindexter, you done overpaid us. You have some money coming back." When my next child was born, James Brown was the godfather.

GEORGE "SPIKE" NEALY: When I first got with James Brown, we were playing in the round — I want to say the Circle Star Theater in San Carlos, California — and the house was full. A bodyguard brought Mrs. Brown to a chair in the round, right behind me. I tried to tell him, "Hey, don't put her there. These sticks of mine break at any time. I don't want to be responsible for a splinter getting into her eye." But he'd left, leaving Mrs. Brown in that seat. The show started. I can't worry about her anymore. I'm locked in. I can't take my eye off Mr. Brown. I've forgotten she's back there. By the time the show was over and we left the stage, she was gone. As she was walking away I saw wood chips in her hair. So I was real quiet in the dressing room. I changed my clothes. There's a knock at the door. Dnt-dnt-dnt! "Mr. Nealy? Mr. Brown wants to see you." "Oh man, oh Lord!" I knocked on his door. "Come on in, son." I saw two people plucking wood out of her hair. I went in explaining: "I told them, 'Don't put Mrs. Brown so close!'" He let me get all that out. "Son, what are you talking about?" I said, "Mr. Brown, I'm talking about the wood chips in Mrs. Brown's hair." He said, "Son, that's not why I called you in here. I just wanted to tell you my wife said if I don't give you a raise, she's gonna fire me. My wife enjoyed every minute. You just keep doin' what you're doin'." That was my first raise.

KELLY JARRELL: My little story is the reason why I will always think of James Brown in a good light, even though I would get so hurt and frustrated and angry with him. It was 1997, and I was engaged to be married. My fiancé did not want me to sing anymore with James Brown. So I quit, but on good terms. Everybody was excited that I was engaged. Huge wedding plans, 300 people. Of course, James Brown would be there, Susan Dey was going to do a reading, the mayor was coming. Three weeks before the wedding, my fiancé called me and said, "I can't go through with it." I was devastated. I was in love. He told me we were soul mates and I believed him. I didn't get out of bed for three weeks. So I'm lyin' in bed, staring at the ceiling and the phone rings. It's James Brown. He said, [*she slips into her J.B. voice*], "Miss Jarrell?" I said, "Oh, hi Mr. Brown. How are you?" He said, "The real question is, 'How are you?'" I said, "Oh, fine." He said, "No, you're not. I'll bet you're lying in

bed right now, staring at the ceiling." I said, "*What?!*"
You see, he knew. He said, "Look, we want you to come
back. We love you. What happened to you is wrong.
And the only way to get over this is to get back to
work." I said, "Mr. Brown, I really appreciate it, but you
know, when I left, I really wasn't making much money
. . ." And he said, "Whatever kind of money you need,
you're comin' back to work." He saved my life. I know
that sounds dramatic, but that's the way I felt. And years
after that happened, I was able to pull him aside and
tell him how much that meant to me. He could be so
cruel to me. "You can't sing, you can't dance, da da da."
Giving me my job back made amends for absolutely
everything. So whenever I got mad at him after that, I'd
always remember that he did that for me.

9/11

I'd been playing my burgundy Les Paul Studio guitar on the James
Brown show and there was a sense that my Les Paul and Keith's Paul
Reed Smith (aka PRS) guitar were too closely matched in terms of
tone. Jeff Watkins could hear the lack of tonal contrast between the
two guitars and he talked to us about it. Plus, the high E string on
my Les Paul just didn't get the same volume as the other strings,
possibly due to an issue with the pickups. The guitar had a slight
grounding issue, too: I'd get unwanted noise if I took my hands off
the strings. I thought maybe the Les Paul had seen better days and
I needed to find something new. I've always been wary of people
fixing my guitars. I'd rather wear out a guitar and then set it aside
than let anybody touch it. I'd gotten the burgundy Les Paul brand

new, and I felt I needed another new instrument, something I could start over with, something with low action, real smooth. Maybe an instrument with a different tone and playability would lead me to different phrasings.

I had been listening a lot to John Scofield and Phish guitarist Trey Anastasio and they both used thin, hollow body guitars, so I had gotten an urge to buy one and pursue new sounds. Maybe a new guitar sound would fit into the James Brown show. And I was thinking about my own sound. All that gigging for James Brown had me thinking about putting together a band of my own, on the side. At first I conceived of a solo gig just to have something fun to do in my downtime from touring with Mr. Brown. But as time went by I felt the need to develop new music with my own band, quite apart from the James Brown trip, and I began to envision a three-piece, instrumental, improvisational band.

I had a vacation day between gigs, so I'd gotten a room at the Sunset Motel on Sunset Strip in L.A., where a lot of guitar shops are clustered. I wanted to see what was on offer, and the price range. The next day I awoke to a weird vibe. As I checked out, the desk clerk told me what had happened — the planes, the madness. Shopping for guitars? Out of the question. I made it over to our bass player Bo's house in Van Nuys and we hung out, talked it over. I didn't even try to get back to Vegas until the next day. By the time I pulled up at McCarran Airport in Vegas in my rental car, hundreds of people were waiting for that car.

We all were aware of the magnitude of events, but James Brown had gigs to play. Nothing could stop James Brown — not even terrorists. Of course, the airports were closed for days. The September 11 attacks took place on a Tuesday, and we had a show set for the Harbor Center in Portsmouth, Virginia, that Saturday. Flights finally resumed that Saturday, and I jumped a series of planes from Vegas to Dallas to Boston to Virginia Beach. My flight into Boston might have been the first plane to land at Logan Airport since the mayhem. All the American Airlines employees were on the tarmac, waving little American flags. The sight chilled me to my bones.

Portsmouth was an outdoor gig, with the stage under a massive tent, by a harbor full of boats — a nice outdoor venue with an open lawn in back for general admission. An older band opened for us, maybe the Coasters. We played an early show for an older crowd. James Brown sang "God Bless America" a cappella by himself at the close of his performance.

We were set to close the annual Blues and Brews Fest in Telluride, Colorado, the day after the Virginia Beach gig. But commercial flights were just resuming. So the organization chartered a 19-seat prop plane bound for Montrose, Colorado, the nearest airfield to Telluride. Not many of the band members wanted to be on that plane. It was the kind where they manually start the propeller in front. I guess that's all that was available, post-9/11, but it reminded us of the James Brown bus — instead of hurtling around mountain roads, we'd be *flying over the mountains*. The band boarded, each of us with our instruments and a little suitcase apiece, and then Mr. Brown's luggage came rolling up on a cart — a couple dozen suitcases and wardrobe cases were transferred into the belly of the plane, which sagged a little each time a bag landed. Tragically, the pop singer Aaliyah had died in a plane crash three weeks earlier in an overloaded prop plane leaving the Bahamas. We were freaking each other out. Pop history is littered with people who went down in an airplane — Buddy Holly and The Big Bopper in 1959, Otis Redding in 1967, Lynyrd Skynyrd in 1977, Aaliyah in 2001 . . . we didn't want to be the next dead celebrities. Or worse: the next dead, anonymous sidemen. Of course, James Brown strolled onto the plane, tickled pink, grinnin', just glad to be rollin' to the next gig. He boarded that overloaded plane singing show tunes. "I dream of Jeannie with the light brown hair . . ." I remember Jeff Watkins saying under his breath, "Man, I want whatever he's on, 'cuz I'm sketched out." This plane had to get from the East Coast all the way to Colorado, then over the Rocky Mountains and down into their midst. We stopped for gas at least twice. Since when do planes stop for gas? Then they'd flip that propeller to get it rollin' again while James Brown is singing show tunes and we're all in our seats, praying and preparing to die because he brought too many suitcases!

HOLLIE FARRIS: Everybody was nervous, for a lot of reasons. It didn't bother Brown — didn't bother him at all. Like when we played in Beirut. Half the band didn't even go. They said, "We're not going. It's just too dangerous." And he went. Just went right on. No problem at all. He just thought he couldn't die, I guess. He went to Vietnam, paid his own way. I understand there was shooting in the background while he was performing. He was fearless.

Of course, we reached Montrose, despite our fears. But then we had to speed through the mountains in a van with a half hour till show time. (The drive typically takes an hour and a half.) We ended up starting two hours late, but we rocked the Rockies, just glad to be alive. The mood was powerful, just five days after 9/11. By the end of the show, it was dark, but we could see the silhouette of the mountains. We'd all left the stage when James Brown popped back out and sang "God Bless America" a cappella. A lot of times, I think he saved his feelings for the audience. His message was togetherness: "We'll be all right. We've got to stay strong." We had a week or so off before hitting the road again.

HARMONIOUS JUNK

The rest of 2001 went quietly. I don't think anyone could avoid thinking about 9/11 constantly for months and, in fact, we played some related benefits and memorials. We played a gig called "United We Stand" at RFK Stadium in Washington, D.C., where we shared a dressing room with Bette Midler, who was cool as hell. You don't forget that stuff. Here's a bunch of half-naked men, changing their outfits, but she was totally cool with it — a complete entertainment professional. Aerosmith showed up to meet the boss, too. Turned out Aerosmith had gone backstage to a James Brown show years before, and Mr. Brown's manager didn't recognize them. I don't know who that was, but according to band lore he told them, "We don't know who you are, go away." RT made sure that didn't happen this time, and Steve Tyler and Joe Perry finally got to meet James Brown. As for the band, we just saw 'em walkin' by.

Somewhere in this kaleidoscope of events — it must have been late September — I managed to follow through on my quest for a new guitar, and I purchased an Epiphone Sheridan, a semi-hollow body guitar with a jazzy feel. The Epiphone has a natural voice, a clarity of tone, and it suited my ambitions for the sound of my own band. I was still looking ahead to what I could do with my downtime outside of Mr. Brown's orbit. But I also wanted to try the Epiphone on the James Brown show. Within a week I had my chance. We had an upcoming gig at the Wild Adventures Theme Park in Valdosta, Georgia. Keith would be absent for his wedding, which he had warned Mr. Brown about a full year earlier to avoid being fired. I broke out the Epiphone. I'd be stepping out on lead guitar that night, while Daryl Brown provided the chank. Well, Mr. Brown let me know that the Epiphone didn't quite have the umpf, the sustain, the power, when he signaled: "We need big sounds now!" I didn't have a backup guitar. Mr. Brown was real cool about it. Generally speaking, he liked a loud, clear guitar tone that could be varied to get that beautiful, funky chank sound or cut through the music on a solo. I knew he liked Fender Stratocasters — he loved the blues — and a lot of his guys over the years played Strats. So he was open to people experimenting, trying to get better tone with better instruments. He gave the band more freedom to explore their thing within his thing than people might think — he'd be open to it unless it presented a problem for him and the overall consistency of his show. I had been looking for a new tone, something cool. The Epiphone didn't work for James Brown, but it didn't cost me anything to try. I went back to the Les Paul for a while. The Epiphone would have its day.

In early November we flew to Toronto for a week to make a cameo appearance in Jackie Chan's kooky Dreamworks movie *The Tuxedo*, also starring Jennifer Love Hewitt. (The movie bombed with American critics, but it earned $100 million worldwide, so how smart is Jackie Chan?) The plot: Jackie Chan saves the day by wearing a secret agent's special tuxedo that allows him to do amazing things, like high-speed martial arts. Mr. Brown and the Soul Generals appear briefly at the end, performing "Sex Machine." In the movie, Chan in his special tuxedo accidentally knocks out Mr. Brown and is forced to finish the song as if he were James Brown. After a week of shooting the producers threw a party at the local Planet Hollywood and we got to meet the stars. Jerry Poindexter accidentally called Jackie "Charlie," as in, Charlie Chan. I was *dying*! I have a great photo of me with Jennifer Love Hewitt to document that I was associated with her for all of 15 seconds. Nice lady. I was kinda starstruck — she's gorgeous — and hanging back when Kelly Jarrell pushed me into position for the photo.

You might think that the Soul Generals got the call to appear in a Jackie Chan movie because we, too, wore tuxedos that made us superhuman. The funny thing is, that *is* how wearing the James Brown tuxedos made us feel, so the irony of appearing in a tuxedo in *The Tuxedo* did not escape me. As anyone who wears a uniform can tell you, it can instill a sense of pride. Our stage tuxedos struck some folks as corny or retro, but they imparted a certain power — an esprit de corps — just as Mr. Brown intended. When we wore the James Brown uniform, we were invincible, in some magical way. We became this gang of musicians and dancers that could not be denied. That show would go over anywhere because everyone had ultimate faith in our leader — faith that he was going to destroy the place. "Rock" Laster used to say, "Nobody's following us, as long as we've got 'Crip,'" a nickname for Mr. Brown. The sheer magnetism of this dude meant that he left a stage like a patch of scorched earth. No one could follow him, even late in his career. And a score of killer musicians in tuxedos laying down a stone groove sealed the deal.

Not every observer saw us this way. The following year a reviewer for the *Winnipeg Free Press* cracked wise about our formal appearance.

> For once, the unmistakably funky scent wafting over St. Boniface last night had nothing to do with Maple Leaf Meats. Across the Red River, American music legend James Brown turned CanWest Global Park into the funkiest baseball diamond on Earth with a show that proved he's still one of the hardest-working men in showbiz. The biggest chunk of the entourage was his backing band, the 13-piece Soul Generals, whose red-and-black suits made them look like the serving staff from Rae & Jerry's steakhouse.

The rest of the schedule for the months following 9/11 was pretty light. The upshot was time off for the band and an opportunity for me to get a little original music going, maybe put together a band. Of course, I couldn't necessarily count on it. If the phone rang, I'd jump on a plane, no questions asked. My aspirations would have to work within the organization's schedule and be set aside if any unanticipated bookings came up. But it was clear that I needed to anticipate life after James Brown. By the time I joined his caravan he was in his mid-60s. How long could he keep traveling the world? How long would he be able to keep performing? Everybody in the band had thoughts about what would be next, if and when the juggernaut stopped.

Earlier in the year, in April, I'd traveled up to Reno and played an Earth Day gig with a jam band that included my old pal, Mike Tuttle. The bass player, Joe Warren (today it's Anderson), was moving to Vegas. We shared an interest in improvisational rock. Back in Vegas I met drummer Dan Paczkowski, who also had similar musical interests. In the late fall of 2001, we worked out some jazzy, jamming instrumentals and got a gig as "Harmonious Junk" at Legends Lounge, the only jam band club in Vegas, on December 7. George Lyons of *The Lyons Den* radio show on 91.5 KUNV, introduced us on stage, recorded the performance, and later played the set on his show. About the name: I love a good play on words. Thelonious Monk was (and is) my favorite jazz musician, the one I consider the most far out. Here's someone who didn't play my instrument, so I could see his music differently. It's complex, a bit over my head. But the things I like about it are the things about him that are unique. He'll wait till the last second in a solo space and you're wondering, "Is he going to play something or not?" and he'd hit these two half-step intervals when it's almost too late, a weird chord that's just perfect. I've seen footage. He'd get up and start dancin' in circles in the middle of a show when someone else soloed, just feelin' it, and return *just* in time to play the melody line. And I loved his name. I always thought it had such a ring to it. Harmonious Junk came to me as an attempt to go in that direction: a jam band instrumentation going in a jazz direction.

Perhaps because I'd grown up playing in other people's bands, I had ideas of my own I wanted to express. And I'd absorbed a few things about being a band leader from one of the great band leaders of all time. I was renting a house with my ex-girlfriend (yes, that's ill-advised), so Harmonious Junk had a place to rehearse. When she was at work we could make some noise. It worked out pretty well, for a while. Harmonious Junk was my band and Joe and Dan knew it. I booked the gigs, put together the promotional material. I made the decisions, musical and otherwise. Now, I'm a hard-ass band leader for one good reason: James Brown had impressed on me the importance of having one person — the band leader — make the decisions. Discussion is good, and suggestions are welcome, but the leader has to make the decisions.

That being said, I learned a lesson of another kind from Mr. Brown — the kind I swore I'd never inflict on another player — that had to do with abusing leadership. I don't recall exactly when this nagging issue popped up, but it never went away. It would drive me to absolute madness. We had three guitar players in the James Brown show at this point: Keith, me, and Daryl Brown, Mr. Brown's son. I sold Daryl my old tuner when I got a new Boss chromatic tuner, the industry standard. It's inexpensive and dependable. Everybody's got one. Back in the '60s, bands had one big strobe tuner at the back of the stage and, one by one, they'd go back to that strobe tuner, tune up, go out on stage and play the show. How many recordings have we heard from that era where the tuning went haywire because they didn't have the digital tuners we have now? (Answer: lots!) Guys like Jimi Hendrix and Albert King were masters at hearing themselves, recognizing when a string had gone flat or sharp and retuning on the fly. The James Brown show offered many opportunities to go out of tune: a dancer might bump you on her way out front, you'd bend a note in the blues, the lights were really hot. You can't fix that on the fly like they did back in the day because it's James Brown's show — and you're not Jimi Hendrix. With a tuner at your feet, you could punch in, take your guitar offline, and tune your instrument without audibly messing up the music. Digital electronic tuners offer many advantages to the performing musician. All such tuners can operate at 440 hertz (Hz), which has been the tuning standard for proper pitch in the U.S. since 1926. You can see that

I'm building the case for the use of modern, electronic tuners — I still can't get this out of my system.

At some point in early spring 2002, we finished a killer show. Grins all around, and we got paid. We're relaxing in the dressing room when Mr. Brown's emissary, Mr. Bobbit, shows up with a message: "You guitarists are all out of tune." Now, I may not be Jimi Hendrix, but I sure can tell when a string has gone sharp or flat. So this pronouncement made no sense. Nonetheless, Mr. Brown began to make this peculiar statement a regular refrain, sending Mr. Bobbit to the dressing room after every show (or so it seemed) to announce that the guitarists were out of tune. The day came when he said, "I want only *one* tuner used by the guitarists," meaning one tuner for all three guitarists, even though we're spread out across the stage. That's a completely unrealistic approach for modern performing. Perhaps Mr. Brown really thought we were out of tune, and he remembered the old days when the entire band tuned off that one strobe tuner. Perhaps something else drove this nonsense. We knew better than to say anything to Mr. Brown about such an irrational demand, so we tried to implement his orders. But when you can't converse rationally with someone, stuff gets swept under the rug, where it festers.

JAPAN AND CHUCK BERRY

The first few months of 2002 were kinda slow for James Brown: we played a couple nights at B.B. King's Blues Club in New York, then we had three weeks off. We did one-offs at the House of Blues in Orlando and the 9:30 Club in D.C. at the end of February. Another three weeks off. I tried to squeeze in as many Harmonious Junk gigs as possible, but in late March, we were headed to Tokyo with Chuck

Berry for two performances, and once May rolled around, we were on the road constantly, summer through fall. That kind of schedule is tough to build a band or a relationship on, effectively dissolving the original Harmonious Junk lineup in April.

I ran into Dr. John — New Orleans's Mac Rebennack Jr. — at baggage claim at Narita Airport in Japan and I just had to say, "What's up?!" The most he could manage was: "Tired." ("Tahd" in his N'awlins drawl.) We'd just made the 13-hour flight from the West Coast, too. (Dr. John should have tried riding the James Brown bus.) For two nights in March, we performed at the Tokyo International Forum, with Chuck Berry as our opening act. First off, when I say we went to Japan with Chuck Berry, I don't actually mean we went to Japan *with* Chuck Berry. Even when you're on the same bill with another artist, you rarely get to meet them, let alone hang out. For all the stars we met and actually hung with, lots of others got away. Scheduling was the usual culprit, because when one band is coming off stage, the other is going on. Your travel itineraries are likely to be different. Whether Mr. Brown and Chuck got together, I don't know. Surely they were acquainted in the old days. (They both appear, separately, on the historic T.A.M.I. show recorded in October 1964, which was filmed, shown in theaters the following month, and released in 2009 on DVD. James Brown gave one of his most amazing performances on that show.)

I learned a lot watching that cat Chuck Berry do his thing. I mean, Chuck's loud as hell, out of tune, and marvelous. Those older guys don't mess with tuners on stage. They'd tune on that backstage strobe tuner and fix it as they go. Old school. With James Brown, we'd hear, "Loud . . . and *wrong*!" Mr. Brown would say that to you, if you were cocky and he wanted to knock you down a couple notches. But Chuck Berry could come in loud and wrong but, that's what flat out rock 'n' roll is all about. As self-respecting professional musicians, of course, we'd all do our best to stay in tune. (Thus our frustration when Mr. Brown wrongly accused us of being out of tune.) Then I'd hear Chuck Berry, one of the original rock 'n' rollers from the '50s, and think, "Geez!" And I began to dig the beauty of that feral out-of-tune-ness. There's just so much conviction in the music that it overcame small problems like . . . tuning. Guys like that came from an era when they didn't really give a fuck. They know the immediate urgency, the depth of real feeling, is more important than being musically correct. And Chuck Berry, like Mr. Brown, had been cranking it out for 50 years. I grew up in a different era, dependent on electronic tuners. We don't have the confidence — maybe the balls — to be that wrong. Sometimes it's good to realize that technology can lead to neutering. Chuck Berry didn't have a set list. He wouldn't even call out a song. He'd just start playing and let the band catch up. I can testify that that's not how it's done in rhythm and blues or soul and funk. But Chuck Berry could pull it off with a barebones rhythm section behind him. The more players on stage, the tighter you've got to be. I remember at one Tokyo performance, he invited a few nice-looking girls from the audience to come up on stage to dance. That did it. Pretty soon dozens and dozens of people jumped on stage and security went nuts. That'd be a scene in the U.S., for sure, but in Japan everything runs meticulously, on-time, as-planned. So this was chaos. Backstage, the Soul Generals were splitting their sides watching the debacle unfold. Chuck Berry wore a bus driver's cap with gold tassels and his jacket had gold epaulets on the shoulders. At one point, I thought I saw him backstage, and I said to Keith, "Wow, that's *Chuck Berry*." But Keith said, "No, that's his manager, wearing the same outfit. I think they do that to psyche everybody out, keep everybody off Chuck's back."

I remember being really hungover one of the nights we played. I was already a fan of sake, but the locals introduced us to Soju, a Korean liquor with an alcohol content that varies widely, from maybe 17 percent to as much as 45 percent, which can lead to some miscalculations. It's like the mother of all sakes. Some band members who had experience in Tokyo took us to this place they called the Soul Bar, in Roppongi District. (Actually, George's Soul Bar is the full name.) They'd been raving about it: "If you haven't been there, you have to go." I think it was Spike, our percussionist, who had randomly found it while walking down the street. The walls were covered with American funk, R&B, and soul album covers. The band was excited to go there. "We haven't been to the Soul Bar in five years!" And it was my first time. The DJ said, in Japanese-inflected English, "Mister Fred Thomas, do you remember this one?" And they'd play a song he'd recorded 30 years ago, one that was only released in Japan. Fred was like, "Damn! Sounds like me. But I don't remember that one." So we had a ragin' time that night, with a predictable hangover to enjoy for the next night's show.

Every time we went to Tokyo, we spent time at the Soul Bar. Those people were super cool and we made a lot of friends. They wouldn't let us pay for anything, and when we presented them with parting gifts, they were very shy about accepting them. While in Japan, we met some funky R&B and soul players from the States. They told us, "We're never leaving. They love us here. We're ragin' five nights a week, making good money, and the Japanese girls love us." (Many years later, after an earthquake and tsunami struck Japan in March 2011, Harmonious Junk played a benefit for the survivors. I prayed that my friend Mizue, whom I'd met at the Soul Bar, was safe and that the owners and patrons we'd met were safe, too.)

We headed to the United Kingdom in May for performances at Leeds University (who can forget *Live at Leeds* by the Who?), the Essential Fest in Bristol and a return to the Hackney Ocean, north of London. We returned home briefly, then set out for a flurry of shows at the Casino Espino in Portugal; a Grand Prix Ball at the Sporting Club in Monaco; a special event dubbed Pavarotti & Friends for Angola, with the opera star in Modena, Italy; Congress Hall in Paris; gigs in Madrid, Milan, and Campione, Italy; and, finally, the Kremlin Palace in Moscow. (Tina Turner had played there three times, and Eric Clapton twice, by the time we arrived.) That tour was grueling. It had long since become apparent that while working for James Brown, I could travel the world and not see a whole lot of it. We'd whisk in, whisk out. I'm not much for walking tours of the castles and cathedrals. If I had time, I got out for a stroll. A group of us would try to get out. But when I was in a new city for only one day — frequently the case — I mostly focused on the business at hand, keeping my guitar together with fresh strings and practicing when I could. Or hangin' with the cats and having a laugh and staying in a good mood. Sometimes the tight schedule and the traveling just stressed me out. We couldn't really go on a sightseeing tour and risk being late or unprepared for the gig. (One time I woke up at a lady friend's house in Williamsburg, Brooklyn, when the band was in New York City. I called in to see what was going on. It was only 10 a.m. They said, "You better get your ass over here, we're leaving two hours early." I panicked and commandeered a very expensive cab ride.)

The Grand Prix Ball at the Sporting Club in Monaco unfolded the night before the 60th running of the Formula One race through the principality's streets. So the international jet set came out in force. Not that it mattered to us. After a 50-minute set by James Brown, the gamblers returned to the tables, the drivers went to bed, and we were on our way to Modena, Italy, the next day, for Pavarotti & Friends' 2002 for Angola gala. That starred the big man himself, plus Mr. Brown, Andrea Bocelli, Grace Jones, Lou Reed, Sting — sometimes the litany of big names you shared the stage with would leave you kind of numb. At one point, Lou Reed and I just happened to be watching rehearsals from the same spot, and he turned to me. He said, "Can you believe we're here *doing* this?!" I could only agree. "Yeah, man, Pavarotti and pop actually works!" Of course, when I met back up with the band, I told everyone I'd been "hanging out with Lou Reed." To which Keith's perennial, one-upmanship response was, "Oh, Lou Reed. Yeah. We spent hours rapping together earlier . . ." No matter who I ever met, Keith claimed to have "been there, done that" before me. (What are friends for?) Our part in the show turned out to be brief, so Keith and Fred and I stayed up till dawn jamming back at the hotel.

Then it was on to Paris, Madrid, Milan, Campione, and Moscow: eight shows in six countries in 11 days. With all due respect, until you've done such a thing, you have no idea what that takes. Madrid was a slammin' show. The band's dressing room had two porta-potties, and one was out of service, so we crammed in there and puffed down on a joint. Wouldn't you know? James Brown suddenly appeared. He had to use our bathroom because his wasn't working. When he comes out, he's smiling and slipped into his just-a-guy-in-the-band mode. "Okay, who's holding? One of y'all's got it." Sometimes we'd send him a jay to smoke, just to be generous, keep things cool with the boss. Sometimes one of Mr. Brown's entourage would come around. "The king wants some crumbs. Anyone got crumbs for the king?" For a laugh, and to keep it all in perspective, someone would say, "It's gonna cost him!"

I'd been to Campione, Italy, four years earlier with Tomi Rae's band, opening for James Brown. At this ritzy casino we were playing at, somebody whispered, "Don't mess with these people's women, or you'll end up in the river." Still, one of my bandmates ended up making out with a woman behind the stage curtain just before our show. (He lived.) Moscow was even less welcoming: it took us five hours to get through customs. Horrible scenario. Twenty-seven bags were "missing," no doubt getting torn apart by customs agents. By the time we got out of the airport I wanted to leave. They treated us like criminals, going through every bag. Outside, unrelenting fog everywhere. All the girls in the hotel bar were way too hot to be there without a man. Then I realized, "Oh, these are hookers." At the gig, Spike accidentally kicked over his timpani and a conga drum at one point and it looked like a disaster in the making. But Spike leapt forward and rode the timpani to the ground like a bucking bronco, creating a spectacle and snatching victory from defeat through sheer showmanship. By our last song, "Sex Machine," Mr. Brown turned to us and, over the house P.A., said, "We're almost going home." We thought, "We can't fucking wait!" Let me put it this way: I have no desire to return to Moscow. Ever.

DENVER

The summer of 2002 took me to Denver for a gig, and I became acquainted with the Mile High City and its musicians — wonderful people and killer players. For a July 3 gig at the Universal Lending Pavilion in Denver, both Keith and I arrived a day early. It was a Monday night. We were staying at the Monaco, downtown, and decided to go out and find a bar and some live music, have a few drinks. We popped into a club called Blue 67. It was "spendy," but the waitresses were attractive, so we hung out. We heard this drummer tuning up in the next room; his name was Zach Pietlock. "Man, you're a funky drummer. We wish you were in our band," we said. Zach's band at that time was Cocktail Revolution. We took a liking to them right away. The keyboard player, Chad Aman, became a good friend of mine. They played warp-speed, acid jazz. They're still around, with a deservedly great reputation. Chad and Zach introduced me to a whole gang of musicians — Melinda Dickson, Byron Shaw, Colin Mitchell, and others. I met so many cool, friendly people, so many good musicians, in one night. So I returned to Denver on vacation, visited all these people, jammed with their bands, and decided Denver was where I needed to be. The city was growing up and had developed a fertile music scene full of hip people. A band could play a dozen towns within a few hours' drive. As far as meeting my James Brown–related obligations was concerned, I just needed a major airport nearby. It didn't take long to make up my mind, and I landed in the Mile High City for good later that September. It had been less than a year since I'd launched Harmonious Junk, and in Denver I set about reforming the band. In fact, Chad Aman soon became the top dog in the band's newest incarnation. With new players, I'd be able to tackle the material I'd been writing on the road.

Anyway, on that first visit, we played the Denver gig and the next day we opened for String Cheese Incident in Steamboat Springs, in the mountains. During the show Mr. Brown mentioned the "Soul Center of the Universe" bridge the town named after him in September 1993. Our sax players sat in with String Cheese. I'd met the keyboard player, Kyle Hollingsworth, at the San Diego Street Scene just prior to 9/11, nearly a year earlier. And I met John Barlow, a lyricist for the Grateful Dead. I said, "You look familiar. What's your name?" "I'm John Barlow." "Oh, you wrote all those great songs with Bob Weir?" "That's me." We were right by the James Brown bus, so he knew I was in the band and we started talking. It's cool to meet your favorite people like that, when they know you're a pro, too. The next day the band drove to Denver and flew home, but Leroy Harper had secured a gig in Breckenridge, Colorado, for his Soul Power Posse, which in that case included Mousey Thompson on drums, Bo Brundidge on bass, Waldo Weathers on sax and my lucky self on guitar. We opened for Papa Grows Funk, then an established band from New Orleans. I don't think we had time to really rehearse any material, so we must have played James Brown's music. But like I said earlier, we all pounced on any chance to get it on outside of the James Brown gig.

Despite the on-off nature of the schedule, the James Brown train never really stopped. Within days of the Denver show, we reconvened at the Greek Theater in L.A., moved on to the Sandia Casino in Albuquerque, and then flew to Europe for the summer swing through the festival scene: Jazz at Montauban in Toulouse, France;

the Paleo Festival in Lausanne, Switzerland; the Gaou Festival in Toulon, France; and the San Sebastian Jazz Festival in Spain. The Paleo Festival in Lausanne, with more than 100,000 people, might have been the biggest. Man, we rocked that one. We arrived at the site in the nick of time, and I volunteered to head out into the festival crowd to seek a joint. With a stage pass around my neck, I walked slowly through the crowd. "I'm with James Brown. We need a couple spliffs . . ." And some nice folks said, "Oh really? *Here.*" That really helped us ditch the traveling blues and get in the mood for our performance. Well, we paid those folks back, big time.

At the end of July 2002, an article on James Brown by Philip Gourevitch appeared in the *New Yorker*. Gourevitch had attended one of our shows at the Paramount in Oakland in June 2001, and spent time with Mr. Brown in Augusta. I thought he had some worthwhile insights into James Brown's show at that point in Mr. Brown's career, and he had a few words for the band worth repeating here.

> While his sound and style are always unmistakably his
> own, he manages in the course of each evening to present
> a sweeping retrospective not only of his own vast reper-
> toire but of all the musical genres to which his originality
> pays homage: from the field hollers of slavery, the call-
> and-response, organ-surging exultations of gospel, the
> tragicomic clowning of minstrel shows, and the boastful
> reckonings and imploring incantations of the blues, to the
> sugary seductions of country balladeers and cosmopolitan
> crooners, the horns of jazz, the guitars of rock and roll,
> and the percussive insinuations of a thousand local beats
> from across America, Africa, and the Caribbean. He has
> repeatedly revolutionized these traditions, discovering
> in them previously unexpressed possibilities. In turn, his

Feelin' it, in Ski Town USA, Steamboat Springs, Colorado,
4 July 2002, when James Brown opened for String Cheese Incident.
In the background, Mousey Thompson. CREDIT: LARRY HULST.

music and dance moves have been so widely studied, rein-
terpreted, ripped off, and sampled by so many artists of so
many different musical dispositions throughout the world
that it has become nearly impossible to say, "This
is where James Brown's influence ends and the rest of
music begins."

The players wear uniforms with . . . a look that places
them about midway on the sartorial trajectory between
zoot-suiters and riverboat gamblers. They come on full-
tilt, cranking a sassy medley of funk hooks.

Although no two nights with him are the same, and
much of what you see and hear when he's onstage is truly
spontaneous, the dazzle of these unpredictable moments
is grounded in his ensemble's dazzling tightness. He
proceeds without song lists, conducting fiercely drilled
sidemen and sidewomen through each split-second transi-
tion with an elaborate vocabulary of hand signals.

That's perceptive writing and, for my money, it rings true.

The pace picked up again in September with a return to San
Diego for the Street Scene; to Colorado Springs to play at the U.S.
Air Force Academy; to Winnipeg, Manitoba, where we had top
billing at the Urban Groove Festival; and on to Suwannee Park in
Live Oak, Florida, to play the Music & Film Harvest with Karl
Denson's Tiny Universe. October took us to a memorable post-
game performance after the Atlanta Falcons played the Tampa Bay
Buccaneers in the Georgia Dome. The memorable part: everyone
left after the Buccaneers crushed the Falcons and we watched from
backstage as tens of thousands of people filed out of the stadium
before James Brown even made an entrance. We had perhaps a
couple thousand people in the audience in a stadium that holds
more than 70,000. Mr. Brown, of course, put on quite a show for

The Godfather of Soul delivering the goods in Steamboat Springs, Colorado, 4 July 2002, where years earlier the town had named a span over the Yampa River the "Soul Center of the Universe Bridge." CREDIT: LARRY HULST.

the faithful and, like pros, everyone forgot the people who'd turned their backs on us.

For our next gig at the House of Blues at Mandalay Bay in Las Vegas, the venue advertised that "The Godfather is Back!" That might have been a reference to Mr. Brown's 22-month hiatus from Las Vegas after the New Year's Eve meltdown of 2000. Las Vegas does not take kindly to artists who displease the customers, but I wasn't privy to whether Mr. Brown had voluntarily exiled himself or actually been blacklisted. Apart from those 22 months, we played Vegas several times a year for years on end, so it's hard to imagine Mr. Brown passing up his bread-and-butter. In any case, my folks came to see the show and, not incidentally, me, as I'd moved to Denver and didn't always have time for a visit when we sped through Vegas. And, of course, my folks were interested in meeting my boss. I'd told them many good things about Mr. Brown and tried to min- imize the downsides. After the show, Judge Bradley — the same guy who pocketed my per diem when I started with the band — told me, "Just wait, he'll see 'em." Mr. Brown's first order of business was to have his hair washed and put up in curlers. After the show, but before I'd changed out of my stage uniform, I walked back out on stage to encourage my folks to wait. I was briefly visible on stage again as the audience dispersed. RT admonished me, rudely, I thought. "Don't take that suit out there after the show!" he growled, as if I was trying to use the tux to hit on women. I cussed all night long about it. In retrospect, however, you always understand more. The tux belonged to "the show" — it's what magically appears after the lights go down and the curtain goes up, and it vanishes when the performers all disappear and the curtain goes back down. It's part of the magic of a live performance. Plus, after the show is when you go backstage and put your hair up in curlers, I guess. My folks waited an hour and a half to meet Mr. Brown, which might've taken a little of the thrill out of it. He was charming, of course. One never knew how things worked in Mr. Brown's entourage and just when he was told that my folks were waiting to say hello. I would never believe that he personally made them wait.

Vegas, of course, overflowed with famous people who were either performing or just having a good time. And when James Brown headlined, famous people clustered 'round like moths to flame. We actually played before a performance by comedian Dave Chappelle at the House of Blues. I say "before" because James Brown didn't like the idea of opening for anyone. Band lore had it that back in the 1980s, Mr. Brown turned down an offer to open for the Rolling Stones. (If you watch the T.A.M.I. show from October 1964 on DVD, you'll see Mr. Brown steal the show, hands down, from the Stones. Twenty years later, the Stones were commercially much bigger. Times change.) In this case, we just happened to play before Dave Chappelle. He's the guy who bailed on a $50 million package deal with a television network because he felt "they" were trying to enslave him. We hung out in his dressing room after his show and talked. He was real cool to the band and extremely funny. The House of Blues in Vegas (and in L.A.) typically brought musicians and actors out of the woodwork. En route to the dressing room one night, I ran into my bandmate, Keith, who said, "Dude, you gotta meet Bill Murray." Keith introduced us. Another real nice guy. The House of Blues is small and intimate and the audience stands right up against the stage, dancing and partying just a few feet away. We stayed in Vegas to headline a private function for the *Wine Spectator* at the Venetian Hotel, then headed to gigs in Portland and the Paramount in Seattle. November and December were slow. Mr. Brown and Tomi Rae Hynie had plans to marry in late December in what we referred to as the "Brown-Hynie wedding." (Sorry, I couldn't resist.) We reconvened to close out the year with gigs in New York and Washington and a gig at Trump Marina in Atlantic City on New Year's Eve.

BEHIND THE SCENES

Most people have no idea what it takes to put on a show of any kind. And when you're talking about James Brown, you're talking about a traveling troupe of two dozen people, sometimes more. The Soul Generals rarely had fewer than a dozen players, The Bittersweet had three to five singers, and we typically had two or three dancers. With R.J. as an occasional walk-on talent, Danny Ray as emcee, and Tomi Rae as featured vocalist, that is a lot of moving parts — all before James Brown arrived on stage, signifying "Star Time." For it all to work, the stars had to align. We had to get from A to B . . . to C to D to E. Spastic choreography linked airplanes to buses to hotels to rehearsals to the actual performances — the purpose of all that traveling.

Typically, the band arrived at a destination much earlier than Mr. Brown and his entourage, which at that time included Tomi Rae, Judge Bradley, Charles Bobbit, and Roosevelt Johnson. Danny Ray and Ronnie Tompkins traveled with the band. Most of us sped to the hotel, and grabbed showers and a change of clothes before heading to the venue for a sound check. Meanwhile, RT, our road and stage manager, and the drummers, headed straight to the venue to set up the drums and troubleshoot the gig. RT was in his mid-60s and, apparently, had started in the business working with Janis Joplin. RT had too many roles, too many jobs, and thus he was rarely in the best of moods. It's typical in the music industry, at least these days, to have roadies who move gear and prepare the stage. James Brown was different in that respect. He ran a lean operation and his organization had externalized a lot of the risk in putting on his show. All we traveled with were instruments and uniforms and

RT. The risers, drums, amps and P.A. were the responsibility of the local promoter. Still, RT had to ensure that what was promised was delivered and quality check the stage and venue. The drummers had to stage their gear just right. By that time the band would assemble and run through a few numbers to check sound and make sure we all had pulses. Keith might lead the band through what he called his "mega-mix," a short medley of key segments of the James Brown repertoire. That'd give the horn players and singers a chance to warm up and it'd give RT a chance to hear the whole band. Cynthia Moore might step out and sing "Respect," so there'd be a vocal mic check. We'd even work on some of our own songs, waiting to see if Mr. Brown would show up. RT wouldn't let us go very long on our own material before he'd say, "Y'all better play some Star Time songs now, or we're gonna be in trouble."

If and when Mr. Brown showed up, we might do a full-fledged rehearsal. He'd apply his trademark banter to knock us into line, one by one. He'd single out someone and demand to know what they were playing. The band would go silent, and you'd have to play your part for him in front of everyone. He'd publicly assess your performance and offer criticisms and admonitions:

> "Whatcha playin'? That ain't *nothin'*. Lay out on this one."
> "That's fair — I can go with that."
> "*Imply* — don't *apply*."
> "Let it *ring*."
> "Cut it *off*."
> "Play *down*. You're playing *up*."

This last admonition applied to the guitarists and bassists. He wanted us to use only downstrokes on the rhythm guitar *and* the bass to get that authentic R&B feel. If he caught you playing an upstroke, he'd fine you. Mr. Brown told Bo Brundidge he'd fine him $50 every time he caught him playing "Damn Right I Am Somebody" using upstrokes on bass. So Bo had to play 16th notes with his thumb — physically, a very difficult proposition — or get fined. To rest his thumb, Bo learned to play upstrokes that *sounded* like downstrokes and to keep his eye on Mr. Brown, so he could switch when the boss was looking.

Over the years, I figured out that my best response to his query — "Whatcha playin'?" — was to say, "I'm playing the part you gave me, Mr. Brown." The worst response was "I'm playing it like the record," because that set up his classic retort: "They cut it wrong!" Trying to please him was aiming at a moving target, apparently by design. Some days or weeks, even entire months, you could do nothing right, musically, according to Mr. Brown. That's when he was at you. You just had to grin and bear it and hope you either did something he liked or that he got bored tormenting you and moved on to someone else. At other times, disconcertingly, you might become the flavor of the month, for no discernible reason. He'd compliment you profusely, feature you more during the show, and sometimes throw you a bonus or a raise. We always knew, however, that whether we were the one being exalted or put under the microscope, it would pass. James Brown had clearly honed his skills at exerting control over his bands through psychological means. His approach mixed a little keep-em-off-their-footing, a dash of divide-and-conquer, and a generous dollop of break-em-down-and-build-em-up. It sounds like boot camp and, indeed, Mr. Brown clearly thought of it in terms of team building. He'd also give you unexpected opportunities to shine. He would take a chance during his show to see whether you could run with the ball if he passed it to you. Knowing that he might call on me at any given time, during any song, to step out and solo in front of thousands of people forced me to step up my game.

Like a good coach, he first laid the groundwork. In one rehearsal, early on, he unexpectedly pointed me in on the solo on "Prisoner of Love." I had to solo over the verse. These days I can think fast enough to not make an utter fool of myself in such a spot but back then, I had to scramble. To play over all those chord changes correctly means executing a fairly rapid succession of arpeggio-like chord tones — single notes within each chord — and they must be timed perfectly to the beat, with a rhythmic fluidity. And you do not want to disappoint James Brown. When he pointed me in on "Prisoner of Love" in rehearsal, I nearly choked. Mr. Brown just said, "Well, that's not bad. Think about that. That might come up again." That inspired a fresh round of thinking on my part: "I'd better figure out how to play arpeggios over the changes in 'Prisoner of Love.'" Occasionally he would ask me to do something that I just could not do, and I'd sound like a fool. That'd be a lesson — I'd swear to myself I'd be more prepared next time. So the next time that song came up in a performance I'd be shitting in my pants, worried he would call me out to test my newfound knowledge. And then he'd hand the solo to someone else and I'd exhale. But I'd be ready. Now imagine Mr. Brown working this way with every single member of the band, until he had us all on our toes. Or on edge. He could be Dr. Jekyll or Mr. Hyde.

JERRY "LOUIE" POINDEXTER: In rehearsal, Mr. Brown would say, "I don't know why you can't get it! Y'all don't sound like *nothin'*!" The band's thinking, "What the hell is he talkin' about? We wupped his ass!" Well, we learned he was playing psychology, because we knew we were kickin' ass. If you do good, James isn't the type to tell you you did good. He'd say, "You ain't playin' *nothin'*!" That's how he kept you focused. James Brown would play games with you. He'd say "You come to me like a man, I'll treat you like a man." James was an old-school, one-upper. If he could get something over on you, if he could scare you, and you didn't comprehend, he *had* you. So I called him on that one time. I said, "Get the fuck outta here! *You* play it. I've been playin' it every night for twelve years and now you're telling me I don't know how to play? *You* play it." Every man puts his pants on one leg at a time. I don't have to stand here and take no bullshit. That's when he started respecting me.

KEITH JENKINS: We'd be doing a festival — maybe three or four bands would have played already — and he'd get up there, turn his back on the crowd and rehearse the band in front of 50,000 people. It was totally embarrassing. In a theater, sometimes they'd hold the doors. But other times, they couldn't. "Let 'em in," he'd say, "We got to get this music right." Sometimes for a year we'd never rehearse, he'd never come to sound check. Some tours he'd come every day and torture us. It's not like we didn't want to rehearse. We liked it when he would come in at a cool venue and want to jam. That could be fun. We'd always be a little tentative because you never knew which guy was going to show up. Would he show up mad and [say] everybody sucked or was he going to show up all cool and laid back and want to have a little fun? Sometimes he'd be both. We called it "chewing nails," when he came in just real mean and nasty and unpleasant and un-pleasant. He'd demand: "Whatchoo playin' on 'Soul Power'?" Like Damon, my trick would be, "I'm playing the part that you gave me." I'd play it. He'd say, "That's pretty good. That's all right." And he might leave me alone. He might come in all shitty, but after 30 minutes, he'd be in a great mood. "Gentlemen, y'all sound fantastic. We're better than anybody in the world. Ain't nobody can touch us. Nobody can do what we do. Let's play something in D minor!" And we'd do a little blues number and he'd leave all happy. "Well, fellas, let's not kill ourselves. Go get some rest and

I'll see you on the gridiron." So you might get Mister Happy or Mister Nasty or both in the same day. It was excruciating but you just had to endure it.

ERIK HARGROVE: He'd hear something he liked, "Y'all *hear* that? That guy's a *genius*! You understand me? He's a *genius*!'" The next song, he would cut that same guy down. "I don't know *what* you're playing, son. I don't even know why you're here!" You had to want to be in that band. For the first year you played with him, you thought you had a sense of how he'd be that night, based on the vibe at sound check. But after a while you realized that you didn't know. You never knew. One minute the song is great, the next minute it's not. And nothing has really changed, at least, to your perception or the band's perceptions. But to him, something's suddenly not right, even when everyone's playing the same way they were just a moment earlier. It was just a realm of unpredictability. Sometimes he was just playing a game — the control game — on the band or certain people in the band. He always kept people on their toes. That could lead to growth. Certainly that growth took place within me. I thought, "What am I doing, messing myself up trying to please this man, instead of just being the musician I am and playing well." Once I learned that was what I needed to do, it gave me a certain confidence to play what I thought was right and what he might want. I had self-confidence and it showed. So even if it wasn't exactly what he wanted, he'd let it go and let it develop and groove. Because he saw that I and the other players were confident in what we were playing. You'd learn that yes, you need to please him, but you still need to be the musician that you are, whether he mentioned that to you or not. Going through all that made you grow in a certain way as a musician.

Once the sound check was over, we might go back to the hotel for a break, returning a couple of hours before show time for the catered meal required by our contract. The meals typically tasted pretty good, but occasionally they were a bit difficult to fully enjoy due to space constraints. Nowhere to sit, barely a place to stand. The promoter's people or a caterer might bring us a big trough of pasta, a big trough of salad and a big trough of ribs. Plastic forks and knives, paper plates. And we're standin' 'round, eatin' ribs, because there's no place to sit. We called it "standin' ribs." B.B. King's in New York had us all crammed into a very small space, and we just had to deal with it. Sometimes it was funny, everybody jumpin' all over each other to get where they're going. It really became a big family scene. But sometimes, the dressing room was just too small. Too many people, too many days on the road. At the Chicago House of Blues, only a few people at a time could fit into the "dressing room." An older gentleman, Mr. Ross, who lived in Chicago, would always come to visit us, inevitably in that dressing room. He was always cool, clever, and had a good story. But he was a large, heavyset man — probably the biggest guy we ever encountered regularly on the road — and he'd take up space enough for three band members, always in the tiniest of dressing rooms. We'd laugh. How does that happen?

When we didn't want to be held hostage to shrinking quarters, Keith would say, "You wanna get away?" and I'd be all in favor. As soon as we would eat, we'd dash and roam the neighborhood until an hour before show time. Grabbing fresh air before show time meant leaving the bubble. Otherwise, James Brown might pop into the dressing room and start holding court, sometimes all the way until show time. Trust me, most of the time we loved hang time with him, but we also craved freedom, if only for an hour. With James Brown in the room, no one could leave. We'd have to hang on to his every word and laugh at the right time. Sometimes he had to get something off his chest about the band. We never knew if he was going to put us on the spot and ask something awkward. A couple years later, in June 2005, during rehearsals in Augusta, Mr. Brown suddenly asked everyone in the band to name their religion. I'd never spent any time in a church. What was I supposed to say? Someone said "Church of Christ, non-denominational," and I thought, "That's my 'out.'" So I said that. I wasn't going to digress into my quibbles with Christianity or whether I believed in a higher power. I wasn't going to say how I really felt, because if that didn't jibe with his perspective at that moment, I'd be landing in a dramatic situation. I respected his beliefs and all that he'd been through, but if I might be subject to probing questions from the boss, that provided a healthy reason to take a little stroll instead.

When the venue offered no dressing room at all, as on a typical festival day, we used the bus. Picture one bus, a dozen men with their tuxedos, and one iron. Mr. Brown would let Danny Ray know which color uniforms he wanted us in; he had maybe eight sets to choose from. New band members didn't get their own suit for years. If the suit had a name on it, I had to ask myself: was that person still alive and, possibly, on tour with me? Finding an unclaimed suit was not as simple as it sounds — we had people coming in and out of the band constantly. I'd been using a certain suit, when, suddenly, that person is back in the band and standing next to me, looking at their suit in my hand. More than once, I heard a voice behind me: "I'm going to need that suit back from you, son." Meanwhile, the clock would be ticking towards show time. At least once, I cracked and just grabbed a suit several sizes too big and spent the night looking like a circus clown. Once, to mess with trumpeter Todd Owens, the band hid his pants, and all the spare sets of big pants, as well as his socks. He had to take the stage late in flood pants and yellow socks and go out front and direct the band, with nowhere to hide. (In Japan in 2003, it would be my turn as victim.) Perhaps the hardest part was ironing a flawless tuxedo an hour before showtime, then waiting around endlessly to play. The moment the previous band finished and cleared the stage, we'd race out there. Everyone handled the pressure of time and tuxedos a little differently.

> **GEORGE "SPIKE" NEALY:** When we were standing backstage just before going on, Mr. Brown would be standing right there, looking. Every shoe must be shining. Every haircut trim. Every wrinkle in that uniform must be ironed out. One wrinkle leads to another wrinkle, which is connected to the money. A few wrinkles and you could be looking at fines before you even go on stage. You learned to be super sharp around him. And you can't get dressed too early. Say you sit down. There's a wrinkle. That one wrinkle could cost you $75 to $100.

> **ERIK HARGROVE:** At first it was difficult to drum in a tuxedo. I hated playing in a jacket. When I first joined the band, we had to wear uniforms that had served past band members. When I came in, I took over for Arthur Dickson, who was a shorter, more heavy-set man. I could wear his coat, it was really big. The sleeves were short, which was fine for me because I don't like my drum sticks getting caught in my sleeves. But wearing Arthur Dickson's pants? No way. They were way too big and way too short. Still, many times I did. I had to make a makeshift belt out of two cummerbunds to let the pants hang low so they didn't look like high-water pants.

> **WILLIE RAY "BO" BRUNDIDGE:** You had to have a certain amount of peace within yourself so this whole chaotic lifestyle didn't drive you nuts. There were times when it was Panic City, but you had to remind yourself, and each

other, "Don't panic, it's going to work out." But you gotta get dressed in five, ten minutes. Bow tie, cummerbund, suit, all wrinkle free.

Before heading out into the spotlights, we'd hold a prayer circle. Many band members were devout Christians and the prayer to them signified their faith. I took it as the sharing of a spiritual moment, a moment to feel the love, to be open to positive vibrations. Considering the vagaries of the road, we had to build a collective band vibe, and a prayer pulled it together. If Mr. Brown wasn't there with us, he'd be having one backstage with Tomi Rae and his manager. It was different for everybody, I'd guess. For the band it felt like a football team in a huddle. Then we'd head out to the stage to do our jobs. Finally. On a several-week tour with all the time spent traveling, killing time in airports, resting in hotel rooms, hanging backstage, we were almost always eager to get on that stage and do our thing. We had work to do.

STAR TIME!

James Brown's audiences typically were warm and welcoming as the Soul Generals hit the stage. Sometimes, especially in the clubs, a party would be ragin' just beyond the lip of the stage. The band would play a short set to warm up the room and get a vibe going for Mr. Brown's entrance, but we never really had to break the ice. People came to the show ready to boogie and jumped out of their seats at the first note. We'd start out with a "grabber" that would get 'em moving. Hollie Farris's "Network" made feet move. Then we'd settle down into a classic James Brown groove. "Soul Power" was a big opener in which two horn players would go up front and play a riff in unison into the vocal mic. Another opener was Bill Doggett's easy-groovin' "Honky Tonk" — instead of a brassy, upbeat number, it was more of a "night time is the right time" shuffle. "Damn Right, I Am Somebody" was my favorite — a really complicated, challenging piece to play. The guitars would play augmented chords and quick chromatic runs with punctuated hits while the band settled into a funky groove, then Fred Thomas would come out front and sing lead vocals.

"If you don't know what we know, you bettah ask somebody . . . Hit me!"

Spike would step out on a percussion solo. Jeff Watkins or Leroy Harper would step out on a sax solo. We'd do Spike's "Give It Up Or Turnit A Loose" introduction, but with a fresh approach. Then we'd slide into the groove of "Make It Funky." Danny Ray would step up to the mic and punch up the excitement. Nothing complicated here — all this work built tension for "The Entrance." It had its roots in vaudeville as well as practicality. Back in the day, bands really did have to break the ice and win over the audience before the front man or woman dared come out. They might even have to actually warm up a cold room. A tough, skeptical audience might need to be loosened up. Plus, The Man doesn't just come out — an audience has to earn it, demand it, call his name, work themselves into a froth. We'd take the groove down to a simmering vamp as Danny Ray began his wind-up.

"Ladies and gentlemen, are you ready for Star Time?"

The audience would give up a reasonably solid roar of approval. Then, as is traditional, the emcee would question the audience's dedication to bringing on the star.

I said, *"Are you ready for Star Time?!"*

The audience would roar again, only louder, more insistently. Then Danny Ray would call out a litany of Mr. Brown's hits and we'd play the unique riff from each song, seguing quickly into the next one. That routine also went back to the '60s and Mr. Brown's groundbreaking live record, *Live at the Apollo*, among others. Danny Ray knew his shtick well and he could only tease the audience so

Foolin' around with Mr. Brown, Caesar's Palace, Las Vegas, June 2000.

much before bringing on the man himself. "It's *Star Time*, ladies and gentlemen! *Star Time!* And heeeere's Misterrrrr Jaaaaaaaaames Brown! Jaaaaaaaaames Brown!" Danny Ray had this amazing way of rolling that first name around in his mouth, taking "Jaaaaaaaaames" for a rollercoaster ride before punctuating it with "Brown" as an exclamation mark. A few of these well-worn incantations would drive the crowd wild, without fail. We'd be focused on the vamp, keeping that simmer going, when there'd be a wave of sound from the audience. The fans would be on their feet, looking somewhere behind me and to one side. Their focal point would start to move and then you'd see the boss in your peripheral vision as he made his way out front, acknowledging the adulation with a dazzling smile, a wink, and a nod to band members as he approached the mic. Mr. Brown would take the mic off its stand as he moved his feet, a rhythmic ripple passing through his body, fingers poppin', feeling the groove we'd be laying down. If I dared glance at the audience and take my eyes off Mr. Brown for a split second, I could read the faces in the front row: "Holy *#@$! It's *James Brown*! For *real*!"

As Mr. Brown hit the stage, the band would be bubbling, threatening to almost boil over. He'd give us a subtle hand gesture that said, "All right now, dial it back, let it simmer." And we would. Whatever he wanted, right? If he knew we were really trying and sounding good, he'd come out and, in effect, with a hand movement, say, "All right, this is good, just bring it down a little bit. That's where we're gonna start from." He liked having a large, powerful band under his absolute command. Not every night began that smoothly. If he came out and he couldn't pick up the groove or thought the groove wasn't there, he'd get in our faces with all kinds of direction. He could be all over one guy. Maybe he couldn't hear the kick drum and, suddenly, he's got an issue with the drummer. And he would not hesitate to address the issue with that person, right there and then, in front of 50,000 people. I learned this the hard way, as did most members of the band, I'm sure. One time, in England, he even held an impromptu rehearsal in front of a festival audience, calling us out by name for our inadequacies, perceived or otherwise. We did our best to not take it personally. Any number of things could contribute to sound issues, especially on those big outdoor stages. Even if our gear met contractual standards, we never really knew what the overall effect would be. Looking back, some of the boss's behavior was understandable. The lead vocalist of any act has a lot of pressure on them.

We'd still be working out on "Make It Funky," watching the boss like hawks, when he'd spin around on the down beat and point to me for the bridge. I'd play the ascending riff, the change part in that song. Then he'd start naming soul foods — "grits and gravy" — and he and RJ would start doin' their thing, dancing, juking around, trading vocal phrases. He'd typically start his set with uptempo dance party tunes to set the evening's tone. Then he'd read the audience and vary the dynamics, which dictated song selections.

A 90-minute set is a lot of time to keep an audience dancing and mesmerized. If he was going to "wear 'em out," as Mr. Brown loved to say, he had to use every trick in the book, some known only to him. (One trick, in his mid-60s, was marshaling his own energy to last a whole show.) Besides the showmanship, it appeared to me that he built an acoustic environment onstage by placing all the instruments where he could conduct the players with ease and where he could arrange the instruments sonically and in nearly symmetrical stereo fashion. He had drums, bass, and guitar on the right *and* on the left, horns stage left, and singers stage right. Our percussionist, Spike, presided from the center of this array.

> **GEORGE "SPIKE" NEALY:** When James Brown put out his hand to conduct the band while he sang, he conducted *two* bands. The instrumentation on his left is the same instrumentation on his right. And a percussionist right up the middle. I was in the perfect spot. My position was like a crow's nest, a watchtower.

In my day, he never used a set list, but back in the old days, according to band lore — some of it firsthand — Mr. Brown would compose a set list and make his players memorize it. And recite it over and over. But in my time, each show had familiar phases, similar slots for the uptempo numbers, the grooves, the ballads. "Make It Funky" might be followed by "Get Up Offa That Thing." Knowing what he wanted to play next required experience with the show, knowing his mind (something akin to group telepathy) and the use of hand signals. For "Get Up Offa That Thing" he'd point to his head and we'd play the show's signature segue riff on the next down beat, ending the song on a G7#9 chord. That gave him the moment he needed to end one song and start another, without any dead air. Or he could add drama to an ending by signaling for a specific riff. To end "Get Up Offa That Thing," for instance, he might point to the side and that meant a staccato series of ascending notes — da-da-da-DA! And the horns would hold that last note, trilling it to boost the excitement. Or he could bring his fist down hard for a big final downbeat: *BOMP!* That's the end. A dozen people had to play in precise unison, based on knowledge, intuition, signals, and a sixth sense. In my time with the band, his sequence of songs often hewed to a pattern. I might anticipate the next song — based on experience, I'd think the next song was probably going to be "Doing It to Death / Gonna Have a Funky Good Time" — but I couldn't count on it. But if he stopped the band, *BOMP!*, and pointed to me or Keith, we'd play that song's signature riff to start it off. Based on the guitarist's timing, the drummer knew when to hit and that enabled everyone else to time their entrance, producing a strong groove leading into the song. The depth of Mr. Brown's songbook meant he had a half-dozen other really funky, original tunes he could break out at the beginning of the show, including "Doing It to Death," "Get On the Good Foot," "Papa Don't Take No Mess," "Papa's Got a Brand New Bag," "The Big Payback," "Super Bad," and "Cold Sweat/I Can't Stand It." The selection depended on whether Mr. Brown was feelin' it. We all had our favorite James Brown songs, but we had to be ready to follow his mood and his cues wherever they led.

We knew Mr. Brown was enjoying himself if he played certain tunes. "Super Bad" was one. That might be at the end of his funk set. If he felt good about it, he might do a big dance bit, really tear it up. The energy would be ridin' high. That'd be the peak of his funk set. He'd give that one hell, knowing we were going to calm it down afterwards. Typically he'd do it early on in his set when he wasn't tired, so he could dance his ass off. "Super Bad" was my favorite, and it was also a highlight in the show. We kept the groove going awhile with different songs, different soloists, different highlights. Then he'd break it down a bit. He might do something jazzy, a piano-based thing, like "Every Beat of My Heart." He'd lead that and take the solos on his Korg keyboard. Or he could play another ballad like "Georgia on My Mind," or "If I Ruled the World" that had complex chord progressions, and which was intense to learn on the guitar. Tony Bennett had put that one on the map. Often, Cynthia Moore — Mr. Brown called her "Soul Sister No. 1" — would come out and sing the bridge on "Georgia on My Mind." She also sang another old cover, "Candy." He'd often do "Living in America" after "Doing It to Death," if he was going to do it that night. At that point he might bring out Tomi Rae, the featured female singer in the show, and she'd do "I Can't Turn You Loose," or maybe one of her original blues tunes. "At Last" was another Tomi Rae tune that became a staple of the show. At the end of the set, James Brown and Tomi Rae developed a cool thing where they'd name various R&B songs — she'd sing a phrase to him, he'd sing a phrase from a different song back to her — and they'd go back-and-forth a few times. The peak of this would come when he'd go into "Bewildered," on the down beat. I'd hit this loud, major seven chord with a volume swell. That was the highlight of that segment, and Tomi Rae's set would be over. Typically, he'd be there the whole time, but if he left the stage, he'd probably return after a wardrobe change. When Isaac Hayes's daughter, Heather, was with us, she had an a cappella bit on the Whitney Houston/Dolly Parton song, "I Will Always Love You." She could really sing, so she'd always get major house with that one. Different people would have different bits. Then the boss would signal for more funk. Towards the end of my tenure, when he'd call "Super Bad," I could tell he felt the show had gone well and he still had the energy to bust out a few serious dance moves and slay the audience with a rare classic. There's a break in the middle when the band stops and the horns play, then the guitarists come in on the super-funky part. I got a break to enjoy the moment, then I had to get funky. That always tickled me.

Theatrical numbers such as "Please Please Please," "It's a Man's Man's Man's World" or "Prisoner of Love" might round things out. "Please Please Please," in particular, provided an opportunity for the famous cape routine, the emotional peak of the show. After James Brown the performer suffered through the heartbreak songs, devastated by loss and completely inconsolable, he'd drop to his knees. Danny Ray would come out of the wings with one of several different colored capes and drape it over his shoulders to console him, protect him, finally to raise him up, and usher him to the wings. Mr. Brown, as he had thousands of times before, would stagger for a moment under the emotional weight of his loss, then suddenly reject solace, refuse help, toss aside the cape, stand erect, defiant, and return to the mic to beseech his lost love to return. In Song Land, she never does, so, eventually, he'd accept the cape, accept Danny Ray's help, and leave the stage as the band played on. As I've mentioned, that made "Sex Machine" the de facto encore. We'd stretch it out and Mr. Bobbit would signal from the wings how many minutes were left in a 90-minute performance, holding up all ten fingers, then five. "Sex Machine" gave Mr. Brown an opportunity to pull any final dance moves, acknowledge the audience with a bow, and thank them. He'd leave the stage to a standing ovation and return to acknowledge the love before departing for the night. No encore. James Brown wanted to wow people with the greatest, tightest show they could imagine, times ten. And leave them wanting more. I remember one exception and his explanation for it. We'd played Arnold Hall at the U.S. Air Force Academy in September 2002 and — lo and behold — James Brown came back out and did an encore. A year later, Mr. Brown was hanging out with the band before a show. He said to us, "You know why we did that encore? We did that encore for the 'gubmint.' There's no 'entertainment business.' It's the 'gubmint.' They let us keep workin'."

MAGIC HAND SIGNALS

The dynamics of a James Brown show would have been impossible without cues. From experience, we knew the emotional and musical arc of the show and that a number of songs could fit each segment. But which ones? Also, a James Brown show rarely let up, so he had developed segues and embellishments for any occasion, which could buy him a moment to decide where to go next. Every performance was fluid and in the moment. He could create a medley of his songs on the spot, in real-time, and call the arrangement on the fly because he had trained the band to watch him so closely. He could go into any song at any time or segue from one song to another after just one verse. He felt he had to keep the show moving at maximum excitement and, should a lull in energy seem imminent, he could punch up the show with the wave of his hand. His presentation aimed to hold the audience's complete attention, whether that meant breaking out a dance step, bringing on the dancers, pointing someone in for a solo, or turning to The Bittersweet for a song. He used everybody on stage and every one of their talents to keep the show moving. Yet James Brown could also use a soulful ballad to touch the audience's deeper emotions and use that connection to keep them utterly engaged. The simplicity of a ballad captivated the listener and he knew how to exploit that moment by releasing all the energy he'd built up with his high-energy funk. Ballads had emotional peaks, too, like in "Please Please Please," when he and Danny Ray would do the cape routine. It's all about the show. We even had Wimbush the magician at one point. We'd break into Grover Washington's "Mister Magic" and Wimbush would take the stage with a couple of tricks. I kid you not.

For cues to work, of course, we had to see them and understand them. That meant everyone on stage focused on him at all times. I'd have to keep track of what the drummer and bass player were doing with one eye and keep the other trained on Mr. Brown. That could be nerve-wracking.

ROBERT "MOUSEY" THOMPSON: The whole key to James Brown was watching him, because a lot of times he didn't know where he wanted to go. But when he went there, he knew you were with him. He'd be like, *"My man!"* You've got his back. He wanted his whole band like that. If you took your eyes off him and he caught you, you were in trouble. Sometimes, I think, he would purpose-fully do things to push you off your game. We called him "Games Brown." Working with Wilson Pickett — I joined his band in 1983 and played off and on with him until I joined James Brown in 1993 — it was soulful and you'd just play *with* him. But Brown was a conductor, an innovator. You played *for* him. You had to watch him. One minute he's doin' one thing, the next minute he might be doin' something else.

ERIK HARGROVE: To play with James Brown in that band, you locked in with him. Once you started playing, sure, you were listening to the rest of the band, and you were laying down what you thought should be played or what he dic-tated that you play. And then you waited for his approval. You were waiting for a signal that what you were playing was correct. Your focus was on him for at least the first 30 seconds. And then you could really listen to what was around you and make sure everyone was locking in to you. If the music wasn't happening, was it okay to maybe shift your timing? If you did, you took a risk. He hasn't said anything yet, that the groove is wrong, that the timing is wrong. So you'd risk changing it to what you think it should be and he might point you out and have the other drummer play. He'd make changes like that minute to minute. If he didn't hear what he wanted to hear, maybe you weren't playing what he wanted, maybe it wasn't coming through the monitors right, maybe he wanted the sound to come from his other ear — because one drum set was on his left, the other on his right. I was always on his right. A number of factors played into why he might switch us. He'd do that with the guitar players, too. He'd tell one to lay out. Same thing with the bass players. Trying to guess the reasons could be very frustrating. So in certain gigs where he was really tense, you just played until you saw that he was comfortable with what you were playing and then you could really listen to what was happening on stage. Other gigs where he was looser about it, you could listen to whichever bass player was playing or whichever guitar rhythm was happening and, usually, everyone was already locked in. But you could play off of it, too, if he was in a playful mood. And he would like that and acknowledge that what you were doing was good.

No matter how much knowledge, experience, and ESP you thought you had, Mr. Brown could surprise you. He could come up in the middle of a show and give you a very specific direction using signals you'd never seen, and you'd have to "cipher it." During one of the last shows I played, he came to me and gave me a brand new rhythm part for "Sex Machine," a part I'd never played before. He walked over to me on stage, got real close, and said, "Aah, don't play that, try something like *this*," and he sang a new rhythm part into my ear. I had to use everything I'd learned to translate his vocalized phrase into notes and intervals in the right scale to make it happen, instantly. You'd think furiously fast. "Does his rhythm start on the I (i.e., the one) or the upbeat after the I or . . ." You'd have to guess, and you might be wrong. He'd shake his head, "No," and sing it to you again. You'd offer a different set of notes. This is live, onstage in front of however many thousand people. But the more you did that with him, the more you had an idea of where he wanted to go. And he *loved* it when you got it instantly. He led that band like a conductor leads an orchestra, but with no charts, just hand signals.

At other times, of course, there was little ambiguity — he'd just point you in for a solo. At that moment, he was essentially entrusting his show to you, handing you the energy, and expecting you to take it higher. So there'd be pressure when he turned to you. As a guitar player, I'd be playing rhythm on all these tight grooves, punctuating them with little riffs. Suddenly, Mr. Brown would whirl around and point me in. The message: "Improvise, *now*." Over one chord for two minutes. And make it interesting. That's not always easy. In line with his taste for theatrics, James Brown generally liked to have his soloists peak on a climactic high note. He'd point to the ceiling. "Heh heh heh heh! Take it *up*, man!" And I'd start to build to a climax, one eye on greatness, the other on Mr. Brown. At that moment he's anticipating his next move. He's poised to take the song back from you and lead the energy back into the show. He'd give you a verse for your solo, then the nod to wrap it up, even if you might not be in that place in a phrase where you're able and ready to reach the peak. So he might extend his cue to you by jumping up and down a bit, telling you to get there quicker. He knows you're not quite ready but you'd better be heading to your climax soon, his body language saying, "'Cuz it's time for me to move on." He never cut you off, though. It was never, "I want it back *right now*." He was always musical and savvy about how to time it. But he'd give you the idea, "Okay, get after it now." Yet you knew you had time to do it gracefully.

WILLIE RAY "BO" BRUNDIDGE: Everything was based on signals. When he called up a song, you had to know the signal. You had to listen and be alert. A new song could begin on the next beat. Whatever song it was, you might play on the intro, and then whoever's song it was would

Hittin' that note, Caesar's Palace, Las Vegas, June 2000.
CREDIT: RICK ANDERSON.

take it from there. Sometimes, for whatever reason, if you were out of tune, Mr. Brown would cut you off and have the other guy play your song. It all depended on what Mr. Brown was feeling. I used to get tested a lot. It's almost like football, where the quarterback throws you a pass to see if you can catch it. Now, if you catch it, he might take it right back or he might throw it to you again. So he'd point me in and out and Fred Thomas, the other bass player, in and out, all within the same song. You had to be watchin' him. He could point you in for four measures, cut you out, put Fred in, cut him off and put you back in, all before the bridge. Just to check the balance of the sound, the balance of the groove. He watched all that stuff. For me, it was the ultimate training. We called it "James Brown University." You had to learn the show from his point of view. It's not correct until he approves it.

ERIK HARGROVE: One signal was a segue signal, to move from one song to another. He would touch the top of his head — he wouldn't actually touch his head, his hand would just go up towards his face, but because he moved his arms a particular way, you knew by watching his body language that he was about to do it. Or something was about to happen. Constant variables were always happening. There were times when he'd turn really quickly and give that signal. And you'd have to catch it. There were times when he was more slow and deliberate about it and you knew it was coming, no doubt about it. You learned these signals by watching, show after show. You didn't get a class on this, a brief, or anything on which signal meant what and what you did when you got the signal. You saw it happen, then you knew, "Oh, *that's* what that is." My whole first year I was still learning the signals and new ones came up all the time. I'd be like, "*Whoa* . . . what is *that*?" When you saw him start to turn towards you, your heart started pounding. You're wondering, "Is this good? Is this bad? Is he going to point me out? What's going on?" Then he'd turn and it'd be either a smile or a frown. You really hoped that it was a smile. Sometimes it was just him — sometimes he just didn't feel it, no matter how great the band was playing. He might start switching instruments. He might cut one song and go to a different song, after only ten seconds. If a song didn't take off he'd give that segue signal to move on.

HOLLIE FARRIS: He was definitely a showman. That's what he was about. He couldn't stand up there and dance all night, so he'd come up with other stuff, change up his songs. We hated that because he didn't realize that people wanted to hear his songs the way he originally did them. So we'd kind of resist that, but he'd still put changes into his music, sometimes for the better, sometimes not. Most of that took place on stage. We kinda knew what he wanted, but he'd signal and we'd just follow along. You had to always pay attention because you never knew what was going to happen. He had to *feel* it. Sometimes he'd get flat out bored doing the same songs for 40 years. He'd get bored with it and he'd try to change it up a bit. Most of the time he was making changes to get that feeling.

THE SIDEMAN'S ROLE

When I mention my own experience in the Soul Generals and place it on a continuum that began and flourished with James Brown's many great sidemen, I'm not putting myself up there. The players I played with are truly great players with soul and chops. They could create and innovate. But playing James Brown's music 30, 40 years after it was invented made me realize that those early guys were the progenitors. They *invented* the funk style; they *lived* it. We *played* it. That's not the same thing. Our living link to that time was my friend Fred Thomas. Funk, supposedly, had been dead since the late 1970s and we were copping its heyday. Even James Brown himself, in a sense, was copping his former self. Yet, with his charisma and arranging skills, he could pull new things out of his music throughout his career. Of course, in the end, for an original artist, it turned out that sticking with your own music, regardless of current styles, was the best choice. Commercially, that made sense. Miles Davis, for instance, didn't do that. But James Brown found that it was his ticket to continued popularity. And it worked.

In the Soul Generals, we had plenty of connections to the continuum that reached from the present into the deep past. A few players in the Soul Generals — Fred Thomas, Hollie Farris, Rock Laster — had been in the band since the '70s or '80s — for 20, 30 years. They'd started their careers with James Brown while some of those older, legendary cats were still around. Take my case. I'd learned a lot from Keith Jenkins, and Keith had learned a lot from Rock Laster. Rock had played with Jimmy Nolen, one of the master stylists of his time, who'd developed the trademark chank in funk music. I knew damn well I held a guitar chair that had been occupied by a long line of greats that stretched back beyond Jimmy Nolen, including Hearlon "Cheese" Martin, Robert Coleman, Phelps "Catfish" Collins, Alphonso "Country" Kellum, Nafloyd Scott, Bobby Roach — I'm sure that list is incomplete. Then there were drummers like Arthur Dickson, Jabo Starks, Clyde Stubblefield, Melvin Parker, Clayton Fillyau, and sax greats like St. Clair Pinckney and Alfred "Pee Wee" Ellis. Then you had the rare cases of break-out stardom, like Bootsy Collins. I'd better stop there because a list of greats is always incomplete. In fact, the more I got into this beautiful music, the more I became aware of all the great people who'd been in the James Brown band — all the great soloists, the rhythm guys, and the parts they wrote that became hits. I realized how many songs were written by the guys in the band and how their individual parts formed the basis for the songs. Clyde Stubblefield's beat on "Funky Drummer" made that track one of the most sampled in music history. Clyde was still trying to get a little recognition for his contributions when he passed in early 2017. I wish guys like Clyde, Jabo Starks, and Jimmy Nolen were more well-known. Those guys invented entire styles of music. Yet there are only three recognizable household names that came out of James Brown's bands: Maceo Parker, Bootsy Collins, and Fred Wesley Jr. I think that's a shame. If you compare Bootsy's total output — he was in James Brown's band for 18 months — against Jimmy Nolen, who spent 18 years with James Brown, it doesn't stack up. Sure, Bootsy is a genius, and he certainly is a star, but being a sideman in a band that spawned the greatest sidemen of all time should not be overlooked. It gave me a little perspective on how much those guys contributed to what we think of as James Brown's music. Consider the breadth of Jimmy Nolen's career: he played for Jimmy Wilson (famous for "Tin Pan Alley," 1953) and he waxed dozens of great R&B tracks for the Federal record label as a solo artist in the mid-1950s. Jimmy joined Johnny Otis in 1957, powered Otis's hit "Willie and the Hand Jive" and others in his three years there. He played for James Brown from 1965 until he quit in 1970, putting his patented chank (aka chicken scratch) guitar on many of Mr. Brown's biggest hits. When Jimmy rejoined James Brown two years later, he put in another 12 years, until he passed from a heart attack at age 49. When he died, his widow called James Brown and reamed him out, according to the story I heard. As I understand it, she told him that Jimmy's dying wish was that she tell Mr. Brown not to treat his band the way he had treated Jimmy. If true, that means Jimmy Nolen literally laid down his life so that players in the later incarnations of James Brown's band would be treated decently.

The thing is, and most everyone acknowledges it — certainly Fred Wesley does in his insightful book, *Hit Me, Fred: Recollections of a Sideman* — most of these amazing players did their best work when they toiled for James Brown. The James Brown tornado took their creativity someplace they perhaps would not have reached on their own. Despite their creativity and talent, maybe these men needed James Brown up front to do their best work. It was, of course, Mr. Brown's talent, charisma, and drive — and his eye for talent — that attracted all those amazing players into his bands, where he ruled them with the proverbial iron fist. James Brown had this attitude that if he wasn't there, it didn't pass his approval. There was no way it could be "James Brown music" unless he personally involved himself in every bit of it. I heard that the *Live in Dallas '68* recording had to have the introductory instrumental section by the band re-recorded after the show. James Brown had not yet stepped out on stage to direct and, thus, it was not "James Brown music." He did the same thing with us when we were in Japan: after a show, we had to hang around and re-record our introductory set in his presence, because if the show came out on CD, he wanted his stamp on the music.

Mr. Brown never relinquished that attitude, whether you want to call it creative control, jealousy, fear of abandonment — elements that figure in almost every theory purporting to explain his behavior. Even in my time, when the Soul Generals worked up some of their own songs and did some recording, we kept it hush-hush. He didn't want his band to be used as a stepping stone for someone's career. If you didn't show 100 percent loyalty, then you were one of *them*, not one of *us*. The issue was control and, given his chaotic, parentless upbringing, one could perhaps understand what drove Mr. Brown. This tightfisted approach could backfire, however, and it led to several entire bands walking out on him, as Jimmy Nolen and his brethren did in 1970. Yet, defections, frequent firings, and other factors created opportunities for new players to come in, as in my case. But some players, even musicians with successful careers of their own, like Tyrone Jefferson, a trombone player, would return. He'd been with James Brown from perhaps 1979 but had been out of the band for years since then. Tyrone was around for maybe six months when I joined, and he sat in on a few one-off gigs in my day. We were lucky to get him whenever he sat in, which must have been summertime, because he'd become a college music professor. He'd be there for special gigs, like the Apollo, because he was one of the heavy hitters.

Leroy Harper, an incredibly talented sax and keyboard player, released his *Painted Man* CD, and a couple of others, in the time I knew him in the band. So while I learned how to lead a band from watching James Brown, I could also see from Leroy's example how one might manage a side career as well. Despite the outward appearance of slavish devotion to James Brown's path, many of us were weighing our next move. He was getting older, we weren't getting younger, and somewhere, someday, the road would fork in two directions.

About this time, we had a change in management. As I understood it, there had only been one booking agency for most of James Brown's career. From my reading, it appears that Clint Brantley, Little Richard's agent, might have gotten to the Famous Flames first, back in the mid-1950s. Apparently, Universal Attractions Agency, founded by Ben Bart in 1949, won James Brown's business in early 1957, but when Ben Bart insisted the group change its name to James Brown and the Famous Flames, some original members left the group. That management relationship lasted 45 years but began to fray by 2000 as Ben Bart's son, Jack, and Jeff Allen, ran Universal and somehow raised James Brown's ire — not a difficult thing to do. In late 2002, Mr. Brown switched to Intrigue Music, run by Frank "SuperFrank" Copsidas out of Fort Lauderdale. SuperFrank formed Seven Decades of Funk Productions, Inc. to handle Mr. Brown's touring business and actually went on the road with us constantly, traveling with Mr. Brown's entourage. That probably meant that James Brown was his single most important client and, clearly, SuperFrank's theory held that his presence would ensure his influence. But Mr. Brown had a deep-rooted mistrust of outsiders, especially those involved in handling his money. He demonstrated this — and, perhaps unknowingly, confirmed where the lines were drawn — when SuperFrank tried to pressure the band into signing a four-page, single-spaced contract. That the contract overreached was established on line two, which identified the territory to which the contract applied as "The Universe." (Apparently, global rights weren't enough, just in case any of us decided to do business on another planet.) Word filtered down through the ranks that James Brown wasn't signing the contract and that he'd told someone in the band, "I wouldn't sign that if I were you." That's all we needed. SuperFrank had given us 24 hours to sign, but no one did. Mr. Brown had let us know that, in the scheme of things, we worked for *him*, not *them*. James Brown could be a very hip dude. He did look out for us, at times. Of course, it's entirely possible that SuperFrank was simply following Mr. Brown's lead. After Dan Aykroyd and John Belushi had cast James Brown as a preacher in *The Blues Brothers*, around 2003, Aykroyd swore he would one day open a House of Blues on the moon, with Mr. Brown at the top of the bill. So, perhaps, Mr. Brown was just thinking big and SuperFrank was just looking out for those extraterrestrial rights. Mr. Brown did used to compliment us by saying, "Y'all goin' to the moon!" Maybe he meant it literally.

When Intrigue came in, things were run more professionally, but at a cost. Intrigue immediately cut each band member's pay by 15 percent, across the board. That memo landed in our laps on January 17, 2003. No doubt management had increased its own profits by taking a bite out of our hides. I had just gotten a raise after waiting two years (and after the last pay cut of 27 percent), so it was instantly negated. The language was not warm and fuzzy.

> *The New Management Company has suggested dismissing 5*
> *people from the group. Do [sic] to the economy and the fact that*
> *I'm performing only limited dates now, [and] in order to keep*
> *everyone as long as we can, we find it necessary to reduce sala-*
> *ries by 15% immediately. Should anyone disagree [and choose]*
> *not to continue in the group we will understand.*
> *Signed, Mr. Bobbit, by order of James Brown*

Of course, this new cut produced a lot of tension and dissention. And now an Intrigue functionary was riding on the band bus. We called him "Alligator Arms" because his were so short. His role on the bus, basically, was to inform management when we smoked and cursed on the bus — a goofy and unwelcome presence. Yet, Intrigue apparently worked with the well-regarded William Morris Agency, a connection that led to large festivals, particularly in Europe, alongside alternative, pop and hard-rock acts. That put Mr. Brown in front of new, young, mostly white audiences, which represented a commercial opportunity to expand his market and allowed us to work enough to make a living. We were having a funky good time and sharing it with hundreds of thousands of people around the world. To my eyes, the glass was still half-full.

ACT THREE
ON THE ROAD AGAIN

By 2003, I'd been on the road for four years in the service of James Brown, dishing up funk, riding the bus, seeing the world. Every day brought something new: traveling to foreign places, new adventures with my bandmates, fresh insights into handling the James Brown enigma. To his credit, Mr. Brown made every performance a challenge, sometimes just by being his demanding self. That suited me — that's why I joined the band. The band itself seemed to be hitting a peak, musically. Around this time, though, a thought began to nag at me: would we continue to break new musical ground or did the range of performances and repertoire established over the past four years pretty much represent the known universe? I'd grown immeasurably as a musician and as a person while working for Mr. Brown. I'd earned my chair in the band, with the help of my bandmates. I'd earned Mr. Brown's respect and we'd survived a little history. On stage, the performances remained a challenge due to Mr. Brown's spontaneity and drive — in fact, in his eyes, it would be categorically impossible to master your job if you worked for him. And any music holds infinite possibilities for one's development, so I was hardly done. Maybe, in the arc of things, I was thinking about my next move like a musician. The phrase "Beyond James Brown" makes me smile, because it sounds absurd. What could there possibly be "Beyond James Brown"? I pondered it, but I made no moves.

After taking most of January 2003 off, we got rolling again with a two-nighter at B.B. King's Blues Club in the heart of Times Square in New York. Our tour itineraries proclaimed this to be the Seven Decades of Funk tour, a phrase that didn't really make sense, although Mr. Brown had indeed turned 70. The late, great Billy Triplett, who'd recorded and run sound for a litany of major artists, joined the tour at this point. (Sadly, Billy passed as we finished writing this book. So did B.B. King.) After B.B.'s, we headed to the ornate Paramount Theater in Oakland. We arrived a couple of days before the gig, and Billy set up a mobile recording studio at the motel, using multiple rooms in our wing. All of us had been writing new material, and we'd been catching brief opportunities here and there to play and record. But not like this. Billy really knew his stuff. I liked him right away. Finally we had professional assistance with our sound from someone who appreciated the band in its own right. He'd help with the stage setup, mic placements, and monitor settings and run the house mix through the front-of-house soundboard out in the audience. Billy had been running sound and working as a recording engineer since the 1970s, starting out as an assistant engineer on Willie Nelson–Waylon Jennings sessions when he was 17. Since then he'd worked extensively for the

Waiting to see what's on Mr. Brown's mind, 2003–2004.

likes of Keith Richards, Eric Clapton, Robert Cray, and Prince, not to mention Oingo Boingo, the Motels, Hall & Oates, Pat Benatar, Heart, Mother Love Bone (before they joined Eddie Vedder in Pearl Jam), Soundgarden, Alice in Chains, you name it. He even ran sound for the late comedian, Sam Kinison, about whom he had great (unrepeatable) stories. When he joined us, he was with the band essentially, so Billy had to wear his own tuxedo, too.

BILLY TRIPLETT: Oakland was where I first joined the band. The bus looked like a tour bus on the outside, but it really was just a Greyhound bus inside. If you'd been in the band for over 25 years you got two seats, one for you, one for your gear. Everyone else had to share seats. And nobody wanted to give up a seat on this bus. In fact, they'd told me I'd probably have to rent a car, I wouldn't be able to get on the bus. But I said, if I'm going to mix this band, I want to be *with* the band, I want to *know* the band, so I just kinda forced my way onto the bus. I walked up and down, I didn't know where I could sit. And the first person who looked up at me and said, "C'mere, sit with me," was Damon. At that time he was considered one of the new kids, even though he'd been in the band for years. We bonded real quick. Then everybody else realized that I was a good guy, we were all on the same team, doing what we loved. When we got to Oakland, everyone was itching to play. The Soul Generals had all these songs of their own. We took over one wing of the Oakland Holiday Inn Express, put the drums and bass in one room, Hammond B3 in another room, guitars in their own room, all the horns and me in another room. We recorded for four days and got some really great tracks. In fact, when we were recording in the motel, I told them we should do this record and call it *When James Wasn't Looking*.

One time we were on the East Coast and everyone was worn down. The organization just hated to spend money. But as production manager, I had money in the budget and if I had something extra, I'd take the band out and treat them like the stars they were. One night I took them all out for this wonderful dinner. We drank wine. We got back on the bus and headed back to the motel and we cranked up AC/DC full blast. And I watched the entire James Brown band sing AC/DC at the top of their lungs. It was pretty sweet. Everybody had been in a really foul mood and I was trying to lighten the whole thing up. And on the way back from dinner everyone was just lit up. They were singing "It's a Long Way to the Top (If You Want to Rock and Roll!)" as loud as they could.

HOLLIE FARRIS: I remember we cut a lot of songs in a motel room. We were hoping we could do something on our own and have [James Brown] just not interfere with it. He had been known to do that. I was with him one time when the band quit and we put together an album. He paid thousands of dollars to stop it. He managed to get a hold of the master and that was it, end of project. Possibly he was worried we'd go off on our own. He'd had several bands quit on him. There was a history there.

ERIK HARGROVE: Billy Triplett was a great guy and an excellent sound engineer — a real professional. He did a great job with the band, considering all the variables he had to deal with, including taking heat from Mr. Brown. Ronnie Tompkins (RT) had a way of throwing the heat off himself. If anything was wrong, it was the musicians' fault. For the longest time I got blamed for not playing the bass drum hard enough. One night in South America, we had this rinky-dink drum set. Mr. Brown said, "You're not playing the bass drum hard enough. You're not giving me enough 'One.'" I broke the pedal in half bringing my foot down on it. And he began to realize some issues were sound issues, not musician issues. Then we started hearing RT's name on stage instead of the musicians' names. So I was glad when Billy joined us.

In late March, Mr. Brown flew to Washington, D.C., with a small unit hand-picked from the Soul Generals, to play two songs for a benefit for the National Republican Senate Committee at the Capitol Hilton. I did not get asked to play the gig, much to my relief. The U.S. had invaded Iraq based on President Bush's lies to the nation only five days earlier. In bold letters, the itinerary thoughtfully added: "WARNING: THERE WILL BE SECRET SERVICE AND HEAVY SECURITY AS WELL AS OVER 200 VIPs." (In other words, keep it clean.) I do remember a gig at the Ritz-Carlton in D.C. at some point where there was a shit-ton of Congressmen. A couple guys in the band had made friends with these Congressmen and they were fans. We wondered aloud to each other: "Are these cats gonna give us all 'Get out of jail free' cards?" Anyway, we did get to see James Brown moving comfortably among the nation's movers and shakers. He had experience. James Brown made no apology for being an American patriot. He had deep faith in America, and he had always preached self-reliance and economic empowerment to all people. In fact, we often flew the American flag or used it as a backdrop on tours overseas. You can imagine that, particularly after the U.S. invaded Iraq, that wasn't always popular. But James Brown wasn't going to shy away from his position. So people could talk about it or, if they didn't like it, they could go on home. I believe that was Mr. Brown's attitude, and I don't blame him. Anyway, everyone knew he was an international ambassador for peace, so flying the American flag wasn't about "USA! USA!" In his mind it was a symbol of freedom and justice, however corny or naïve that may sound. And he certainly wasn't all about America. Like any great entertainer, when he traveled to another country he learned to speak a little of the language. He'd say something onstage in the local language, and they'd know he was a friend of theirs. Mr. Brown and the Soul Generals were invited to play at the White House around this time, but the arrangement on offer called for a ten-by-ten-foot stage, which of course did not even offer enough space for Mr. Brown, a microphone, and a few dance moves, let alone a band. Mr. Brown occasionally performed at awards ceremonies or on television without the Soul Generals or with just one half of the band, but he wasn't heading to the White House without some soul power. The White House didn't budge on the size of the stage. Mr. Brown passed on the invitation.

Taking a solo, with Ray "Bo" Brundidge on bass partially obscured, and Hollie Farris, trumpet, listening intently, sometime in 2003–2004.

Despite my passing thoughts about the future, 2003 was developing into a fun year. I have delightfully absurd images in my mind from a brief tour of Texas. We played Dallas, rode the bus to Houston that night, and arrived at 3 a.m. By two in the afternoon, we were rousted out of our rooms and bused to the gig. Again, after the show, we jumped on the bus and arrived in Austin at 3 a.m. The next day we performed at the Travis County Exposition Center, which is basically a rodeo arena. No doubt we were all a little punchy. While the band played its intro, we waited for the singers to arrive, but the grounds were dirt — it was a rodeo arena — and the stage sat in the middle of it. The women couldn't walk out there in their high heels and dresses, so they had to be driven to the stage.

We were vamping on this intro long past the point when the horns would've heralded the singers' arrival. We just had to keep it simmering for their entrance. No vamp in history has ever gone on that long. Typically, a stage and curtains create a little drama for an entrance. That night, the audience saw everything. A car pulled up to the edge of the arena. Five good-looking women in dresses and heels got in. Then came a long, slow drive through the sand and dirt to the side of the stage. Someone helped each singer out, then they negotiated a stretch of sand to reach the stage stairs. Finally, they were in position — the crowd roared. Next? Same routine with James Brown. By the time we needed him at the mic, they had just put him in the damn car. We just kept vamping while the star was driven, seemingly in slow motion, to the stage. We delivered the usual razzle-dazzle performance. At the end of the show, Mr. Brown hustled down the steps, dashed toward the stands, and actually ran around the entire rodeo grounds in his suit and boots, high fivin' the fans as he went. That kind of direct fan contact was really cool to see, and they loved him for it. We loved him for it, too — we got to see another facet of his personality that night: the unabashed, crowd-pleasing showman who was still having the time of his life. Moments like those inspired our loyalty. I can still see him running around that huge arena. It made me appreciate that he was pretty fit for an older guy. I mean, on stage he never stopped moving. That's a good cardio workout. Then a run around an entire rodeo arena at full clip? The more he performed, the more fit he became.

In my case, at this point, the more time off we had, the better for me and my own band. By April 2003, I had the lineup that would record my first CD, *Space Cadet*, that fall. That lineup stayed together for about a year and a half: Chad Aman on keys, Mario DiBona on drums, Jack Alterman on bass, and Justin Jones on sax. All great musicians who helped me realize a dream. At that point I was just getting it together as a band leader and learning to sing. We played mostly instrumentals, but I would add vocals where I could manage them reasonably well and I just started to build from there. I'm not a natural singer and I don't have much range, so I've learned to sing and play in keys that work best for me. The amazing thing is that if you continue to work on it, your range grows. I get another note every six months or so.

Spring meant outdoor shows, which were usually a lot of fun. We played Sunfest in West Palm Beach, Riverfest in Little Rock, CityFest in Montgomery. We rode the bus clear from Montgomery to New York City for the next gig. (Only 18 hours by bus.) What a contrast. We played a free show in New York's Battery Park as the city kicked off its River to River Festival, dedicated to lower Manhattan's recovery after 9/11. The Antibalas Afrobeat Orchestra opened with some funk of its own. The next night it was black tie at the Jacob Javits Center for Elton John's Robin Hood charity, with Billy Crystal emceeing. We watched Elton John do his thing for an hour, then we did our thang. A couple nights later, in Asbury Park's Conventional Hall, they were having trouble with the sound as Patti LaBelle opened for us. Out on stage, Patti struck a pose for some of us in the band as we snapped pictures from the wings. When the sound problems persisted, she hissed into the mic: "Y'all better fix the sound for James Brown or he's gonna *cut* somebody!"

Before setting off for the usual round of summer festivals in Europe, we played a few here at home. First we hit Bonnaroo, a giant hippie scene in Manchester, Tennessee. We got there the night before our gig and caught Widespread Panic up close. (I still don't understand their draw.) But Warren Haynes and Robert Randolph sat in, so that rocked. I met up again with Chet Helms, who remembered me, and we hung out together for a late-night set by Medeski Martin, & Wood with Robert Randolph and Luther Dickinson sitting in. Chet was taking pictures and he got some great shots of James Brown and the Soul Generals in performance. The next day, we opened for the Dead — formerly the Grateful Dead — on the big stage to about 80,000 people. The Soul Generals killed it that day, and we came off the stage in the blazing Tennessee summer heat only to find the bus locked. We couldn't change out of our sweaty uniforms and the hired driver was nowhere to be seen. We were milling around the bus and, because of that, I saw Phil Lesh walk by. I intercepted him. "Hey, man, I've seen you play a million times since I was a kid." Phil said, "You guys played great!" Across the way, we could see the Dead's setup: each band member had his own primo bus parked backstage. And James Brown's entire crew showed up in one of those rented Coach USA buses, with a hired driver who's locked the bus and gone to catering to hit on women. *Thanks, Bus Driver*. It worked out, though, because I got to meet Phil Lesh.

James Brown was due to receive a Lifetime Achievement Award from Black Entertainment Television (BET) later in June, and our schedule was packed tight, so we flew from Tennessee to Oakland so we could use the Luther Burbank Center in Santa Rosa, California, for a rehearsal. (No one missed the 2,400-mile bus ride.) We dashed north the next day to a gig at the Mountain Winery in Saratoga, California, another gig outside Medford, Oregon, and then hopped on a bus to Hollywood for the actual BET rehearsals. (A mere 700 miles, covered in 10 hours.) When we stepped out on stage for the real thing the following night, we could see all the biggest names in black entertainment right there in the front rows. Steve Harvey introduced us. Backstage he was brimming with jive. "Y'all bettuh be strong, cuz I'm gonna bring you out like a motherfucker! You bettuh be goood!" You know how Steve Harvey, can be. The band was thinking as one man, "Shut the *fuck* up! We got this!" But we liked Steve Harvey and that's his thing, messin' with people. So we're up there, killin' it on "Sex Machine." It's near the end of the set. James Brown dropped to one knee, bowed his head, and signaled the band to stop. *BAM!* We stop. Danny Ray came out and threw the cape over him. Right then, someone started heading toward us from the wings. He looked familiar. I remember turning to Bo standing next to me. "Is that #$%@ Michael Jackson?" Bo goes, "I think so." Michael looked good, like he'd been working out. He hit the stage hot, doin' the glide. Suddenly we realized that *he's* the special guest who's going to present James Brown's lifetime achievement award. Danny Ray grabbed the cape, James Brown kicked the band into the bridge for "Sex Machine," and he and Michael Jackson started dancing, throwing moves back and forth. Mr. Brown looked inspired. He handed Michael the mic and Michael gave a trademark James Brown howl. Then Michael headed off stage to give his speech. Mr. Brown sent Danny Ray racing after him to tap him on the shoulder. "*Put the cape on him,*" he said. Danny Ray draped the cape over Michael Jackson's shoulders and the place went berserk. Then Michael gave this tear-filled speech about how he learned so much from his idol, James Brown — how to dance, how to sing, how to put it over. Mr. Brown accepted the award fairly nonchalantly. He didn't really say much, then he turned to us and kicked us back into "Sex Machine." Finish the show!

It all looked spontaneous, yet it went pretty darn smoothly for a truly serendipitous moment. If my friend Kelly Jarrell is right, there'd been a bit of planning for this moment.

KELLY JARRELL: Whoever was stage managing the BET awards show went up to Danny Ray just before our performance and said, "Mr. Ray, we have a special guest, a secret guest who's going to drape the cape over Mr. Brown." "No, no, no, absolutely not, that's *my* job. I don't part with the cape," he told 'em. "Mr. Brown would *kill* me if I let someone else handle it." You know, the cape is Danny's big moment. They said, "We can't tell you who it is — it's a secret special guest." "No, no, no, I'm sorry," Danny Ray said. Finally, Michael Jackson appeared and said, "I want to put the cape on Mr. Brown." Danny Ray perked up. "Oh! *Michael!*" So then it was okay! You can see the moment in the [YouTube] video when Mr. Brown bends down and Michael Jackson puts the cape over him and we all moved back, star-struck. It was this giddy rush.

Two thousand three saw the band perform a lot of great shows. The band got squeaky tight, Mr. Brown minded his Ps and Qs, and the shows improved with Billy Triplett mixing the house sound. Like any support person in Mr. Brown's orbit, Billy played a lot of roles, eventually. Not only did he run superb sound, he got the band through airports and booked into hotels more efficiently — simple tour stuff that he had a lot of experience with. That must have taken some weight off RT's shoulders. But Billy's major contribution was mixing the band from front-of-house, out in the audience, where it mattered. Prior to Billy's arrival, RT had to do it all, but no one person could do it all, and our sound suffered for it. That's not maligning the dead — RT has passed — he simply couldn't devote enough attention to the Soul Generals' large, dynamic sound, and he might not have had the skills for it. That's where Billy came in.

BILLY TRIPLETT: When I started, the main challenge was "RT," Ronnie Tompkins. I had to figure out how to do things, diplomatically. Then he started trusting me. It took months. I'll never forget walking across a field at Bonnaroo to reach the stage. There's this long line of black guys following RT and then there's me. Someone asked, "Who's *that* guy hanging out with *those* guys?" And RT just said, "That's my *dawg*!" Once I overcame RT's resistance, things started happening.

I think we had 48 mics for most shows. At the BET Awards at the Kodak Theater, I think I used 56 channels. To mix a band that big and dynamic, you have to keep your eyes open. It's a baseball game and that ball could be comin' right at your head! That's where the rush comes in: you never know what's going to happen. James Brown would wiggle one finger and it meant, "Switch the rhythm section." The band had two: one funky, one solid. He'd change it around with a finger wiggle. And if you missed that signal, you were dead. That was the world's tightest band, really. They'd say, "What will we do when James Brown goes?" I told them, "You guys are the greatest band in the *world*. You can do anything you want." That's why I did those recordings with them, apart from James Brown. I said, "We should do nothing but your music." They wanted to record and see if Mr. Brown wanted to do something on top of it. I told them, "You don't need him, you guys are *so good*." We all knew he wasn't going to last forever.

I'd talk to Mr. Brown, but seldom. He'd definitely talk to me, especially if he thought the drums were too loud. He'd say, "Watch 'em!" He was straightforward on what he wanted. But I kept my distance. I never wanted to be the star's personal friend; it gets weird. I think Prince was harder to work for. Prince was real moody — there's a fine line between genius and insanity. I was more the band cheerleader, hanging with the band. I'd make tapes of the shows and play them at night on the bus and they were all blown away. They'd never heard the bass and drums [in a concert mix].

After a week's break, we reassembled in Duanesburg, New York, for the Gathering of the Vibes, another big hippie fest. I barely made it in time. I'd rushed home to Vegas to see my uncle Don, who'd suffered a heart attack and, in the end, never regained consciousness. He called me "Damon Van Halen" ever since I was a kid and started playing guitar. Funniest guy I ever knew. I still miss him. Anyway,

I was the last band member to reach the Vibes festival site, where I ran into my bandmate Keith, who, true to form, immediately said, "Hey man, you gotta come meet Dickey Betts." So we hung out with Dickey Betts on his bus. He said the same thing a lot of people said when they met us on the road. "Geez, we never really believed that all you guys rode a bus like that from gig to gig." The minute the gig was over, it seemed, we were boarding a plane for London.

The very next day, nearly 3,500 miles away, we played The Royal Albert Hall — the same stage where the Beatles, Bob Dylan, Cream, Hendrix, and other great musicians had performed. Our complete focus on James Brown kept our awe in check long enough to deliver a great performance. What a room. After the gig, I was walking to the bus and saw people waiting to meet Mr. Brown. I said, "Where's the party?" A young woman said, "Our house!" She was with her brother and their mom. The mom said, "My husband wanted to be here, but he's on the road." I said, "Who's your husband?" She said, "Steve Howe." (That's the guitarist for Yes, one of my all-time favorite bands.) I told them that sometimes during a show Mr. Brown would say to me, "Play that little Irish thing," and I'd play the beginning of "The Clap," by Steve Howe, from 1971's *The Yes Album*. Their dad wrote the song the day his son, Dylan, was born, only months before I was born. Small world.

We moved on to Liverpool, the Beatles' hometown, and then crossed the North Sea to play the Pori International Jazz Festival on the west coast of Finland, where we headlined on the main stage. Then we headed south for another sprint through Italy: Perugia, Rome, Naples, Bari, Verona, Caldiero, Sardinia, Sicily, and Palermo — nine shows in 11 days. That's hard work. But when you map out those gigs in sequence, as I did years later, it looks like someone knocked over a bowl of spaghetti — a crazy mishmash of bus rides running in every direction, then back again. Those Italian tours were always crazy. I'll never forget Rome — actually the Piazza del Porto, Civitavecchia, northwest of Rome.

Keith Jenkins, me, and Erik Hargrove pose for a publicity photo,
3 May 2003, at the House of Blues in Orlando, Florida. The
photo was taken in case the trio could get gigs on the side.

We played well past midnight in a tent in the plaza of this port on the Tyrrhenian Sea. By the time we headed to our hotel, it was three o'clock in the morning. We were dead tired. Turns out our "hotel" is a convent, courtesy of the promoter. And it's locked. To a person, the entire troupe was pissed off. "Why are we staying here?" RT called the promoter to no avail. We banged on doors and created a ruckus until we were finally admitted to our rooms. When we woke up, we were surrounded by nuns. Billy Triplett told me he was getting coffee and said, "Good morning" to a nun, who retorted, "Fung-gaa!" as in, "Fuck you!" And she flicked her fingers under her chin at him. I guess they didn't like it any more than we did. We had to wait in the courtyard for the bus, and we couldn't help noticing that the turtles in the fountain were all humping each other. The promoter had basically screwed the band and the turtles were all screwing each other. Somehow, on the road, things like that seemed to make sense. And we had seven more shows to do. You can be sure Mr. Brown did not stay in a convent that night.

> **KELLY JARRELL:** All those Italian tours were run by this crazy promoter, who was kinda shady. Sometimes we'd arrive at a piazza in some little town and nothing would be set up. Then, little by little, a stage would get built. There might be a tent for us to sit in until they threw a piece of bread at us. It was always so sketchy.

Everyone goes to Italy to eat, right? But when you're confined to a bus on the highway between cities and gigs at odd hours of the day or night, Italy could mean mediocre bread, pasta, red sauce, and a little cheese. Very infrequently, a salad. On tour, the notion of a balanced diet is out the window. That's hard on your body. There were times when, for one reason or another — it was late, our hotel wasn't near a restaurant or grocer, we were broke — we could find nothing to eat at all. My bandmates had funny ways of coping. On my first tour, I had knocked on Fred Thomas's door. Strange smells wafted from within. "What are you guys doing in there?" Fred was ironing Spam he'd brought from the States. Everybody's yukking it up, eating Spam. Apparently, this was a long-running tradition in the band: the iron that came with the hotel room would double as a hot plate, putting a crease into the Spam. (Woe to the next guest who tried ironing clothes after that trick.) Jeff Watkins would use the hotel room coffee maker to cook hot dogs. Once you realized the potential for almost literally starving, you'd take precautions.

> **FRED THOMAS:** I did a lot of things to survive on the road. You'd always carry something: Spam, crackers, something. That saved a lot of cats. You could be starving to

death. You're coming off a gig and nothing's open, hotel kitchen's closed. What are you going to do when it's three, four in the morning?

Wherever in Civitavecchia Mr. Brown was staying while we cooled our heels at the convent, things apparently weren't too cool at his end, either. Somewhere in this run of shows, Mr. Brown sent Tomi Rae back home. All we knew was that she and her part in the show were gone. Per the usual, nobody asked any questions. Later it came out that this was when James Brown discovered that Tomi Rae's first marriage had not been annulled at the time he married her in December 2002. A few weeks later, a full-page ad appeared in *Variety*:

> Due to Mr. James Brown and Mrs. Tomi Rae Brown's heavy demanding tour schedule, they have decided to go their separate ways. There are no hard feelings, just a mutual show-business decision made by both parties.
>
> Mr. Brown says, "We both love each other but it has become difficult to function together. With love and affection we both reached this decision. We were a great team and we both have a great future."

That announcement inevitably sparked a bit of chatter but, again, no questions were asked. After nine shows in 11 days in Italy, we flew to New York and rode the bus directly to Atlantic City to play Boardwalk Hall before we got a break. (Think about the traveling covered in that sentence.) Soon we were racing across the country again, from Michigan to New Mexico (a mere 1,600 miles by bus). We had ten days off, reconvening for a theater show on Long Island, then heading south to Chastain Park in Atlanta. Photographer Chris McKay of Concert Shots snapped pics from the lip of the stage and wrote afterwards:

James Brown proves that getting up in years doesn't prevent getting down onstage. The Godfather of Soul lived up to every expectation of mine, which was a relief considering I've been let down by so many 'veteran' acts I've seen lately. 'Make It Funky' was the opening song and the recipe for the night. James did one-legged shimmies across the stage that seemed to defy gravity while belting out shrieks and screams that shouldn't have been possible from a human. "Get Up Offa That Thing" had the diverse crowd doing just that. Everyone was dancing and cheering. . . . Just when [the show] had almost reached its moment of perfection, the unthinkable happened. Everyone's dancing, the lights are spinning, the band is rocking, and James is smiling when all of the power and lights shut off unceremoniously. I looked at my watch. We'd reached the 11 o'clock curfew. The crowd booed and hissed at the disrespectful ending to a great night.

You can only imagine how rude that was, cutting off power to a 20-piece band in mid-flight, like coitus interruptus or something. Then we were off to Japan again, my third trip there. They say third time's the charm and, certainly, that was true for me. Unfortunately, Billy Triplett didn't come with us.

BILLY TRIPLETT: I only worked for them until just before they left for Japan. There was a break. James Brown didn't have gigs booked. So I filled in on a Goo Goo Dolls tour when a friend lost his father. I'd be back in time to go to Japan. And the organization got all pissed. They didn't want me to go out with someone else. I said, "Well, you're not working. And you're not going to pay me a retainer. So what's the difference?" But the management didn't like it. SuperFrank said they'd hire

Feelin' it on the fly, with bow tie typically askew. CREDIT: ODETTA

someone else. It was their control thing. And they went through four or five guys after me and no one stayed.

I'll tell ya, though, I mixed James Brown at The Royal Albert Hall and the Soul Generals *rocked* it.

KICKING UP A STORM

My first trip to Japan had been overshadowed by Mr. Brown's unpredictable behavior. The second trip, with Chuck Berry, had included my initiation into the joys of Soju — the sake-on-steroids — and was too brief for me to get to enjoy my surroundings. The third trip, in October 2003, was the Goldilocks moment — just right. We were there for ten days, long enough to shake off jet lag and really enjoy it. We were not there to relax, of course. The day we landed, we rushed into TV Asahi studios to perform a short set. Mr. Brown and Tomi Rae must have reconciled because she came along and performed her guest spots in the shows. We played a couple of nights at the famed Nippon Budokan in central Tokyo, which was initiated as a pop music palace by the Beatles in 1966 and has hosted just about every artist since, from Bob Dylan to Cheap Trick. We moved on to the Sun Palace in Fukuoka, the Festival Hall in Osaka, the Nagoya Shimin Hall in Nagoya, and the Sapporo Concert Hall Kitara in Sapporo. On the second day at Budokan, for some reason now long forgotten, I'd been pissy all day — "Mr. Attitude and Won't Shut Up" — and the entire band conspired to hide my pants just before show time. Then everyone watched with amusement as I puzzled over their absence. I had to wear the wrong color pants, because mine were just plain gone. I thought, "My god, did I not put them away after the last gig, after partying?" At the last minute, when we'd all gathered in a circle for our ritual prayer

From left to right, during an evening out in Tokyo, 2003:
Jeff Watkins, Erik Hargrove, soundman Todd Harris, Yonna
Kari, Me, Sara Raya, Keith Jenkins, Leroy Harper Jr.

before hitting the stage, Jeff Watkins had them in his hand all wrinkled up. He threw them at me, like, "There are your stupid pants, bitch." And I had to run and change really quick while everyone laughed hysterically at me. Everyone got the treatment at some point, and that time *I* deserved it.

Near the end of the tour, I visited a head shop where they made elixirs. Legally. I tried one. The result, believe it or not, inspired a couple of songs for my first solo CD, *Space Cadet*, scratched down on the hotel stationery. And I had another inspiration. I was always searching for something to blow James Brown's mind. (Without falling into the obvious trap of getting caught up in the hype.) One night everyone had gone to a party, and I stayed behind, "in the zone," working on all these song ideas. I had time alone, a luxury. All sweaty and nasty in my hotel room, suddenly, my room seemed confining. So I grabbed my electric guitar, took the elevator to the lobby of this posh Sapporo Park hotel and walked out into a sprawling park. I'm out on a little dock on a pond there, thinking. How could I possibly pull some sort of bold move during the show? It'd be fun to top off the tour with something kinda wild. I was thinking martial arts, a kick of some sort. I thought, I'll have to lead with my left leg on the kick, because the body of the guitar is slung over my right leg. I'm figuring this out while, frankly, I'm tripped out. In my mind, I tried to time a kick with a certain note at the climax of a solo. As I strummed a few chords, I heard a hand drummer across the pond practicing. So I'd stop and listen. Then he'd stop and listen and I'd play. I finally figured out how to do this kick I created without falling on my face. I just invented it on the spot. I'd heard that in the band's past, "Sweet Charles" Sherrell had done a karate kick, but not with his bass guitar. I just wanted to get *crazy*. The next night was the last show of the tour. At that point, I hadn't told anyone what I had in mind, except my friend Erik, the drummer. Mr. Brown threw me my solo in "Doing It to Death" and as he stepped forward from his keyboards to take back the reins, I took two steps forward and did this high karate kick at the climax to a screamin' solo! Behind me, Erik timed a cymbal crash to my kick. We'd worked that out before the show. Typically, Mr. Brown woulda yelled my name after my solo but, instead, he's *shocked*! He threw up his arms and started running around the stage, cracking up. Then he came around, gave me a high-five, and I could see it in his eyes. "That was *cool*!" He *loved* it.

The highs could be so high onstage. Nobody could let their personal shit get in the way at these moments. Despite the rough patches, to see the look on James Brown's face when I unleashed my new kick — well, I treasured that moment and still do, just knowing I'd surprised and delighted him. Of course, once you do something cool in the show, he's going to kinda destroy it by making you do it over and over again. From then on, he'd make me do the karate kick at the end of my final solo of the night. Guys in the band told me, "Didn't we ever tell you that if you do tricky shit, you'll have to do it *all* the time?!"

GEORGE "SPIKE" NEALY: James Brown taught Damon how to pull not just a little from the audience, but to take them to the frenzy point of the solo. So when Damon came up with that karate kick at the peak of his solo, James Brown was like, "*Now* you got it!" From then on, Damon had to end every night with that kick. You're locked in! You're part of the frenzy now. One particular night I decided to spin my sticks at the end of a solo — go around my entire rack of cymbals and hit each one as I spin my sticks. And, boy, when I saw James Brown's face, I said, "Oh boy, I might as well get ready to do that spin every night when he calls for it." He wanted that big close out.

HOLLIE FARRIS: That karate kick would make Bruce Lee jealous. Just blew everybody's mind completely! We didn't know Damon could do anything like that. But from then on, that was part of the show. It had to be done every night. Mr. Brown used to bring me out front and make me imitate his dancing. That was embarrassing. He wanted to do that a lot so I had to learn to dance like James Brown. I did some of his moves! He'd just do crazy stuff and if it worked once, it was in the show.

Inspired by the developments in Japan, I returned home and completed writing songs for my solo CD, *Space Cadet*. During a tour break in early November, I booked studio time in Denver to record with my band. I was proud of the result and looked forward to sharing it with Mr. Brown to see what he thought of what I was doing with what he'd taught me.

DANNY RAY

At the end of November 2003, we played two nights at the hallowed Apollo Theater, where James Brown had made his mark 40 years earlier. Danny Ray had met Mr. Brown sometime in the early 1960s at the Apollo and expressed his desire to serve the cause. This might be the right moment to say more about Mr. Brown's right-hand man on stage, our emcee, Danny Ray. His full name was Danny Ray Brown, no relationship to James Brown. But if your last name is Brown and you work for James Brown, you gotta lose it! I mean, the universe — let alone our organization — wasn't big enough for two Mr. Browns. So he became "Danny Ray." I believe he'd served as an airman in Korea. On the road he had many responsibilities, including the show's wardrobe, so he'd be muttering under his breath the whole time, sometimes erupting into a highly stylized tirade if things weren't going just right. Cussing and fussing was his shtick, especially after he'd had a couple drinks. Band lore had it that one time out on the road, Danny Ray slipped on ice and fell hard on his butt. But he came up smiling — he hadn't spilled a drop of the glass of brandy in his hand. Danny Ray had a catchphrase for everything. When he saw an old car or anything that could potentially break down, he called it a dice game, because it was a game of chance. Naturally, at discreet times, that reference included the James Brown bus, which he rode in with the band.

We had great times with Danny Ray. He is a true classic, bless his soul. Every little thing that he would do in his day, just going about his job, was *classic*. He'd make us laugh *and* he'd drive us crazy. If your coat was wrinkly and you had not ironed it, he'd be on you. (Danny Ray would say things akin to: "Mr. Brown don't wanna see no road maps on those uniforms." Or: "Y'all better iron those uniforms so I don't hear it from him. 'Cuz he'll be up my ass if y'all lookin' unkempt and ghetto in them suits.") He was known to cuss and point. He had all these giant wardrobe bags with all the tuxedos in them that he was accountable for, and he needed them moved around. And he's a little guy, so he's not moving those things himself. We might get the uniform bags off the bus and onto a cart for him, then he had local porters at the venue to help him. He'd tell them what he needed done, and his instructions would be laced with profanity, but in a charming way. Us, them, whomever — Danny Ray was an equal opportunity cusser. Whoever helped him would love him by the end, in most cases. A friend of mine, Deb Pastor, at the House of Blues in Chicago, was in charge of hospitality for the band. She *loved* him. He was always impeccably dressed, and was always charming the ladies. Fittin' in with the plan. He's the kind of guy who'd bring a dozen roses into the bar to hand out to the ladies just to be cool — not trying to bed one of them, just hanging out. He had stories. He knew Jimi Hendrix before he became a star. He knew the singer, Sarah Vaughan — "The Divine One." From what I understood, Danny Ray and Mr. Brown had gotten together at the Apollo Theater in the early 1960s, and after that they probably put in something like 45 years together on the road. Mr. Brown would say, "Danny Ray been with me 20, 25, 30 years. And he ain't but 29 years old!" Danny Ray attended sound checks to work his emcee shtick into the show, developing new things to say. The cat had to be as spontaneous as any musician and more so because, at times, the entire show pivoted around his emceeing. His interplay with James Brown and a microphone was something to see. When he'd call for *Star Time!* and the boss strode out to the crowd's adulation, Danny Ray had to retreat gracefully and scoot out of the spotlight. Later, at the end of the show, Mr. Brown would toss the mic aside and walk off stage, and Danny Ray, somehow, always caught the mic and went into his emcee number — "Jaaaaaaaaaaaaames Brown!" — as

Mr. Brown walked offstage to cheers from the throng. They both had slick moves and interaction that was totally spontaneous. They could roll with it any which way. Backstage, hanging out, Danny Ray would often say, "It's God, the job, then me," to describe his priorities. He was an entertainer and he loved attention. And if you gave him the attention he craved, he might go on and on and on. Sometimes that'd get on your nerves, but he made us laugh and we couldn't help but love him.

> **BILLY TRIPLETT:** Danny Ray is one of my all-time favorite people. He is magical. He'd say "I'm-a gonna have a hamhock sammich!" That man was the only one who'd show up on the bus fully dressed in a three-piece suit. Always tight. You never ever saw that man with a wrinkle in his clothes. Never. In fact, the band taught me how to iron. I'd never ironed anything in my life before that. We all had to wear tuxedos, even me. That was one of the first things I had to do: go out and buy a tuxedo. With James Brown, you had to have the look and Danny Ray exemplified that.

THE STRATOCASTER

Thanksgiving was around the corner, but we jumped on a plane to Amsterdam to play the Heineken Music Hall. On Thanksgiving Day, we played the Philharmonic in Cologne, a sumptuous, state-of-the-art modern theater. A day later we landed in London to play the Rainbow Trust Children's Charity Ball at the Natural History Museum, a gala fundraiser for seriously ill kids. The people associated with the event included the royal family and lesser mortals.

So I learned later. At the time, we just rolled in, ironed our suits, grabbed our instruments, and delivered a show. With us on the bill were a few names: Sting, David Byrne, Brian Ferry. Needless to say, James Brown headlined. The next day the BBC taped an exciting show of ours at the LSO St. Luke's in London's East End. It was part of the BBC Four Sessions; you can catch it on YouTube. (In that vein, I should mention that a professional outfit also video-taped us performing at the House of Blues in Anaheim, California, which would become the concert feature on the biographical documentary DVD, *Soul Survivor*.)

Jeff Watkins had never stopped trying to convince me and Keith that if one of us went to a Fender Stratocaster that we'd have a more complementary blend of guitar tones. "You guys both have a mid-to low-range tone," he told us. "For a funk band, a higher-range tone would go better with the mid-range. It'd cut better." Jeff was right. Keith played a Paul Reed Smith, whose humbucker pickups and resonant tone sounded a lot like my Les Paul, which also used humbuckers. There's so much personality in a Stratocaster, and it offers a wide range of tone. In a Strat, you have this single-coil pickup sound that kind of pops out. It's not all about sustain, it's about the personality of a single note. That one note might ring all day on a Les Paul, where it'll fade away on a Strat. That means that sometimes you need to dampen more actively on the Les Paul to maintain control over its sustain, where you've got to really fret that note on the Strat, give it some vibrato to make it ring out. Besides, as Jeff pointed out, I had the wah-wah parts in the show, and those single-note lines cut through the band's big sound nicely on a Strat. You could get a lot of mojo out of a Strat, once you got used to it.

That was our thinking, and in December 2003, I decided to buy the damn Strat. (Hey, it only took two years of thinking about it . . .) I was ready for something new. I wanted a new axe, a new sound, a new way of playing guitar. At this juncture, with effort, I could afford to spend $1,000 on a new instrument; though, as a working stiff in the Soul Generals, buying a new instrument wasn't a casual move. We had most of December and early January off, so I tried out Strats at various stores in Denver until I found one that played just right. All I was thinking about was tone and playability. I kinda ignored the fact that the Strat had a floating bridge and stock saddles for the strings. The floating bridge accommodates a whammy bar that the player bends to make a note or chord go sharp or flat. That adds a range of possibilities to your playing. The downside is that, if you break a string, all the other strings go out of tune and there's no way to recover, other than to change the string and retune all six strings. The saddles on the bridge keep the tension on the strings at one end, while the nut, at the tuning peg end of the fretboard, keeps the tension at the other end. But stock saddles could have sharp edges and lead to strings breaking, especially considering how hard we played.

The fact that I used a relatively stiff pick was also rough on strings. The health of my strings was on my mind. After all, I'm the guy who'd compulsively changed them for every show for years to ensure they wouldn't break during a performance. (Eventually, I'd install the more forgiving Graph-Tech String Saver saddles on the Strat.) The first night I played the Strat in the James Brown show was a February 2004 gig at the House of Blues in West Hollywood. I left my trusty Les Paul at home. We were on the band's bus outside the House of Blues on Sunset Strip. Dan Aykroyd was hanging with us, as usual. We'd never know who else might be in the house. Before the show, I thought, "Damn, am I gonna get through the night with the strings I have? Or should I change them?" I was uncharacteristically indecisive. I decided I wouldn't change them, but looked 'em over to make sure there weren't nicks in the strings at the saddle that could lead to one breaking. Keith and I had crammed a piece of cardboard under the Strat's floating bridge to make it more like a stop-tail. But in my haste and concern, I replaced the back plate — the plate that covers the springs that give tension to the bridge — on backwards. That plate has holes in it, so you can restring the guitar without removing the plate by passing a string through the designated hole, back to front, then taking it up to the tuning pegs to wind it and tie it off. I realized my mistake just before we went onstage. If I'd broken a string in that situation, I'd have to leave the stage, take four screws out, remove the plate, restring it, retune it, and replace the plate. In show business, leaving the stage is definitely not done. Leaving Mr. Brown's stage — well, a chore like that would have taken me out of the action far too long for my own good. So, with moments to go before taking the stage, I returned the back plate to its proper position. And, wouldn't you know, with that stiff pick and in the heat of battle, I ended up breaking a string during the show. I changed it right there, with the band cooking away beside me. That's how close we lived to the edge. No backup guitar on stage. No guitar tech to help. Do it yourself. And if you're not ready for a key part in the show that belongs to you because you're changing a string, you're going to get dirty looks from the boss, at the very least. My obsession with the health of my strings was well founded.

The evening had another twist, perhaps understandable only to guitarists. I've got my new Strat, my new tone, my new direction, after playing a Les Paul every night for a decade. And three of the biggest Les Paul legends in the world — Jimmy Page, Slash, and Joe Perry — turned up in the house that night, witnesses to my string breaking and my onstage repairs. Erik Hargrove ran into them at the bar after the show. It's pretty exciting when you don't know who's out there, and it's better that you don't know. You wanted to have your shit together. Mr. Brown accepted the new guitar. Of course he would: many of his guitarists had wielded Strats.

By this time, I'd completed mixes on most of the recording sessions with Harmonious Junk. I had a demo disc. I knew it was a risky proposition to share it with Mr. Brown. He might easily view it as a lack of dedication to the cause or even as treasonous. Still, I couldn't help but be jazzed to have him hear my stuff. The new CD reflected my own thing: modern, funky rock with lots of improvisation. It also reflected everything he'd taught me about being melodic and keeping it tight. I'll never forget the moment I planned to take a chance and give him the demo. We finished a four-day tour in late January 2004, at the House of Blues in Vegas. We thought all had gone well, but Mr. Brown sent Mr. Bobbit back to the band room. "You guitar players are all out of tune." We knew we were perfectly in tune. But he sent me home on a down note, with a feeling that my efforts in his band were fruitless. Looking back, this was Games Brown talking. Knowing his ridiculous claim would get under our skin, he must have used it just to keep us off our footing. In his mind, at least, this meant he had the upper hand. Maybe he thought Keith and I had grown too close or that my karate kick moment had gone to my head, or maybe he did this stuff instinctually just to sow chaos. The sheer mindlessness of this tuning jive made me say to myself, "I don't even want to play in this band anymore" — echoes of my feelings in Visby, only many years later. At such moments, my buddy Keith would tell me, "He's gonna give this money to somebody, it might as well be you." Of course, we'd all vent to each other that he must be crazy, because his complaints didn't make sense. But my interest in having him hear my new recordings simply evaporated.

A brief digression is all that's necessary to sum up the dynamic balance of joy and frustration that went with working for Mr. Brown over the years. James Brown was one of the most charming individuals you'd ever meet. He had the power to make you feel unbelievably great. Onstage and off, he could be funny, generous and lovable. But he also had the power to chip away at your dignity just by what he made you endure every day. Though none of us in the band were judgmental types — and this memoir is 99 percent composed only of what I saw and heard firsthand — still, we couldn't ignore the occasional, troubling newspaper report. In fact, exactly one week after he pointlessly put us down regarding our (perfect) tuning, he was arrested for domestic violence. I hate to repeat it here, but it's a matter of record. The disconcerting thing? He and Tomi Rae were together again at the next gig, like nothing had happened. None of my business? In a way. But Tomi Rae had been a friend. The equation — whether the good times were worth the hassle, plus this added moral dilemma — became harder to balance. I had to admit, to myself at least, that I was a mercenary, concerned with my own best interests. At some point, we all face choices. You can take a stand, but there's always someone else ready to replace you. Or you can narrow your field of concerns and compartmentalize your ethics. We all do it, every day. And now I was doing it, and I knew it.

When Mr. Brown was arrested at the end of January for allegedly pushing Tomi Rae to the ground during an argument — according to the papers, it was never addressed by the organization — we were rightfully appalled. Yet, I think most of us immediately wondered how the situation might affect our livelihoods. The answer was swift and, as mercenaries, we accepted it: within a week we were back on the road, headed for a two-night stand at B.B. King's intimate little club in Times Square, and within days we were on a flight to play Le PROGT, a festival in Cayenne, the capital of French Guiana, just north of the equator on the northeast coast of South America. Just when I thought I couldn't be surprised, we were flying to French Guiana. Being near the equator, the climate was sweltering. Fortunately, we soon hopped on a plane to perform in Fort de France on Martinique, then Gosier on neighboring Guadeloupe, in the eastern Caribbean. Cool sea breezes soothed us, at least for a day or so. February in the Caribbean sure beats February in New York City, though our stay lasted all of 48 hours — just enough time for a plane flight, a bus ride, a meal, a performance, some shut eye, and a chance to do it all over again further on up the road. I needed a work visa for New Zealand and we flew down at the end of the month for a show in Auckland. Los Angeles to Auckland is a 14-hour flight. In retrospect, it's not surprising that my buddy Keith Jenkins reached the end of his tether when we landed.

KEITH JENKINS: Damon and I were still rooming together at that point, when just about everybody had their own room. We got to New Zealand, and our tiny room has two little single beds pushed together. I'd had enough. I'd been in the band ten years. So I called over to Mr. Brown's hotel. "Mr. Bobbit? This is Keith." "What's goin' on, kid?" I said, "I just have a question for ya." "What's that?" I said, "Did you want me to burp Damon after I feed him? Or did you want me to change his diaper first?" He said, "What're you talkin' about?!" I said, "Well, I just didn't know what to do since y'all got us in these baby beds." He said, "Oh, I hear ya." I said, "Do you? *Do* you hear me?" I said, "Let me tell you something. I've been here ten years. You've got people that've been here ten minutes, and they've got their own rooms. Enough is a damn 'nuf." He said, "I understand. I'll take care of it." And from then on, we had our own rooms.

Of course, I'm listening, just rolling on one of those baby beds, laughing my ass off. Once again, I admired my friend for speaking up in no uncertain terms. (I'd have to give Mr. Bobbit props for handling his end of that conversation, too.) The incident showed that if you woofed a little sometimes, you could make things happen. Woofing to Mr. Bobbit, that is. Just like woofing about the bus, you didn't want to go woofin' to Mr. Brown about no baby beds. Even though we spent a good deal of our time on tour hanging out in each other's rooms, having a little space to yourself was good for your sanity. I thanked my brother Keith for woofing on that one.

The next day, we hopped a plane across the Tasman Sea to Australia and across the entire continent for a date in Perth, on the west coast. We returned east for shows in Melbourne and Sydney and at the East Coast Blues & Roots Music Fest in Byron Bay in New South Wales. Young people seeking "the lifestyle" made Byron Bay something of a mecca. I confess, we didn't see much of the lifestyle, despite our interest. We had to be back in the States for a nearly uninterrupted series of shows from mid-April until June, when we were set to depart for a monumental tour of Europe.

Within days of getting home, we raced to gigs in California, Arizona, Washington, and Michigan — mostly casinos — in the Deathmobile. I mean, the James Brown bus. At the Celebrity Theatre in Phoenix, the jazz organ maestro Jimmy Smith sat in. He was a true legend, having come up in a similar era as Mr. Brown, recorded prolifically for Blue Note records in the 1950s and '60s, and dubbed himself "The Incredible Jimmy Smith." Anyone who knows anything about Jimmy Smith knows he was irascible and just as quick to challenge others. That night we had two monumental egos on stage at the same time. By the time he stepped up, Jimmy Smith somehow had already ruffled Mr. Brown's feathers. For me, however, the moment was old-school cool. I was positioned next to James Brown's keyboard, and here comes Jimmy Smith. This guy really made his mark on the Hammond B-3 organ, and he'd played with giants. In the early days, that included Wes Montgomery, Kenny Burrell, George Benson, Lee Morgan, and Stanley Turrentine. In later days, his collaborators included Frank Sinatra, Quincy Jones, Etta James, B.B. King, Dr. John, even Michael Jackson, if you can believe that. Anyway, James Brown stepped away from his keyboard to let Mr. Smith do his thing, and I'm standing there while Jimmy Smith played a solo in which he does trills on either side of the keyboard while playing with his teeth in the middle. By then he was in his late 70s. Less than a year later he was gone forever.

HOLLIE FARRIS: James tried to sabotage Jimmy on stage by telling him the wrong key to play in. Brown might have been upset. I heard Jimmy ask him for cocaine before the gig. James wouldn't *think* of touching cocaine.

Testimony to Mr. Brown's continued ability to bring it — and bring it doubly hard in the face of apathy — came in response to a show at the House of Blues at Mandalay Bay in May, as Spencer Patterson reported for the *Las Vegas Sun*, in a May 24, 2004 article titled, "Brown can't get crowd to 'wake up'":

> Apathetic crowds are hardly rare in Las Vegas . . . But when you buy a ticket to see the Hardest Working Man in Show Business, you've got to be prepared to do a little work yourself . . . Whatever you do, don't force Brown to beg, as he did midway through Friday's show: "Wake up, wake up, wake up," he implored, to no avail. Even longtime hype man Danny Ray — who has made a career of working audiences into a frenzy for Brown — seemed fazed by the crowd's disrespectful take-it-or-leave-it attitude.
>
> Give Brown tremendous credit, though: Despite his relatively listless surroundings, the man conjured up a supreme effort, proving that he remains a viable live act some 50 years after breaking into the business. Though he never did the splits, Brown pulled out most of his other familiar dance steps, spinning, shaking and bouncing his microphone stand away from his body and back again in perfect sync with the beat.
>
> Unable to draw strength from the crowd, Brown instead looked to the ultra-tight ensemble onstage with him, the Soul Generals, to liven up the proceedings. Saxophonist Jeff Watkins led the way, heating up versions of "Make It Funky" and "Get Up Offa That Thing" with

raging tenor workouts. Guitarist Damon Wood, whom Brown identified as a Las Vegan, also stood out, contributing a funky solo during "Doing It to Death."

We were set to depart for England in mid-June to play a handful of monster gigs on a double bill with the Red Hot Chili Peppers, the funk-tinged rock band from L.A. that was then enjoying a surge of popularity in the U.K. They were on the cover of every music magazine while we toured with them. I wasn't a particularly big fan, but they had a big sound. George Clinton had produced one of their albums, and they knew how to bring it. Just before we left the country, we played the House of Blues in Chicago one night and the next we entertained with other artists at the 43rd annual International Achievement Summit at the Field Museum. We're up on stage, two stepping in our impeccable uniforms, boogieing for a black-tie audience that included (so I learned later) former President Bill Clinton, Archbishop Desmond Tutu, Coretta Scott King, and dozens of heads of state — like locals Mayor Richard Daley and New York Mayor Michael Bloomberg, along with filmmakers, writers and musicians such as George Lucas, Norman Mailer, and Bonnie Raitt — the works. Honestly? We could see we were in nice digs with a high-end crowd, but of course we didn't recognize faces from the stage, nor did we attempt to mingle. In fact, we played only three songs, warming up the stage for Aretha Franklin. I'd guess Mr. Brown accepted the slot because we had to get our beauty sleep before flying overseas for a grueling, month-long tour. Plus, I mean, Aretha Franklin, right? James Brown could be a gentleman, and Aretha certainly demanded R-E-S-P-E-C-T on his level.

CHILI PEPPERS IN ENGLAND

We landed in London a couple of days later and got right into it with a huge show opening for the Chili Peppers at Commonwealth Stadium in Manchester, a venue that holds 48,000 fans. The Chili Peppers' audience fit the new business model — the kids who came to see them were not necessarily tuned to James Brown's thing, but the band and its crowd really dug James Brown once they caught him in action. That's the thing about younger audiences: they're open to good sounds. If they liked the funkiness of the Chili Peppers, they'd "get" that one of the originators of funk was James Brown. Subsequently, they might buy one of Mr. Brown's iconic records or even seek out one of his solo shows. For the Chilis' tour, he streamlined his show to an hour of high-energy music, to keep the kids' attention. Our efforts were well received. I met some people at that first show and invited them back to the hotel to hang with the band, but the security guard at the hotel wouldn't let me bring them in. I guess the hotel people had seen it all before and non-paying guests weren't welcome. Manchester is a wild party town, and its soccer fans are notorious rioters, I knew that much.

When we returned to London to play three shows in Hyde Park on June 19, 20, and 25, 2004, it was in front of 258,000 concert-goers over all three nights. I learned later that those shows earned the distinction of being the highest-grossing concerts at a single venue in all of history — more than $17 million for three nights. (The Chili Peppers released a double album from the three shows a month later, and it shot to the top of the U.K. charts.) The promoters must have taken care of Mr. Brown, because there was no squawking, à la Visby, about the enormous crowds and their relationship to his fee. Hyde Park had a bit of history with live rock 'n' roll, dating back to a free Rolling Stones performance for 250,000 people in July 1969. I believe the park still hosts live pop music to this day. The opening act before we went on — Chicks on Speed — was atrocious. Apparently, the Chili Peppers' lead singer's girlfriend's sister was in the band or something. This was their big break. I remember one song they shouted in their Cockney accents: "We don't play gitaahs! We don't play gitaahs! We don't play gitaahs! We don't play git-aaahhs!" That did not go over well with the audience, judging by the hail of heavy nine-volt batteries that were hurtled onto the bandstand. (They say the audience at the Apollo is tough . . .)

I got a little wild at the second Hyde Park show. The first day I didn't get a solo, so I told Danny Ray that if I got a solo the next day I was going to do something crazy at the peak, like jump off the stage. "*Do* it, man!" he said. "You gotta make a *bold move*, man!" He loves that crazy stuff, and people eat it up. So I went for it. Just below the main stage, about six feet down, was a huge riser for video cameras projecting the show on big screens. So as I hit the solo's high note, just as Mr. Brown was about to snatch it back, I leapt from the stage to the platform below — I was caught up in the hype. I had to hand my guitar back up to the band, and Mr. Brown himself helped me climb back up. I ended up with a big bruise on my leg where the guitar landed on it. But you gotta create some excitement sometimes, you know what I mean? Mr. Brown musta dug it, because he smiled that bright white smile of his when I got back on stage.

We went to a couple of parties while we were in London, and here's where I understood the difference between old school jazz, rock, blues, and funk artists and the new breed — at least one of them. I ran into Anthony Kiedis, the Chili Peppers' lead singer, and said, "Hey," in passing, like, *hey, it's cool to be on these gigs with you.* He just looked at me like, *who the fuck is this guy?* and walked off. To be fair, he probably had no clue that I played for James Brown, but, hey, people are still people. Later, I spoke to the guitar player, John Frusciante, as we walked by each other backstage. I said, "Hey, man, I play guitar for James Brown. It's been an honor, thanks for having us." He said, "Cool, man. We're hoping he might sit in with us today; we're really excited." I said, good naturedly, "Good luck with that." But I thought, "Cuz you'll need it." Mr. Brown had his manager, SuperFrank, check it out. "What do you want him to do? He's not gonna want to come out while you guys play punk rock." SuperFrank told the Chili Peppers or their go-between that they'd have to talk to Hollie Farris, our trumpet player and band leader. And they said, "Why do we need to talk to your trumpet player about Mr. Brown sittin' in and yellin' '*Haaaa! Get down!*'?" That's all they wanted. They wanted him to pop out, yell "*Get funky!*" pull a dance move, and split. So they could say James Brown sat in with their band. They wanted a little glow from his stature, his legend, his presence, his brand. Being old school and a true showman and musician, Mr. Brown just wanted a little something spelled out. That's not too much to ask. But I could see their point too. "Why do we need to go through someone else to talk to you to get you to sit in?" Apparently, Mr. Brown's message was: "Well, you got to talk to my man about these notes and chords and things." Besides, just because you're on the same bill as another band, you're not necessarily mixing. If you're singing in a ton of shows, you can't be sociable with everybody. You have to save your voice. You could talk yourself out and have nothing left for the show. *They* want to meet *him*, no matter how big they are, not the other way around. Eventually, they got SuperFrank to describe to James Brown what they wanted him to do. Later, one of our entourage paraphrased the exchange for us, in a cartoonish way. Supposedly SuperFrank said, "Well, Mr. Brown, they want to start it off with a drum beat for about four bars, and then the bass comes in for about four bars, then the guitar players starts playin' for about four bars, and then you come out and do whatever you want — like scream "*Haaaa!*" Mr. Brown's response? "Naaah . . ." Sure, he appreciated the tour money and playing in front of a few hundred thousand British kids, but doing some goofy cameo to please a young band he didn't really know? Beneath his dignity. Plus, the man needed his rest.

During the Hyde Park shows we stayed nearby at The Kensington Hilton with Mr. Brown. This time, we didn't mind being in close proximity to the boss, as it appeared to be one of London's finer establishments. Not only did I write a couple songs on the hotel stationery, but we ran into all sorts of people there. We met the singer for Modest Mouse, an indie rock band from Seattle that became pretty famous. We ran into a cat whose name I don't recall who had played guitar on Michael Jackson's *Thriller*. He told us how Quincy Jones, the producer, came in and erased this cat's guitar parts and replaced them with parts by one of his own studio guys. When Michael Jackson listened to the tapes, he said, "Hey, where are those funky riffs my guy laid down?" Michael Jackson was feeding off those riffs for his own performance and, suddenly, they were gone. Apparently, MJ stood up for his guitarist and demanded that he return and re-record his parts. "Michael had my back and that was cool," this cat told us. As sidemen, we appreciated stories like that. We also met Rick Rubin, the producer, who handled Johnny Cash's last few albums. Johnny Cash went out strong. Keith's got the balls to talk to anyone, and he buttonholed Rick Rubin. "Man, I wish you could do an album with James Brown, like you did for Johnny Cash." Keith tried to pitch him that if James Brown would cover AC/DC's "Back in Black," they'd have a hit. Rick Rubin (no kidding): "Have his people call my people." Who knows what could have happened if, late in his career, James Brown had put himself in someone else's hands, just for one album. But I don't think James Brown had the temperament for that approach. Producers are there to push the artist around and get something new out of them, and I don't think Mr. Brown would've allowed it. Whatever the producer's supposed role, they'd still be working for him. So, predictably, that pipe dream went nowhere.

Between the second and third Hyde Park shows, we took off by bus for Cardiff Millennium Stadium in Wales west of London for another performance with the Chili Peppers. On the Cardiff jaunt, we discovered that the drummer for the Chili Peppers, Chad Smith, just loved James Brown. We ran into him at a dinner someplace, and he sent our table a bottle of wine. Everyone liked him a lot. When we played our first Hyde Park show, he had staked out a spot in front in the photographers' row. The Chili Peppers' show in Cardiff was powerful. They came out rockin'. The energy was explosive, and the bass player, Flea, went out to the lip of the stage and pulled his pants down. He was swinging his bass . . . and everything else. We were in the wings, just cracking up. Let's just say it provided a bit of contrast to the Soul Generals tuxedos. Flea had established a reputation when the Chili Peppers closed Woodstock '99 by playing the whole set completely nude. They'd been known to perform with the entire band dressed only in socks. And to think Jim Morrison of the Doors got busted in 1969 for just suggesting he was gonna pull his trousers down. Things change . . .

The next day, James Brown and the Soul Generals flew over St. George's Channel for a return appearance at the Vicar Street festival in Dublin. A day later we were back in Hyde Park in front of 86,000, if you can believe that. The day after the third Hyde Park show, we played the Olympic Torch Concert on the Mall. Bo Brundidge remembers this one better than I do.

WILLIE RAY "BO" BRUNDIDGE: They had the Olympic torch going back to Buckingham Palace. We got a call: would we like to open the torch festival at Buckingham Palace? We were supposed to have a day off, but we all agreed to do it. It's another rainy day. As we got off the bus — there's like 18 of us — we each had our own personal attendant to hold the umbrella and get us to the dressing room, which is like a little house. There's a little sign, "James

Brown and band." Another sign said, "Osbourne." I'm thinking, "Ozzy Osbourne?" After we came off stage, returned to our dressing room, [and] there's Ozzy, his wife, Sharon, the kids, Jack and Kelly, their friends [sitting at] a table full of wine. They'd just watched our show through the monitors. They said, "Fabulous show, come have some wine!" And we're like, "Wow!" We grabbed glasses, pulled up a few chairs, and we're hanging out, drinking wine with Ozzy and the gang. As we're doing that, we saw Ron Wood and Rod Stewart heading out to do their thing. How cool was that?

We moved on to the Glastonbury Festival in Pilton, England, performing in front of a crowd 150,000 strong. Pretty heady stuff, even after following the Godfather of Soul around the planet for five years. Backstage, Kelly Jarrell introduced then-16-year-old singing sensation Joss Stone to Mr. Brown, which sowed seeds that still bloom today.

KELLY JARRELL: I met Joss Stone backstage. I said, "I work with James Brown," and she said, "*Oh my god!*" And she started singing "Man's World" to me. Mr. Brown was in a great mood that night, so I dragged her over and said, "Mr. Brown, this is Joss Stone, she's only 16 years old, but she's the biggest thing over here. Let her sing this song for you." Joss started singing "Man's World," and he got so excited. So when they were both on Jonathan Ross's BBC show in June 2005, he remembered her and he made her come on stage and sing that song with him, unrehearsed.

The next day, we wore 'em out at Bridgewater Hall in Manchester and two days later, we did it again in Glasgow, Scotland. We'd had performed ten colossal shows in 13 days, but the tour had only hit the halfway mark. We played the Carling Apollo Hammersmith Theatre in London, then flew to Paris for a performance the following day at the Palais de Congress. Mousey really captured the feeling of racing from city to city across Europe at this juncture, playing in front of 50,000 people here, 100,000 people there.

> **ROBERT "MOUSEY" THOMPSON:** At that point, I'd been on so many stages, it seemed like the same audience going around the world with us. You'd get that feeling, that wind, coming off the audience and just touching you. You'd think, "I know I'm *here*, I just don't know *where* I am! I've seen places I never thought of as a kid or even dreamed of from history books. The schedule was pretty tight, though. If you could rest up, you'd go out and see places. Sometimes I wanted to get out just to touch the soil. I wished I'd documented more, gotten more of an understanding of things. But I was still like a little kid, excited to be out, playing with J.B., making people happy.

Amazing side trips sometimes got crammed into our travels, despite their frenetic nature. On this trip, when we arrived back in London from Glasgow, a handful of us jumped in a van and went straight to the Power House, a studio in the West End. The Black Eyed Peas — an American hip-hop band then gaining some success en route to platinum-album status — had laid down basic tracks for "They Don't Want Music," for their next CD, *Monkey Business*. They'd arranged with James Brown Enterprises to have Mr. Brown funk-ify it. To put his stamp on it, Mr. Brown brought along guitar, horns, and singers to help out. When we arrived, Will.i.am met Mr. Brown and said, "Nice to meet you, James." (He didn't get the memo.) Mr. Brown coolly stepped back, Mr. Bobbit stepped in, and Will.i.am received the memo on how to properly address *Mister* Brown. Mr. Bobbit was real smooth at that stuff. The actual recording process turned out to be an in-the-moment studio happening. If I remember right, the Peas had taken a guitar sample from Mr. Brown's tune "Mind Power," Mousey played a drum groove to it, which they sampled, I played a riff that they sampled before I even knew it was being recorded, and Jeff did a solo in an isolation booth, for some reason, accompanied by Mr. Brown. Fergie and the whole band were watching when I tried to play the riff Mr. Brown requested. It didn't sound right and I said so. Mr. Brown told me, "Just play the part I gave you," which was in D (Dorian) minor, his favorite key. While he hunched over the board with the engineer, I transposed the riff to E minor, the correct key for the song, and laid it down as instructed. Mr. Brown turned around. "*Now* you got it." Will.i.am was mixing on the spot, using a laptop, which opened my mind for the first time to the possibilities of compact digital recording. The Black Eyed Peas were already pros in the studio. At one point, Will.i.am's eyes lit up. Pleased with his newest mix, he jumped up and ran over to Mr. Brown for approval. The star was on the couch, eyes closed, possibly napping but definitely exhibiting no interest whatsoever in his surroundings. It's funny. That tune is about people not having any substance in their music, just *boom boom boom*. And that's exactly what the Peas became, later. (A side note on Mr. Brown's favorite key, D (Dorian) minor: it involves only white keys on the keyboard. Keith told me Mr. Brown asked him what key his own song, "Body Heat," was in. Keith said, F sharp, and Mr. Brown said, "Oh no, too many black keys.")

From London we moved on to Paris, where the audiences really dig funk. Parisians are true James Brown fans. We always tried to really "bring it" there, to reciprocate their love. The other beautiful thing about Paris was that the band repeatedly had opportunities to perform after hours in a small club. The long run of giant shows that summer made us appreciate the rare opportunities we had to get it on after the main show, in a place where we could relate to people, face-to-face. You can get big energy from a big crowd, but it's also kinda diffused when they're 15 feet below you, behind security fencing. My friend Rob Schuder, from the Las Vegas Jam Band Society, and I had connected back in 2001, and Rob's brother, Scott, owned the Mazet, a bar in Paris. So if the Soul Generals wanted to play, we had a place to do it. Needless to say, a core group of us headed to the Mazet that night after our performance at the Palais de Congress. We had to borrow a drum kit, which we all helped carry down the street to the club, where we played our asses off for a couple hundred Parisians til the wee hours. It was a paid gig, but in stealth mode. No one told James Brown the band was out on the town as a unit. Plus, we could not advertise that James Brown's Soul Generals were appearing after hours, especially if the main show didn't sell out. The proprietor, Scott Schuder, and his people fed us Champagne and took care of us. What a night! The next day all we had to do was get on a bus and sleep for 500 miles as the French and German countryside rolled by.

We headlined the Tollwood Festival in Munich, and the next day we rode a couple hundred miles to top the bill at the Zeltmusik Festival in Freiburg. We had a blessed three days off, which included our travel time to Flanders in Belgium to play Rock Zottegem west of Brussels. (Yes, sometimes our days off were spent riding a bus to the next gig.) We caught our breath and got out of the James Brown bubble for a day or so. Then we beelined for the North Sea Jazz Festival in The Hague. Someone shot video of "Make It Funky," which has cool shots of me and Keith flanking Mr. Brown up front. (You can see it on YouTube.) It's a great visual and it speaks to his color-blindness when it came to getting the job done. The tour took us to the Museumplatz in Bonn, Germany — there are clips of that on YouTube as well — followed four days later by another headlining appearance at the Umbria Jazz Festival in Perugia, Italy, our last stop. Umbria Jazz was another of those multi-day festivals where the lineup of dozens of bands included a mind-numbing litany of big names, including B.B. King, Keith Jarrett, Hank Jones, Alicia Keys, George Clinton, and others too numerous to mention. We got in and out on our own schedule, as did all the performers. In this case, the chances of meeting these music giants were slim to none — we were all like ships passing in the night.

That tour might have been our toughest yet. We played 18 shows in 16 venues in eight European countries in 31 days. In Perugia, backstage before our show, Mr. Bobbit walked up to me and Keith and said, "Ah, Keith and Damon. Put 'em together, you've got one good guitar player." We're thinking, "What the hell did he mean by that?" He was just messin' with us I guess, but at the time I got a little hot under the collar. I came out on stage that night on fire. I'm thinking "Give me a solo, I'll show ya something." And James Brown said to me, "You play well under duress." Later, I realized that Mr. Bobbit probably was only riling us up for the stage.

GOOD ADVICE AND GAMES

We had a month off at home before the madness began again, so I rounded up my band and played a fun gig in Vail, Colorado. I wanted to put together a few gigs in a row to see what the band could do, but the opportunity proved fleeting. Within the week, James Brown and the Soul Generals were back in the air, en route to play the Laugardalshöll in Reykjavik, Iceland, where the fans' reception during and, I must say, *after* the show was warm and enthusiastic. Three days later, we made a return appearance at the Vicar Street festival in Dublin for two nights running. Before the second show, Mr. Brown hung out with the band, and at one point he took me aside and talked to me one-on-one about soloing.

He gave me some of the best advice I ever got from him — or from anyone, for that matter. Musicians, in general, and guitarists, in particular, tend to play too many notes, thinking we have to fill a lot of space. Backstage in Dublin, as I remember it, Mr. Brown said to me in a collegial tone, "When you solo, think of it as a conversation. In a conversation, I say something, you hear what I say, then you say something. Then I add something more, and you respond. So in your solo, have something to say, and leave a little space." The gist of his rap, as best I can recall: When the audience hears your statement, let them have a moment to take it in, so they'll be interested to hear more. Don't overwhelm them with too many notes. You're trying to reach people on an emotional level, you're seducing their sensibilities. You have to develop what you'd like to say and, to do that, you have to use space. And when you use that space, you allow yourself to feel the energy of the moment. You're giving yourself time to decide where you're going next. And you're taking the audience with you. A solo should not be a pre-conceived blathering of notes. Just as a horn player must craft a phrase to leave space in order to breathe, a guitarist has to use space to allow the audience to digest his statements. Phrasing solos in this manner lends itself to being melodic and the best initial phrase often is just a statement of the melody, of the vocal phrase in the verse or refrain. You follow that up with a restatement, a variation, a new place to take the conversation. If you can phrase a solo melodically, it'll be memorable, something the listener whistles on the way home that night. To this day, I try to remember that lesson every time I step out to solo.

Sure, some of the funky music Mr. Brown played didn't necessarily require melodic soloing, but the ballads, blues and the R&B he played definitely lent themselves to this approach. I was touched that he took the time to guide me as my playing developed in his service. Despite the ups and downs, he still gave a damn about my work.

We flew on to Prague for this brief tour's fourth and final date. To play those four gigs for Icelandic, Irish, Czech, and German fans, we flew more than 10,000 miles — a far cry from the days of Jimmie Van Zant, a motor home and a biker rally. I've heard bands say they're paid to travel, because that's how you spend the majority of your time. The gigs seem almost incidental, even though that's obviously the reason you're traveling. On that short tour, we probably spent a total of six hours on stage for four gigs that required ten days' time. While we went home to rest, Mr. Brown went to Cambridge to receive the Harvard Lampoon's Wheelwright Award for "outstanding contributions to human life." We caught up with Mr. Brown the next day at the Roseland Ballroom in New York City, where Slash, lead guitarist for Guns 'N Roses, jammed with us at sound check. He turned out to be a regular guy and played on our show dressed up in his trademark top hat and leather pants. We had Lenny Kravitz on the bill, too. This was all part of Miller Brewing Company's *Rocking Through the Ages* promotion.

In October 2004, Mr. Brown took a stripped-down version of the Soul Generals to play the month-long Night of the Proms, a series of performances at the Sportpaleis Antwerpen in Belgium, a massive venue built for sports in the 1930s but now largely devoted to music. (Videos of these gigs are on YouTube.) This long-running, indoor festival paired international pop music icons of the day with a local orchestra. For a month, we shared the stage with Joe Cocker, The Pointer Sisters, Cyndi Lauper, Shaggy, and a host of European pop artists. Every one of the 23 shows sold out. James Brown's music had to be coordinated with the orchestra, so we played the same four songs every night. The orchestra played for a while, then Joe Cocker closed the first set. The second set opened with the orchestra, then Shaggy took the stage. When the orchestra played "Bolero," that was our cue. We'd get tucked in amongst the orchestra, ready to play our four songs: "Living in America," "I Feel Good," "Sex Machine," and "It's a Man's Man's Man's World." Easiest gig ever.

Mr. Brown's wrong-but-somehow-right reasoning about guitar tuners won a level of vindication on this run, at least in his mind. He'd been beating this dead horse for some time. Using a single tuner for two or three guitarists made no sense technically — digital tuners are identical. It practical terms, it made performing vastly more difficult. As it turned out, however, the orchestra in Antwerp tuned to 442 Hz, not 440 Hz, which is the standard guitar tuning frequency in the U.S. This is about pitch. I don't know the reasoning, but orchestras tune a little bit sharp. In a weird way, in James Brown's mind, this supported his contention that we had to use a single tuner. He talked to the orchestra leader and came back and he said, "See? Y'all got to tune to fo-fo-tee-two." In his mind, this established that not all tuners were tuned the same. We're like, "Damn!" It was kinda cute in a way. He was right, in a jive-y, twisted way. We let him have his little joke, but it grated on us.

During the five-week Night of the Proms gig, the band lived in the Astrid Park Plaza Hotel, along with Mr. Brown and his entourage. As I've mentioned, proximity could be dicey. We typically played four nights in a row, then we had three nights off. Even on the nights we played, we'd be off work early and had time to ourselves. That gave me a chance to do some writing for my second CD, *Too Cocky in Nagasaki*, and the band really got into working on its own tunes. We often used our free evenings to record different ideas and even lay down tracks on an iMac, instead of partying. Without the constant travel, we had time for creativity and most of us were writing either with the band in mind or for our own projects. After weeks of living in this hotel, playing an easy gig or having the whole night off, we became accustomed to our digs. We couldn't afford room service, so we'd bring food and beer back to our rooms, stash them in the fridge, and then convene in someone's room to hang out and maybe do a little recording.

One night after we'd played our set, we returned to the hotel, and I changed into jeans and flip-flops, grabbed a large beer out of my fridge, popped the top, and headed down the hall to the elevator to join my bandmates on another floor. I pushed the Down button. Suddenly, I heard voices on the elevator coming up. Mr. Brown and his entourage! I'm standing right outside the elevator door in my jeans and flip-flops, clutching one of those triple-proof Belgian monastery beers. If there had been a stairway nearby, I'd have run for it. If there'd been a hallway around the corner, I'd have ducked into it. Had there been any means of escape, I'd have taken it. As it turned out, there was nowhere to run, nowhere to hide. I just stood there as the elevator doors opened, steeled to my fate. Typically, I would've greeted Mr. Brown and his entourage. "Great show tonight, Mr. Brown." But not now. The doors of the elevator slowly opened and Mr. Brown was standing there in his three-piece suit. Mr. Bobbit and Tomi Rae were with him, still dressed up from the show. Mr. Brown looked me up and down and just started shaking his head. He wasn't smiling. "Son, you were doin' *so good*," he said evenly. "You don't want to ruin it with that. Don't let me see that again." I wasn't sure if he meant the jeans, the flip-flops, the beer or the whole package. I should have had the sense to apologize and say, "You're right, Mr. Brown. It won't happen again." But I said, "What? Don't have a beer?" He said, quite sensibly, "If you want a beer, go down to the hotel bar and have one. Just don't run around the hotel with an open beer." Busted, big time. At that point I moved to a different floor from Mr. Brown's suite, because my new girlfriend, Jennyfa, came to visit from Germany, where we'd met at the Zelt-Musik-Festival in Freiburg in July. We needed some elbow room. But I'd learned a lesson and, not incidentally, taken my place in the band's deep lore.

GEORGE "SPIKE" NEALY: Everybody in the band knows that story. It's a good story because you already know James Brown's reaction. You know when that door opened, there was so much wrong in James Brown's eyesight.

You can't do much. He'd just shake his head. He just sees so much wrong and all he can do is say, "Son, have a nice day." He was our boss and everything, but at the same time, he was pure man and he was human. Everybody got one chance. In *his* mind, you must have lost *your* mind. You would know without a shadow of a doubt that you have really been caught in a predicament. And you'd know that as long as you're with his band, you'll never be caught like that again. Like I said before, when you travel with Mr. Brown, you're on stage all the time. Still, he understood. He told me once, when we were coming home, "Son, once I'm behind my gate, I get a chance to be 'Grand-daddy.' But when I come out of my gates, I have to be 'James Brown.'" He expected us to step it up, too.

We'd had a week off at home when we started a punishing winter tour of Canada in late November and December. Ten shows in 14 days. That's a lot of time on the road in serious winter conditions. We played Halifax, Nova Scotia; Montreal, Quebec; Toronto, Kitchener, and London, Ontario; Vancouver and Kelowna, British Columbia; Edmonton and Calgary, Alberta; and ended the tour in Saskatoon, Saskatchewan. The day we left Halifax, we picked up a newspaper, which featured a photograph of me next to James Brown onstage and a positive review. That should have been a good omen, but by the time we reached Vancouver a week later, trouble had raised its ugly head again. We were at the Queen Elizabeth Theatre in Vancouver in mid-performance when Mr. Brown decided I was out of tune. Only Keith was allowed to have a tuner now and he stood in the middle of the stage. I'm stage left. Mr. Brown actually stopped the show, announced aloud that I was out of tune and that I needed to go tune up on Keith's tuner. This is dead air, right in the middle of the show. James Brown called me out in front of 4,000 people, announced that I'm outta tune, and directed me across the stage to Keith's tuner. Hey, it's his show he's messing with, so if he needed to berate the band a little, we put up with it. So I unplugged and walked over to Keith in the middle of the stage. "Uh, Keith, may I use your tuner?" "Oh, sure, man." We both feigned casualness, but my bro had to know I wasn't enjoying the joke. And the audience? I could only wonder. I mean, "Welcome to the James Brown show!" I plugged into Keith's tuner and, as I suspected, each of my strings triggered a green light, one after the other, meaning that I was already perfectly in tune. In front of 4,000 people, I said loudly, "Thanks, Keith" while Mr. Brown was half talking to the audience, making a joke, and checking me out in his peripheral vision. I don't know if he saw that I hadn't touched one tuning peg. But I reported back. "I'm good!" "Thank you, son!" he said, as if the incident had been necessary. And off we went with the rest of the show. The incident itself was no biggie, but the mindlessness of this game was taking its toll. I'd had a lot of experiences in the band by this time and knew how to balance the petty, everyday stuff with the good times on stage. I mean, typically after a show, we'd talk about how great the boss had been that night. Keith would say, "Did you see when he busted that one dance move?!" We were as much his fans as his little whippin' boys. So the senseless BS only hurt our genuine admiration for the man. The fact that he'd sacrifice the audience's experience to try to rub my face in something that silly, and just plain wrong, bothered me. He'd found a way to dispirit me. He'd found a button to push. And he knew it.

RECOGNITION

I tried to brush this stuff off. It was about Mr. Brown, not me. I had a musical identity and a life outside Mr. Brown's orbit. My first Harmonious Junk CD had been out for a couple of months when *Westword*, Denver's alternative weekly, ran a positive review — a real shot in the arm for me at that juncture.

"While difficult to hang a genre on this coaster, it's hard not to like the musical product of James Brown axman Damon Wood and company," wrote Nick Hutchinson in vintage *Billboard* style. "Wood struts his road-tested guitar stuff on *Space Cadet* and demonstrates creative songwriting ability from track to track, weaving funk, blues, reggae, soul, and psychedelia into a musical throw rug that recalls classics such as SRV, Billy Preston, Jimi Hendrix, Albert Collins, and even Jimmy Herring. Despite these mostly dated influences, the music feels fresh, with a personality all its own. Keywork by Chad Aman (also of Denver's Cocktail Revolution and Byron Shaw Projex) simmers and shines throughout, while bass ace Jack Alterman keeps the low end tight as a new pair of loafers. The disc goes out with a bang, not a whimper, stringing together four solid butt-kickers."

When the James Brown machine took a break in January 2005, I got the new version of Harmonious Junk into Denver's clubs and Colorado's mountain towns, building a name and an audience. Finally, doing my own thing, with my own band. No games. It felt good and people were responding. I'd made a wise choice to live in Denver and get my thing moving with the great musicians who lived there. I'd told Nick Hutchinson, the *Westword* writer, earlier that year, "It's nice to come home and get in my own band." But the moment to savor personal success proved to be brief. James Brown Enterprises and the road soon beckoned.

In February 2005, we began a six-week odyssey. Mr. Brown started off on his own, accompanying Usher on stage for "Sex Machine" at the annual Grammy Awards in L.A. Then we all flew south to Mexico City to play the Auditorio Nacional. We flew east for a gig in Santurce, Puerto Rico, then north to Miami to catch a plane for the 11,000-mile flight to Jakarta, Indonesia. We lost an entire day to time zone changes. As I learned later, even though Jakarta is on the equator, the flight from Miami actually traveled north over North America and across the Bering Strait before turning south over Russia, China, and Korea to reach its destination. You're in the air for nearly 24 hours and looking out those tiny windows, you might think you're flying anywhere. We boarded in Miami and deplaned in Jakarta countless hours later, an inch shorter and mildly confused. Who really knew *where* we were? We focused on reviving ourselves for the next gig.

The schedulers were wise to give us a day to recuperate and rehearse before headlining two separate days at the first Jakarta International Java Jazz Festival. The festival featured more than a hundred local acts, as well as George Duke, an amazing composer and multi-instrumentalist who had worked with one of my favs, Frank Zappa. The Tower of Power's former guitarist, Bruce Conte, was on the bill with a new outfit and I remember hanging out in his hotel room at four in the morning with him while he showed me and Keith a few guitar tricks. Those chance encounters on the road could make blowing through time zones worthwhile. Everyone's experience might be different, however, and not everyone loved Jakarta.

KELLY JARRELL: Jakarta really stands out in my memory. When our car pulled up to the hotel, they used a mirror on the end of a stick to look under our car, searching for bombs. It was a scary place to be. The caste system was in place. You were either really, really poor or really, really rich. We stayed at the Hilton Plaza International, which was connected to the Jakarta Convention Center, where we were playing. When we walked down the halls to get from the hotel to the convention center, the people who were working the festival were sleeping in the hallways. It was too much to go all the way home and come back for their next shift. So they'd camp out with the clothes on their back. That looked really rough.

Apparently, the fact that Mr. Brown hadn't taken two drummers to the month-long Night of the Proms in Antwerp grated badly on my friend, Erik Hargrove, the drummer who had to stay home. After sitting home for all those weeks, he decided he could do better and left the band of his own accord. Erik subsequently moved to Singapore for many years and has been involved in so many cool musical adventures that you should look him up on Facebook to learn more. Tony Cook returned to take Erik's chair. Tony had worked for Mr. Brown between 1976 and 1993 and departed to work on his own Trunk-o-Funk project.

ERIK HARGROVE: Java Jazz in Jakarta was my last gig. I let Mr. Brown know on that first date in Puerto Rico that would be my last tour. He was very surprised, judging from the look on his face. He shut that down, put on a normal look, and told Mr. Bobbit to call another drummer. I found out later that he was deeply hurt that I left. But I didn't leave him. He left me. I wanted to be a part of that band and be on stage with him, but I had to make a decision to move my life along. I really did want to stay. But at that point, I said, "That's enough." It was painful. I loved traveling, being in different places. Even though the touring was hard the way we did it, just being some-place new — I loved that part of being in James Brown's band. When it came to the stage, there were great times connecting with other musicians, as well as Mr. Brown. Damon would take a solo, and he and I really connected rhythmically. It was times like that you got this huge high. You forgot there was an audience out there. It's about what's happening on stage, what's happening in the music. That connection between musicians is what makes it. I've never been involved in anything so exciting since. And I never will. That was unique to James Brown, and the energy from him and the people in that band. James Brown was a super complex guy. [For the most part,] the downsides were overcome by the good times. There was nothing like it in the world. It was probably the best high you could have.

When we returned from Jakarta, I had a solid week off before we flew to Buenos Aires, Argentina, and on to Vina Del Mar, Chile. It's one of the vagaries of traveling the way we did, as well as memory and time, that aside from the ecstatic receptions we always received overseas, I don't remember much about those gigs.

HOLLIE FARRIS: We played Luna Park in Buenos Aires a couple of times. Anytime we played anywhere in South America, it was a madhouse. They loved Brown. It was like he was on top of the world, like he was The Number One Artist in the World at that moment — that's the vibe we got from the audience. They'd be beside themselves. One time we played there, Brown was really, really sick. He was so sick he was hooked up to IVs, catheterized, the works. And he pulled all that out and went out and did a two-hour show, then went back to the hotel and got re-IV'd.

By May 2005, I'd been in the band nearly six years. Not that such a milestone mattered to anyone else. The only thing that mattered was your consistent ability to bring it to each and every gig. In fact, Fred Thomas, the band's longest-serving member, had put in five years for every one of mine. Yet I felt that, on my terms, I'd put in quite a bit of time in Mr. Brown's service. Erik Hargrove had been the first of my contemporaries to depart but, as usual, there wasn't much time to dwell on it. Soon we were off on a jag of a dozen gigs, from Massachusetts, New York, and New Jersey down to Mississippi, Georgia, and Florida, playing in posh theaters, casinos, urban clubs, outdoor venues. We had some time off scheduled in June, which was healthy, considering that after that we would embark on a monster, six-week tour of Europe. I had Harmonious Junk booked for a couple gigs in Denver when I got the call to fly immediately to Augusta. Mr. Brown had suddenly decided he wanted to go into the studio. I did what I had to do: I canceled my band's two gigs and hopped on a plane. And it cost me. I had a nice, 6:30 p.m. slot at Denver's LoDo Fest in front of thousands, and we were heading into a new club in Evergreen in the foothills and I had to cancel both gigs at the last minute. That's terrible for business. We lost our booking agent over it, and it sure didn't help our push to cultivate a following. Still, I got a chance to play on a record with James Brown.

Upon my arrival in Augusta, I learned that *Rolling Stone* was sending a writer, Jonathan Lethem, to hang out at the sessions and write a feature. The city had just unveiled a bronze statue of Mr. Brown on Broad Street, near James Brown Boulevard, just a stone's throw from Twiggs Street, the crater of poverty from which he had escaped. The city and its famous feral son had made peace — at least temporarily. Lethem was cool, we all liked him. He was obviously a big fan and respected James Brown. Lethem told me that *Rolling Stone* publisher Jann Wenner gave him his choice of three people to write about and he chose Bob Dylan, Willie Nelson, and James Brown. He typed away on his laptop the whole time he was with us in the studio. James Brown would say, "Whatcha writin' over there, Mr. Rolling Stone?" Pretty priceless stuff, looking back. I mean, James Brown was a very complex cat and, after a while, Lethem started tapping into the layers of his personality — even the dimensions of his personal reality and how Mr. Brown was like a time traveler constantly traversing all the different eras he'd lived through. From the resulting article, which ran a year later, it's apparent that while Mr. Brown was on his guard, he couldn't resist showing off. James Brown didn't have the greatest relationship with *Rolling Stone* over the years. I'm guessing he was flattered by the attention and understood the possible implications for the business side of things. But at the same time, he instinctively kept Lethem at arm's length. He knew the press could spin things. Artists *should* be wary with a writer in their midst. *Rolling Stone*, in his mind, did not regularly feature black artists on its cover — at least, it had never featured *him* on its cover. When I read Lethem's article much later, however, I found that he had written a true and fair story. He came off as a fan who respected James Brown, but he also drilled down into the man's presence, his complexities, and the band's almost menial status. It's one of best pieces of reportage and analysis on James Brown published at that time, so with Jonathan's permission, I'd like to share a few of his insights in his June 29, 2006 feature in *Rolling Stone* on "Being James Brown: Deep Inside the World of the Godfather of Soul."

> When James Brown enters the recording studio, [it]
> becomes a stage. It is not merely that attention quickens
> in any room this human being inhabits . . . The band,
> hangers-on, the very oxygen, every trace particle is
> charged in its relation to the gravitational field of
> James Brown.
>
> James Brown is dressed as if for a show, in a purple,
> three-piece suit and red shirt, highly polished shoes, cuff
> links and his impeccably coiffed helmet of hair . . . When
> we're introduced, I spend a long moment trying to con-
> jugate the reality of James Brown's face, one I've contem-
> plated as an album-cover totem since I was thirteen . . .

I find it, truthfully, terrifying to have that face examining mine in return . . . I'm also struck by the almost extraterrestrial quality of otherness incarnated in this human being.

Mr. Brown proceeded to fuss obsessively over a vocal overdub, rapping aloud over abstractions only he understood (but that Lethem jotted down) and kept the band on its toes for several hours straight. Lethem wrote, later:

> Throughout these ruminations, the members of James Brown's band stand at readiness, their fingers on strings or mouths a few short inches from reeds and mouthpieces, in complete silence, only sometimes nodding to acknowledge a remark . . . A given monologue may persist for an hour, no matter: At the slightest drop of a hand signal, these players are expected to be ready . . . His bands have always been the Hardest Working Men in Show Business, the longest-rehearsed, the most fiercely disciplined, the most worn-out and abused . . . These men have been indoctrinated into. . . a purely Pavlovian situation, one of reaction and survival . . . Their motives for remaining in such a situation? That, I'll need more time to study.

Damn, this cat Lethem saw it all. After a full day of painfully pure James Brown — long monologues, over-staged vocal dubs, repeated playbacks, and that Pavlovian attention and silence from the band — Keith whispered to Lethem, "You've got to tell the *truth* about what goes on here. Nobody has any idea." (And Lethem jotted that down, too.) Afterwards we kinda grabbed him and said, "Hey, hang out with us," and we took him to a bar and did some 'splainin', no doubt helping Lethem with his study of our motivations. Later, Keith captured it when he told Lethem: "We're like a blade of grass trying to push up through the concrete."

The mere publication of the article in June 2006 established how much Mr. Brown's attitude had rubbed off on me. Lethem had made me and Keith prominent participants in one long passage. The day the article came out, my drummer called me. He said he couldn't make our practice that night. I fired him, instantly. I told him, "Hey man, I have to let you go." I had just seen my name in *Rolling Stone* and decided: "I can't put up with this bullshit!" (Yes, I know what you're thinking, but that's what I did.)

There was a postscript in Lethem's piece for *Rolling Stone*. He'd joined us on a gig at The Sage in Gateshead, Newcastle-on-Tyne in England, during the six-week tour of Europe that followed the recording sessions in Augusta. He finally understood why we did it.

> Bumbling along with the red-costumed tribe in the tunnel to the stage, I find myself suddenly included in a group prayer — hands held in a circle, heads lowered, hushed words spoken in the spirit of the same wish I've just acknowledged privately to myself: that a generous deity might grant them and Mr. Brown a good night.
>
> Now I can hear the sound of the crowd stirring, boiling with anticipation . . . Danny Ray, every impeccable, tiny inch of him, pops onstage. He says, 'Now comes Star Time!' and the roof comes off. Under Danny Ray's instruction, the crowd rises to its feet and begins to chant its hero's name. When James Brown is awarded to them, the people of Gateshead are the happiest people on Earth, and I am one of them.

After the show, we went our separate ways. I'm pretty sure Lethem stayed at his hotel and, probably, so did Mr. Brown and his entourage. But for some reason there weren't enough hotel rooms in Newcastle for the Soul Generals, The Bittersweet, and the dancers, so we all piled onto a bus (not *the* bus, fortunately) and rode the 300 winding miles back to London that night, arriving just before dawn. We'd just begun a tour that had us playing 22 shows in 20 cities in eight countries over six weeks of summer. To get a feel for that sort of tour you have to glance at the itinerary.

21 June 2005, fly to London from the United States

23 June 2005, Civic Hall, Wolverhampton, England

24 June 2005, The Sage, Gateshead, Newcastle-on-Tyne, England

26 June 2005, The HMV Forum, north London, England

27 June 2005, Forum, London, England

28 June 2005, BBC TV show, *Friday Night With Jonathan Ross*

29 June 2005, Heineken Music Hall, Amsterdam

1 July 2005, Volkspark, Mainz, Germany

2 July 2005, Galapagar, Madrid, Spain

4 July 2005, Palais de Congress, Paris, France

6 July 2005, Live 8, Murrayfield Stadium, Edinburgh, Scotland

9 July 2005, T in the Park, Kinross, Scotland

10 July 2005, Oxegen Festival, Naas, Ireland

12 July 2005, Stadtpark, Hamburg, Germany

14 July 2005, LB/BW Jazz Open, Mozarthaal, Stuttgart, Germany

16 July 2005, Piazza Duomo, Treviso, Italy

17 July 2005, Blues Di Marca, Fermo, Italy

20 July 2005, Piazza Cattedrale, Trani, Italy

21 July 2005, Castello, Otranto, Italy

23 July 2005, Summer Festival, Piazza Napoleon, Lucca, Italy

24 July 2005, Festival, Olbia, Italy

26 July 2005, Piazza Del Mare, Genoa, Italy

28 July 2005, Sporting Club, Monte Carlo, Monaco

29 July 2005, Sporting Club, Monte Carlo, Monaco

31 July 2005, Estadio De Les Folletes, Benidorm, Spain

1 August 2005, return to the United States

I'm still simply in awe of what we accomplished on that tour. We managed to have some fun, and there were interesting turns in the road. On the BBC TV show, *Friday Night with Jonathan Ross*, the new British singing star, Joss Stone — who Kelly Jarrell had introduced to James Brown the year before at the Glastonbury Festival — sang a duet with Mr. Brown on "It's a Man's Man's Man's World." (Yes, it's on YouTube!) Years later, after Mr. Brown's passing, Hollie Farris and Jeff Watkins toured the world with Ms. Stone. The band wasn't needed that night, so we flew to Amsterdam ahead of the next gig. I roamed the cafes, sampling the local treats. The next night we played the Heineken Music Hall. I hadn't had much sleep. I'd been up all night tripping and wrote a song as dawn arrived. At that night's performance, when it came time to peak on my solo and do my karate kick, I biffed it and almost fell into the audience. Mr. Brown looked at me like, "Whaaaat?!" and the singers were laughing pretty hard. Clearly, that was my bad — I had stumbled, literally — and we had four more weeks to go on the tour.

On Independence Day, we returned to play the Palais de Congres in Paris and by all accounts we put on a great show. As I've mentioned, the Parisians truly dug James Brown and his music, and we were treated like superstars. We did another after-hours gig after our main show. I think DJ Pari organized it. DJ Pari and his Soulpower organization had produced a host of James Brown-related artists, including Marva Whitney, Lyn Collins, Bobby Byrd, Maceo Parker, Fred Wesley, Vicki Anderson, Pee Wee Ellis, Bootsy Collins, Clyde Stubblefield, John "Jabo" Starks and "Sweet" Charles Sherrell. So it made sense that he'd put something together for us. And working with all those former James Brown sidemen, he had to know of our collective frustrations and how an after-hours gig for the band would do wonders for our souls. As we arrived, a line of people stretched around the block, waiting to see us. I believe the performers included most of the band and Danny Ray, who traveled with the band and would emcee our after-hours gigs. We all took turns singing our own songs or James Brown material. We did Keith's "mega-mix" that night, the sound check trick of taking the band through 20 songs in 20 minutes. I'd written the changes for "Get Real With Me" for my next CD, *Too Cocky in Nagasaki*, and Fred Thomas sang it that night. It was a real band effort: Keith wrote the lyrics and Waldo and Hollie had written the signature horn lines. I mention that because it shows that the Soul Generals really was a band in its own right. There's killer video of this gig, with all of us sweating like crazy in this tiny club. Danny Ray hung out on stage, cool and crisp and un-rumpled as usual in his white three-piece suit. After the first set, I retreated backstage and actually had to wring out my shirt. Keith had stripped down to a tank top. Yet Danny Ray remained cool as a cucumber in his three-piece suit. (How does the man *do* it?) We had serious fun that night, up close and personal with the fans, just as we liked it. And the opportunity to step out on our own, as the Soul Generals — without Mr. Brown and his harsh criticisms — went a long way towards soothing our collective soul. We played our hearts out, with heads held high.

At one of the festivals on this tour, I was in a backstage bathroom, shared by the star and his band, combing my hair, lamenting that I'd begun losing my hair on top. Mr. Brown came in, overheard me and took me aside. "Castor oil," he said quietly, as if confiding a secret. "Put castor oil on your head." I nodded, deferentially, in agreement. To myself, I thought, "Castor oil? I'd rather just lose my hair!" I didn't say that, of course. You could never say anything, really. He could see that I was losing my hair and he'd been there. He was sincere; he was helping me out. Despite the years, the miles, the hassles, we still had that rapport. He said, "Son, I lost my hair two, three times." He got it to come back, apparently, with the aid of castor oil. That was a bit too far for me. He also told me to eat lots of bananas. "Potassium! It's good for yo' hair!" His other advice was to always take a bath, never a shower. He told me: "Water can rust iron. What do you think it's doing to yo hair?!" He said this just to me, like a little side note. Who knows? Maybe he had something there. But I just started wearing hats.

Mr. Brown could be such a strange mixture of your friend and your tormentor. On any given night you might think you knew which one he would be, based on pre-show scuttlebutt — but you'd be wrong. It was around this time that Mr. Bobbit arrived backstage after a show and indicated that Keith and I had a "bench warrant" and were required to see the king. Mr. Brown said, "Mr. Bobbit, whatever Keith is making, you give that to Damon now, and whatever Damon is making, you give that to Keith." Imagine how massively rude that was to Keith — he's a band leader with five more years' experience than me. He was my best bud in the band — in fact, as the two guitarists, we were like a unit within the band. We'd been tight from day one, both personally and in performance. Naturally, Keith was making more than me before this switch, and I offered to split the difference, at least. Keith thanked me, but turned me down. He could handle it, he said. I admired his attitude toward a clear attempt by Mr. Brown to drive a wedge between us. Looking back, part of Keith's success must have been his ability to either confront Mr. Brown or simply ignore his tactics. This was yet another reason I promised Keith (and, silently, myself) that I'd back him to the hilt if the shit ever hit the fan.

A week or so later, after we'd played Live 8 in Edinburgh, T in the Park in Kinross, Scotland, and the Oxegen Festival in Naas, Ireland, we performed in the Stadtpark in Hamburg, my then-girl-friend Jennyfa's hometown. She came out and danced onstage, with Mr. Brown's permission. That night we found another place to do an after-hours jam and blow off steam with the locals.

I like 'em kinda wild, and Jennyfa did not disappoint on that score. She traveled with us to Italy, where we played eight shows in 12 days. But Jennyfa's wildness began to grate on me — she gave me no rest from her antics — and by the time the tour ended, she was rooming with Sara Raya and barely speaking to me. We played the usual, insane Italian tour, criss-crossing the country. First Treviso in the north, down the Adriatic coast to Fermo, south to Bari, back up the coast to Trani, back down the coast to Otranto, then a full-day bus ride northwest to Lucca, west of Florence and, finally, Genoa, further northwest, on the coast, halfway to our next two-night stand at the Sporting Club in Monte Carlo, Monaco.

KELLY JARRELL: I remember one night at the Sporting Club in Monaco Mr. Brown was singing "Georgia," which gave me a moment to scan the audience. And I said to myself, "Look at the bright, violet shirt and the lime green tie on that gentleman. *Holy shit!* That's *Elton John*!" And it freaked me out so badly that I missed my steps. The Bittersweet were swaying to the left, I was swaying to the right. I lost my timing. After the song, The Bittersweet left the stage and I said, "Look, look, that's Elton John!" The girls said, "We were *wondering* what was wrong with you." Later, Elton John got up during "Sex Machine." I thought he'd be able to take the song and run with it, but he didn't really know the words. He seemed caught off-guard, but he was a good sport. It was "Sex Machine" — "*Giddon up . . . Giddon up . . .*" — right? He couldn't really ad-lib.

By this time we were rag dolls. Our day off was spent on yet another epic 12-hour bus ride along the Mediterranean coast to Benidorm, Spain, south of Valencia, where James Brown & company closed the Benidorm Music Meeting '05, a three-day affair in a soccer stadium with Jamiroquai, Echo & the Bunnymen, and dozens of others. Finally, we reached Madrid and flew home. Kelly Jarrell resigned to get married.

KELLY JARRELL: I'd just gotten engaged. And I let Mr. Brown know that was my last tour. He assumed that meant I was never coming back. I *was* telling everyone it was my last tour, but I probably would have stayed on if he'd made any overtures. He didn't. After the tour we flew into Columbia, South Carolina, not far from Augusta. Mr. Brown said, "Okay, Miss Kelly, Mr. Bobbit's got some money for you. Mr. Bobbit, give Miss Kelly a bonus." And Mr. Bobbit looked at me and said, "I don't have any money." Real rude. I thought that was not only anti-climactic but it hurt my feelings. Mr. Brown had a hard time with anybody leaving. He had to be the one to tell you good-bye and that way he could give you permission to come back. He ruled by intimidation. He focused on your weaknesses. The other side of it, of course, was that that was the ride of our lives. Being in that band meant experiencing a wide range of emotions, and I think you had to be a certain type of personality — just dysfunctional enough to continue to do that year after year. Not everybody could handle it. Road life is hard under the best of circumstances. I'll bet Damon had a harder time than he let on, because he seemed to be loving and easy-going. That's what I picked up.

We returned home virtually unscathed by the longest tour we'd ever done. When I reached my apartment, I had a nice surprise waiting. *Relix* magazine, a niche publication devoted to groups such as the Grateful Dead and the Allman Brothers Band and jam bands in general, had written a positive piece on my *Space Cadet* CD. Under the column, "Artists too New to Know," writer Mick Skidmore called my new music "making jazzy funk fun," which worked for me. Skidmore added that the CD was "superbly crafted," which felt good. I had worked really hard on the arrangements, the sounds, and the mix. "*Space Cadet* . . . sees the band exploring a plethora of instrumental textures with some unusual twists," Skidmore wrote. "Not surprisingly there's an underlying funk edge but in a jagged sort of psychedelic fashion: Witness the sassy opener 'Sweet Delight' and the percolating riffs of 'Bubbledown.' Elsewhere the band flits from melodic jazz-rock (not unlike Steve Kimock) to the beautifully haunting title cut, which features pirouetting leads counter-pointed by delicate piano work that really highlights the sophistication of this ensemble." Between my hometown *Westword*'s kind words and *Relix*, which had a national reach, the word was getting out. In fact, *Westword* readers named my band "Best Jam Band in Denver" in 2005. Locally, Harmonious Junk was gigging with the help of a booking agent. We weren't playing a ton yet, so *Space Cadet* really helped put some buzz behind the band.

THE BREAKING POINT

Thankfully we had a couple weeks off after living on the road for six weeks. But there'd be no rest for the wicked. We all met up in Bend, Oregon, in late August and played three California dates in four days, including a return to the Greek Theater, and the next day we performed in New York City as Hurricane Katrina devastated New Orleans. After a short break we flew to Hong Kong to perform for conventioneers of some sort. My itinerary read: "Hong Kong — day lost." I remember a boat trip around one of the islands. Everybody who jumped in to go swimming got stung by jellyfish. Some of us bought custom suits on the cheap. Jeff Watkins got all pimped out in a suit that went psychedelic-iridescent when you got up close. His inner-bargain-hunter came out and he bought *seven* suits, and he's been wearing them ever since. We flew south over the South China Sea and Vietnam to reach Kuala Lumpur in Malaysia.

Caution was the watchword. In Malaysia, they had just sentenced to death a guy from China who was in Malaysia illegally and got caught with two pounds of marijuana. The judge said, "At the time of your arrest you gave no information. Then, later, you wanted to come forth and say you were holding this for another man. You are sentenced to death." Kinda gets your attention. Still, we managed to find "mash," as we called it. And I met a girl there. We had an interesting time.

Within 72 hours of our appearance on a stage in Kuala Lumpur, we were onstage at the Farris Center in Conway, Arkansas, a good 8,000 miles away. And we followed that up with gigs at Eastern Illinois University in Charleston, Illinois, and an outdoor amphitheater in Sunset Hills, Missouri. The touring was no less frenetic than when I jumped on the James Brown train seven years earlier. How a 70-something artist like Mr. Brown managed all that traveling and performing, I will never know — and I doubt that modern science will ever explain it. He clearly tapped into the audience's energy and thrived in the spotlight. That worked for us, too, but hurtling through a Time Tunnel and popping out for a gig could be mind-blowing.

Despite making a lot of the same stops over and over, we still played some exotic new places each year. In 2005, that included Mexico City, Santurce (Puerto Rico), Jakarta, Buenos Aires, Vina Del Mar (Chile), and half the stops in Europe that summer were new — Edinburgh, Wolverhampton, and Newcastle (England), Mainz and Stuttgart (Germany), and nearly all the towns we'd hit in Italy. I'd made my first (and perhaps only) visits to Bend, Oregon, and Charleston, Illinois. (Woo-hoo!) Every venue and every locale was different, and that kept us interested, even if the experience on the bus, if you will, was grindingly familiar. Mr. Brown's mood always fluctuated, so I couldn't put my finger on any real change there. Could racing around the world, backing a superstar, ever get tiresome? Would it ever end?

I hadn't really imagined it myself, yet we all knew the James Brown gig couldn't go on forever. Hell, I knew that when I joined in 1999. And according to Billy Triplett's recollections, we'd been openly discussing it since 2003. Yet Mr. Brown showed no real signs of slowing down. The stage was his home. And many performers might tell you that the stage can be a trouble-free zone as far as life's other hassles are concerned. When you're out there, it's all about the music and the performance. The rest of the world and life's little hassles are at bay for the duration. So, we all lived for that moment of glory, and the way the energy flowed back from the audience. At this juncture, I couldn't see voluntarily stepping away from the action. I was making a living, I had a band going on the side, and Mr. Brown seemed to be in a good place.

November sent us back to California: a club in San Diego, House of Blues in West Hollywood, the Bob Hope Theatre in Stockton (hadn't been *there* before), the ornate Paramount Theater in Oakland. Four 90s, five days. After Christmas we played out East: the 9:30 Club in Washington, D.C. (NPR taped the show), House of Blues in Atlantic City, and two shows on New Year's Eve at B.B. King's in New York. New Year's Eve was marred somewhat, not by Mr. Brown's behavior per se, but by a reminder of the band's "place." We all understood the economics of touring: big band, big overhead. We accepted that the star's digs should be premium, the band's less-than-premium. But this New Year's Eve, the boss was in New York at Trump International, 1 Central Park Avenue, and we were staying at a Days Inn somewhere in Newark, New Jersey, on some superhighway, sandwiched between 14 lanes of traffic with nothing within walking distance. We had no means of transportation. We'd been parked here, to cool our heels, for *days*, because it was cheaper than sending us home right before the New Year's gigs. When it was time for the gig, a totally beat-up, airport express van with a cage in the back picked us up. Our accommodations and transportation were our world for an overly long weekend, and the desultory conditions were just a little too much. Why were we staying in the middle of Newark, surrounded by highways, when we're going to play Times Square? I know New York hotels are expensive, but the Days Inn nestled in the freeways of Newark was hardly the only solution. To be fair, this could not be Mr. Brown's doing (theory), nor would it be possible to address it with Mr. Brown (fact). The organization's tour scheduler just didn't give a damn about the band. It was time to woof. And it was my turn. I got on the phone to the office. I said, "Hey, Claudia." She said, "My name is Claire." I said, "What are we *doing* out here?" And I held my cell phone out to the traffic for a minute so she could hear the incessant roar. Nothing came of it. We just rode it out like everything else. But sometimes that treatment would rub you the wrong way, big time. It wasn't James Brown, it was Intrigue Music, nickel and diming the band.

Perhaps fortunately, the schedule allowed no time to dwell on indignities. The James Brown train left the station again 48 hours later. We had no time to return home, so from our four-day sojourn above the highways of Newark, New Jersey, we jumped on the bus to the Potawatomi Casino in Milwaukee. Remember, it's early January. We headed further north for a two-nighter at Casino Rama in Ontario, back south to the House of Blues in Chicago, then northwest for another two nights at the River Rock Casino in Richmond, British Columbia. Our route described a jagged suture across the U.S.-Canada border. Fortunately, the shows went over well and garnered respectful reviews. Jane Stevenson at the *Toronto Sun* gave the first of two Casino Rama shows four and a half stars.

> The Godfather of Soul . . . was decked out in a glorious
> forest green suit, trimmed in sparkling silver sequins, with
> a matching green shirt and green boots . . . as if the Jolly
> Green Giant suddenly got funky . . . The 72-year-old
> Brown was back in fighting form last night . . . [And] an

extended, jam-happy version of 'This is a Man's World'
. . . clearly demonstrated The Funky President had indeed
returned to office. This was an old-school soul revue all
the way . . . and the audience couldn't get enough of it.

Mr. Brown might have sensed our own, deteriorating mood, or he might have been oblivious to it, but he invited the band to his hotel room that night to watch a video of the previous night's gig, which was a pretty rare occurrence. We snacked and drank Champagne together, and it was one of the coolest James Brown-and-his-band evening hang-outs. The tour was due to tie off at Bimbo's 365 Club in San Francisco, and that's about as far ahead as I could think. About this time, unfortunately, I heard from someone with firsthand knowledge that the boss and his wife were at odds, if you will, once again. A year earlier, during the Night of the Proms, Joe Cocker's keyboard player had approached me to ask if everything was okay. He'd heard my boss and his wife rattling around in their room. All this heightened my moral dilemma, even for a mercenary. This time it felt downright shitty to be part of that operation. The highs and lows were getting more extreme.

Tension crackled as we zig-zagged across the Canadian border. Keith woofed on the band's behalf and actually got each of us $500 apiece because we'd played two shows on New Year's Eve at B.B. King's. He was one of the only people who would stand up and say whatever had to be said about the treatment the band was getting. Given my indignation in Newark, I'd say Keith's attitude was rubbing off on me and, to be honest, everything was rubbing me raw — just as he had prophesied years earlier. On one of these shows, I remember Mr. Brown got pissy about the band's response to a hand cue. Being kind of over it, I hit a sour note on purpose, as if to say, "Oh yeah? You want to fuck with *me*?" And he looked back at me, like, "Now you're going to *sabotage the music*?" I never did it again, and I admit it was unprofessional, but that's how bad it was getting.

At our second night at the River Rock Casino in Richmond, British Columbia, I got backstage early and Mousey was already there, on his job. But Mr. Brown was back there too, messin' with him. I came in and sat down, and Mr. Brown asked me, "Did you tune up?" I said, "Yes, Mr. Brown, we tuned up at sound check. And we're gonna tune up again before the show." (He *had* hired professional musicians, after all.) Looking back, I guess for whatever reason he just couldn't help himself. "Well, y'all need to use the same tuner." He couldn't stop from beating that dead horse for the umpteenth time. That stupid crap had been going on for two years now and just the sheer senselessness of it was a downer. Not to mention that using one tuner made performing unnecessarily difficult for the three professional guitarists in his service. In a carefully calibrated voice, I said, "Mr. Brown, these tuners are all the same." I'd probably never talked back to him until this point, if you can call a simple statement of fact *talking back*. He even used to say that he liked me because I "didn't make no trouble." And, judging by his mood, this would not be the best night to introduce new behaviors. But I was finally to the point where I needed to speak up. "Mr. Brown, this is a new technology. These tuners are all the same. They're digital. All set to 440 hertz. I can tune up on any one of these and they'll be exactly the same." He said, "Heh heh heh, son, you real new at this." So I said, "Yeah, twenty years. Twenty years I've been onstage using tuners. I'm real new at this." What he meant was: "Don't you get it? You're not supposed to argue with me." He couldn't say, "Prove it," because he wouldn't risk investing his time in being proven wrong.

We went out and played the show. But under the surface, the unease persisted. We had recently learned that instead of receiving a full week's pay for six days on the road, our checks were being pro-rated at six-sevenths of a week's pay. On my last check, I'd been out seven days because I'd traveled to the East Coast from Denver. So I was paid a full week's pay. But everybody from the East Coast was shorted one-seventh of their paycheck because they'd been out only six days. Back when I started, if we were out on the road for a long weekend we got a week's pay. Now Intrigue Music was chiseling us nickel by nickel, when anyone will tell you that six days on the road is a damn week's worth of work when it comes to putting on the James Brown show. I was so pissed off that I went to James Brown in his dressing room and told him about the shaved paychecks. It was too much. A couple people came with me. I tried to be diplomatic about it, not disrespectful. I was drinking a glass of red wine, though, and I didn't care that he saw me drinking. But I kept my cool. I very respectfully said, "Mr. Brown, we trust *you*. But we *don't* trust the people who handle the money." Although it wasn't my direct problem that night, I'd get my turn at the same treatment if I didn't step up. Trouble is, if it's not someone's direct problem, they don't say anything. And if it *is* their direct problem, they just bitch and never do anything about it because they fear getting fired. At this point I didn't care anymore. I had had to listen to people talk about him and Tomi Rae fighting. I'm getting ground down by the repetitive goofiness over tuners. There's no new music coming in. The show hadn't evolved in the past six months. I'm exhausted by all the traveling and the tension that went with it. But instead of breaking down, I stood up. And I told James Brown face-to-face, "You know, every time we get paid, there's like one-seventh shaved off our pay. We're tired of dealing with it. We're out here on the road, everybody's doing their job." He said, "You better watch out. You're gonna end up like Kelly." (Kelly Jarrell had left to get married.) I said, "Like what?" I was gonna call him on his jive. "Well, she ain't doin' *nothin'*." I said, "Wherever she is, she's doin' *somethin'*." What I meant was, "She's got a life, she's just not working for you." That was a rough exchange. I honestly don't remember exactly how it ended, probably because it was eclipsed by subsequent events.

We must have flown to San Francisco, because that's a 1,000-mile jaunt and there was only 20 hours until the next show. We all got to Bimbo's 365 Club, near Fisherman's Wharf, early that evening, eager to do the gig and get home. But it was way too small a space for us all to be crammed into at the end of any tour, let alone this one. The place is tiny, maybe 500 seats. We've got a little dressing room. He's got a little dressing room. When we got there, he was already there, already in a bad mood from the discussion the night before, and he's saying stuff to deliberately push our buttons. The pressure cooker had to give; steam had to escape. At the sound check, Keith started playing Black Sabbath riffs, loud. Between sound check and show time, James Brown fired him. Early on in my tenure, based on all that he'd done for me, I'd told Keith that if he ever got fired, I'd quit. Well, that night, it took all of two seconds after learning that Keith'd been fired that I walked up to James Brown and asked, "Is Keith fired?" He said, "Yeah, Keith's fired." I said, "Then I quit. I thank you for everything." And I shook his hand before he even comprehended what I'd said. He said, "Son, just play the show." I said, "No, I won't play the show. You can play the show yourself." Now we're having an argument. I said, "People devote their lives to you. You can't listen to anyone. You won't hear the truth from anyone." I can't be sure I accurately recall his response, but I remember that he said either, "I don't need to listen to the truth," or "I don't need to listen to anyone." It was one of those two comments. My response was equally confrontational. "Well, people don't need to devote their lives to you when you don't give a fuck about anybody else." Suddenly, he wanted to fight me. His eyes were on fire. In his mind, I'd dissed him. Somebody got between us. And that was it.

Keith and I went out drinking that night, and we naturally gravitated back to the show, where we'd left our guitars and gear. I was in a rotten state of mind and started booing, but Keith got me to cool it. After the show, I was still pissed. Someone in the band had brought in a friend of his to fill in on guitar, which upset me at the time, I gotta say. I had finally stood up to James Brown to make a point on behalf of the band. But some people would back him no matter what. It wasn't my place to try to change James Brown's mind about anything. But he could've bought loyalty so cheaply, just by acting like he cared that the band was getting skinned. "They're doin' what?!" Or something like that. You can give a man dignity just by lending an ear, and you can rob him of dignity just by shutting him down. Anyway, I made an ass out of myself backstage, collecting my equipment. That's how it ended. I yelled. "Where's my fucking tuner? Where's my one motherfucking tuner?" My apologies to the cat who sat in for us on guitar. That might have been his one and only night playing with James Brown and he had to wonder, "What's wrong with *that* guy?" I just didn't want to see him up there. The next day I went home and I didn't work for James Brown anymore.

AFTERMATH

My departure was messy and traumatic. The confrontation with Mr. Brown had seemed to cross a line and things had reached a point of no return. I drummed up gigs for Harmonious Junk and put out my shingle for guitar instruction, though my thoughts and feelings remained a jumble for weeks. I was excited to start a new life, to pursue my own fortunes, to create my own opportunities. Having served somebody for the better part of a decade, enjoyed the highest highs, and endured the occasional boot on my neck, I was finally free. Getting off the road for the first time in nearly eight years was a huge relief. The phone wasn't ringing. I wasn't dashing to the airport with guitar and valise. I didn't have to turn the other cheek for the umpteenth time. Still, the turn of events left a void. I deeply regretted leaving my bandmates in a lurch, and I missed their camaraderie. I missed Danny Ray. Damn it, I missed James Brown and all that went with him.

Then the phone *did* ring. "We're going to China in a couple of weeks, and we don't have anybody." It was Mr. Bobbit. "What's it going to take to get you back?" Jesus! What had been a life-altering trauma to me was, for the organization, just another little dust-up in a nearly 50-year continuum of staffing the band. I might have pissed off Mr. Brown one night in San Francisco, but I had a passport and I knew the show. "Hire Keith back," I replied instantly. "That's the only reason I quit. Hire Keith back and I'm good." Mr. Bobbit said, "Okay." When I hung up, my thoughts and emotions resumed their civil war. *What was I doing?* Did I want to be brave and make my own way, like Erik Hargrove had done? Or was I just going to go back to the same old deal with Games Brown? I called Mr. Bobbit back, but the call went to voice mail. So I left a message. I said, "Oh, and by the way, I want to be paid for those recording sessions in Augusta last year. We were never paid to record." We had gotten rehearsal pay, which was not our real pay. We were never paid proper session fees. My indignation rose and, consciously or not, I added a deal killer. "I want about four thousand dollars. That's my pay. Then I'll come back." I never got a call back. Keith went back. He had a family; he needed his job. As for me, my demand for four grand was my way of putting the kibosh on going back. I thought, "That was too easy. Why did I just let them get me back that easily?" I didn't give a fuck about going to China. So I ladled on the demand for money I knew they wouldn't pay and that was that. It was very sudden and it could have gone either way. At least I had created opportunities to which I could now turn to. I had other things I wanted to do with my life — things that didn't require inner turmoil from being ground down. And I'd learned a thing or two about leading a band: only one person can make the decisions. A band leader can't be soft. A band leader can't be held back by his band. And, it's not about hanging out with your friends. I had learned that much from Mr. Brown, and I work that way to this very day.

Of *course* I had second thoughts about leaving James Brown.

Later, I called Mr. Bobbit and left a message. I let him know that I was sorry how things went down, and I asked him to let Mr. Brown know that I really appreciated everything he did for me, all the opportunities he provided me. My years with him had been the ride of a lifetime. After my thoughts and feelings had battled to a truce, I had nothing but love for everyone involved. Mr. Bobbit didn't return the call. Later still, I called Mr. Bobbit again. I asked him whether, if the band ever hit Denver, I could sit in. To his credit, Mr. Bobbit got back to me. The word was, Mr. Brown said that'd be okay. James Brown and the Soul Generals were all over the world that year, mostly hitting the same old venues, cranking out the same old show. They never made it to Denver. I never did get a face-to-face with James Brown to apologize, nor did I get to speak with him again, which would have provided some closure.

I had dreams, later. When I was in the band, I had nightmares about the show. Nightmares that I couldn't find my stage outfit, my pedals, my cables were all the wrong sizes and the show was underway. I'm seeing all this from some crazy distance, somehow paralyzed, unable to act. Then, when I wasn't in the band, I had dreams that he let me come back, and I wondered in my dream whether he was going to send me home or let me play the show. And I'd wake up, but by that time James Brown had passed away — there'd be no resolution, no closure. It was that deep — not easy to leave, not easy to stay, not easy to move on, not easy to find peace, not easy to shake my dreams.

EPILOGUE

For Christmas 2006 I drove from Denver to Las Vegas to spend the holiday with my family. That's a long drive, and I slept in on

Christmas Day. I awoke to news that James Brown was sick, that he had been hospitalized. To me, at first blush, that meant that he was okay and being cared for. Then my mom said she'd heard on the news that Mr. Brown had passed. The phone began ringing. Friends, bandmates, and the media were calling. People tend to remember where they were when a truly meaningful event tore their world apart. So it was for me. But the reality of Mr. Brown's death didn't really hit me until I was driving home to Denver. How could a man — *The* Man — just vanish from this Earth? I thought of the arc of his remarkable life, how he'd raised himself from nothing to global superstardom and turned the world onto funk and soul music. And how he took me with him on some small part of that great journey and changed my life.

I crossed Utah in a violent blizzard, then crept over the Rockies on Interstate 70. As I later learned, the authorities closed the highway behind me. As I descended from the mountains to the plains, the snow turned to rain. And as the wiper blades swept the rain from my windshield, more rain blotted my vision. The radio kept playing James Brown, over and over. I was close to home when I broke down and cried. I couldn't tell the rain on my windshield from the tears in my eyes.

A couple of weeks later, I wrote an epitaph that helped me process my thoughts and emotions and might explain why I've been moved to share my story.

REST IN PEACE JAMES BROWN

The world lost maybe its greatest living performer on
Christmas day '06, the incomparable James Brown. Having
had the wonderful opportunity to play with him for almost eight
years is something I will always feel blessed and thankful for. He
was an unending source of strength and determination with an
incredible energy and a great sense of humor. People will always

speculate on his personal battles, but I will remember the man
who rocked so many houses, so many towns, so many countries,
and I will remember the smiles and the tears on the faces of
the fans he loved and lived for. I will remember the laughter
he could generate in a single moment on stage or off with his
silliness and charm. He gave us all so much good advice over the
years, I just hope we can remember and carry on in his tradi-
tion. I know I will try my best in his honor. We send all our love
to James Brown, his family, the band members current and
past, and the extended family and fans across the world. See you
on the gridiron, boss. The world will never forget you.

With love and respect, Damon Wood, Denver, January 18,
2007

Over the years since Mr. Brown's death, I've learned that my experience wasn't all that unusual. I've met and played with the "Funky Drummer," the late Clyde Stubblefield, who quit James Brown before I was born. We had very similar stories to tell about our time with the man. Undoubtedly, Mr. Brown saw me grow from someone hungry for opportunity, eager to learn, someone who wouldn't "make no trouble" despite Mr. Brown's behavior, into someone who had grown musically and personally, gotten tight with his bandmates and, finally, someone who would no longer gloss over the bullshit he threw my way. I think he had to find something he could use to keep me in check — just like everyone else who ever worked for him. He was forever, in his mind, prepared to quell an insurrection. He could tell that foolishness about making the guitarists use only one tuner hit me hard. I want to think that his hardscrabble beginnings, his mother's abandonment, drove him to be forever haunted by issues of trust, even while he strove to be magnanimous and kind. In the absence of real trust, maybe he felt he had to maintain the upper hand in all his relationships, including his band. Maybe it was the numbers: one man in need of two dozen other people to keep the bright lights on. That makes you vulnerable. Most of what James Brown did, he did through sheer willpower. His drive to overcome, to succeed no matter the obstacles, culminated in the man I worked for. He was a tough cookie. But sheer willpower couldn't do it all. So he had to play games, too: divide-and-conquer, manipulate, pump 'em up, kick 'em down, keep 'em off balance. Make 'em believe that their only choice is to stay with the show. Looking back, as I have done here and continue to do from time to time, I might have been among the fortunate few who decided to step away when the equation no longer added up. I had grown as a man and as a musician and, ultimately, I chose to pursue my own path before Mr. Brown's passing forced me to do so. But I wrote this book, didn't I? Like everyone who ever worked for Mr. Brown, I can't help but look back to the days when he pushed us to our limits and beyond and shared the sheer joy and the pure excitement he conjured out of thin air with a holler and a dance step and a big sound. Not only did this man rise above the crater of Twiggs Street, he and his music forever changed the world. As I said at the beginning of the book, working for James Brown was the hardest thing I ever had to do. And through good times and bad, it's still the greatest thing that ever happened to me. So far.

ACKNOWLEDGMENTS

DAMON WOOD

James Brown, for giving me a chance, showing me the world and sharing his talent, drive, humor, and wisdom. Thank you, Mr. Brown. It was the ride of a lifetime. Phil Carson, for being a real brother, a great writer, bluesman, musicologist, and JB fan, and for having the vision, skill, patience, and dedication to see this project through. My JBU family that contributed their personal memories and feelings, I can't thank you enough: Keith Jenkins, Fred Thomas, Erik Hargrove, George "Spike" Nealy, Hollie Farris, Jerry "Louie" Poindexter, Robert "Mousey" Thompson, Willie Ray "Bo" Brundidge, Kelly Jarrell, Yonna Wynne, Jimmie Lee Moore and Billy Triplett. Everyone who was part of the show, onstage or behind the scenes, for their friendship, grace, strength and love, and for sharing the time of our lives. Jonathan Lethem ("Mr. *Rolling Stone*"), for the epic piece on JB, getting my name in *Rolling Stone*, help with publisher ideas, and overall inspiration. Mom and Dad, your support has always meant the world to me. Aunts Jolyn, Anne, Nicki, and Grandma Merle, for the harmony singalongs around the kitchen table when I was a kid. Grandpa Woody and Uncle Frank, for tolerating their shenanigans . . . from the den. Danielle, Michele, and Toni, for braving my early performances. All my musician friends and family that have shared the journey, you know who you are. Thank you: Harmonious Junk Band past and present; Brian Efros, Rob Buehler, Gary Herrera, Ron Roelofsen, Erik Norland, Steven Smith; Rick and Eleanor Anderson; Patrick Sites and Whitewater Ramble; Jay and Phil Bianchi, Sancho's, Dulcinea's, Quixote's; Pete's Monkey Bar, Jim Shields & Snake River Saloon; ECW Press for helping us make this happen; Catherine and Grommit, my loves.

PHIL CARSON

I can't say for sure when James Brown entered my life, but enter it he did, when I was young. I got hooked on "I Got You (I Feel Good)," from 1964, the first hit I clearly recall. That voice, that howl, that sinuous rhythm, got me goin'. In 1964, my dad bought us a handheld, AM transistor radio and, at that time, if you turned it on, it returned the favor. Later, when I saw video of JB performing "Prisoner of Love" on the October 1964 TAMI show, his dancing, singing, mic handling and his sunglasses-bedecked band exuded the fever and coolness of funk — it's still the hippest performance ever. Even as a white suburban kid, I always respected how JB and Muhammad Ali spoke for their people in 1960s America. Thanks, Mr. Brown!

To James Brown fans everywhere, but particularly those outside the United States: I'm grateful that you kept James Brown in your hearts and kept him working into the 21st century.

I chose Damon as my guitar teacher in 2010 because of his affiliation with James Brown. Damon always went the extra mile to ensure I understood my lessons. When I finally prevailed on him to share a few stories from his days working for the Godfather of Soul, I started recording his reminiscences. I knew we had *something*. I'm not sure Damon ever believed it (I *am* a journalist, after all), but I helped him put this book together to pay him back for those lessons, and for sharing stories that gave me a clearer, more intimate view of Mr. Dynamite himself.

I'd like to thank everyone in the Soul Generals, particularly those interviewed for this book, including Erik Hargrove, George "Spike" Nealy, Keith Jenkins, Jerry "Louie" Poindexter, Jimmie Lee Moore, Hollie Farris, Robert "Mousey" Thompson, Willie Ray "Bo" Brundidge, Fred Thomas, Kelly Jarrell, Yonna Kari Wynne, and the late, great soundman, Billy Triplett. By extension, I thank all sidemen and women everywhere: they are popular music's unsung heroes.

Thanks to Jonathan Lethem for early advice on finding a publisher and for reading the book prior to publication, to Sam Cutler, whose memoir of life with the Rolling Stones and the Grateful Dead inspired me to contact ECW Press.

As always, I thank my father and late mother for their gift of life and their guidance, even if I didn't always follow it.

A heartfelt shout-out to my hometown crew, who always supported my writing, my music, and my urban and backcountry adventures and kept Haven Industries running smoothly: John Kippley, Rob Selleck, Steve-o Brereton, Rick Roseberry, Bobbo Z. Shaffer, Keith Kramer, Jeff Mason, Joe Cesare, Jim Whalen, Mike Gorzelanski and the life-sustaining blues band, the Delta Sonics (John Butler, Al Chesis, Bob Pellegrino and their fans).

Thanks to Barb Moulton for advising us and to the patient crew at ECW Press, who believed in the book and improved it along the way: Michael Holmes, Laura Pastore, Crissy Calhoun, Jessica Albert, and Erika Head.